Towards Asian Community
Peace through Education

Edited by **One Asia Foundation**

Towards Asian Community
—Peace through Education—

Edited

by

One Asia Foundation

Copyright © 2018
by One Asia Foundation, All rights reserved.
English translation right arranged with One Asia Foundation.

Printed in Japan.
ISBN978-4-7556-1298-5

One Asia Foundation
#405 Station Plaza Tower, 2-22-1 Nishi-Nippori,
Arakawa-ku, Tokyo, 116-0013, Japan
TEL. +81-3-5615-5500, FAX. +81-3-5615-5501

Ashi-Shobo Publishing Company
2-5, Tsukasa-machi, Chiyoda-ku, Tokyo, 101-0048, Japan

Prefatory Remarks

Today, the nature of the state and the individual is under question, and we are called upon to seek the essence of what it is we should pursue, the direction in which we should take, and the issues which we should either reform or overcome. This means continually questioning not only those issues which float on the surface of the various phenomena that compose society, but also the essence which lies at the root of these issues.

Today, globalization progresses at a rapid pace in a wide range of areas. Globalization casts its shadow over the individual's way of thinking, over their sense of values and their worldview, continually transforming people's sense of solidarity with the community. Given that we are in a global age, many of the various issues confronting the individual are connected with issues of global scale. Problems at the individual level may not even be resolvable through visions at the state or national level, but would rather require a global viewpoint to find solutions.

One Asia Foundation roots itself in such a global viewpoint, with the policy of being unconfined by state, nation, religion or ideology, and being disengaged from politics. Looking towards the future, we are developing a diverse range of activities which will help overcome many barriers of the past which still tower before us. Specifically, the *Courses of Asian Community* is one example of such activities. By sharing our dreams of the future with thousands of researchers who are part of the Courses, we are working to help all people break free—or we coin the term, "graduate"—from many barriers which exist in today's society.

One Asia Foundation has been supporting the establishment of the *Courses of Asian Community* in universities since September 2010. This initiative has blossomed to the point where the courses are currently available in 520 universities in 48 countries and regions across the world. The Foundation holds an annual One Asia Convention for researchers from universities running or preparing to run these courses. This annual convention provides a forum of exchange and research presentations that go beyond the traditional frameworks of regional and specialized research.

The Seventh Convention was held in 2017 at Nagoya, Japan. Divided into three sessions, the Convention featured 32 research presentations. While the research themes were diverse, all were united towards the broader theme of creating an Asian Community.

This publication gathers these research presentations together into a single volume. It contains hopes and dreams for the future from researchers across a wide range of disciplines, while it also highlights many issues. It has not been an easy task to compile such a number of diverse research themes into a single book. But it is unmistakable that all of these papers are connected by the common theme of the One Asia Convention Nagoya 2017—namely, "Peace through Education." This theme has given the publication its name, *Towards Asian Community - Peace through Education*.

The articles are compiled in the same order in which they were presented at the Convention. In addition, the authors have submitted their articles in English. The authors have different first languages, and some expressions and uses of language may vary and may prove to be difficult to understand, but let us be tolerant on this matter.

Through repeated cycles of trial and error, humanity has pursued freedom and equality, along with happiness, comfort, and a secure environment. The nation state was also created in pursuit of these goals. Moving forward, by deploying new tools and interpersonal networks, we must seek to achieve a community that can provide a free and satisfying environment beyond national boundaries, on a global scale.

The papers included in this publication respond to a wide variety of global issues, while simultaneously offering a diverse range of perspectives whereby eliminating negative phenomena including conflicts between nations and individuals, and inequality. Moreover, the papers provide a gesture toward creating a freer, symbiotic society in the context of a shared vision that transcends the local and the state.

Finally, I wish to express my thanks and appreciation to the academics who have supported this initiative with their manuscript submissions, despite the limited nature of the time available. Motoharu Nakayama, President of Ashi-Shobo, also willingly gave us his cooperation, in spite of the difficult requests we made of him. We should also acknowledge the major role played by the Foundation's Nozomi Taira, who has been responsible for this volume from conception to publication. Let me take this opportunity to express my heartfelt thanks to you all.

August 3, 2018

Joon Kon Chung,
Representative Editor,
One Asia Foundation

Contents

Section 1
Proposal for Peace through Education

Chapter 1
The Politics of Peace through Education: Classrooms, Streets and 'Dark Tourism' in Japan *13*

Chapter 2
The Significance of Health among Human Conditions in Asian Communities: Peace through Education *23*
1. Ordinary Understanding of Health *23*
2. Philosophical Examination of Health: Consideration of Hans-Georg Gadamer's *The Enigma of Health 24*
3. Prerequisites for Health *25*
4. Conclusions *26*

Section 2
Reports of the course on Asian Community

Chapter 3
Interculturalism in Communication and Education in the Courses of the One Asia Foundation *31*
1. Introduction *31*
2. Theoretical Background *32*
3. Research Methods: Intercultural Values and Education *36*
4. The Results *38*

Chapter 4
Practice of "Asian Community Theory" *41*
1. History of the "Asian Community Theory" course at University of Sanya *41*
2. Current results and problems *42*
3. Participation in conventions and visiting other universities *44*

Section 3
Perspectives towards an Asian Community – Part 1 Politics, Economics, Environment and Social Matters

Chapter 5
The Idea of Community and the Transformation of World Politics: Perspectives from IR Theory *49*

Chapter 6
Multi-level Governance and Regional Economic Cooperation: Case of Northeast Asia *65*
1. Rethinking New Regionalism and Its Influence *65*
2. Sub-regional Community Building and Its Challenges *69*
3. Development of Micro-regional Economic Circles *72*
4. The Prospect of Great East Asian Integration *76*
5. Conclusion *79*

Chapter 7
'East Asian Safe Community' Drawn in 'Nagoya': War, Disaste, Calamity *85*

Section 4
Perspectives towards an Asian Community – Part 2
History, Education, Thought, Philosophy and Religion

Chapter 8

Sharing and Accumulating Understanding of Neighbor Countries and Their People: A Foundation for Asian Community *95*

1. Asian Community and Understanding of Neighbor Countries and Their People *95*
2. Various forms of the Understanding of Asian Neighbors *97*
3. Expanding the understanding of Asian Neighbor Countries and Their People *102*

Chapter 9

Interreligious Dialogue between North and South Korea to Build a Peace Community *105*

1. Introduction *105*
2. Inter-religious dialogue and experience in traditional Buddhist Teachings and *Won*-Buddhism in Korea *106*
3. Inter-religious dialogue and cooperation among North and South Korean religious leaders *110*
4. Conclusion *113*

Chapter 10

Asia Seen from a Mongolian Perspective *119*

Chapter 11

New Asian Youth Peace Education in the Fourth Industrial Revolution *137*

1. Introduction *137*

2. The necessity of peace education and the actual situation of youth peace education in Asia *139*

3. The role of the Asian Foundation for New Young Adult Education *145*

4. Conclusion *153*

Chapter 12
Research on the Culture of the Formation of General Geographical Places Name in the East Asia Chinese Character Culture *157*

1. Introduction *157*
2. Examples of General Geographical Name Used to Decribe Place Form of the Nature *158*
3. Examples of General Geographical Name Used to Decribe Place Form of the Humanities Category *163*
4. Conclusion *168*

Chapter 13
Promoting Global Citizenship Education, Multicultural Education, and Civic Education to a Peaceful Asian Community *171*

1. Introduction *171*
2. Conceptual Review *173*
3. Methodology *175*
4. Findings and Discussions *176*
5. Conclusion *183*

Section 5
Perspectives towards an Asian Community – Part 3
Culture, Arts and Media

Chapter 14
Hybrid Food Culture through Migration: Case of Ethnic Koreans in Central Asia *189*
1. Introduction *189*
2. Migration of Koreans and Making *Koryeo saram* foodways in Central Asia *190*
3. Re-migration and globalization (1991–) *195*
4. Conclusion *197*

Chapter 15
Forming One Asia Community: Asian Value and Growing Up Research Atmosphere *199*
1. Introduction *199*
2. The Preparation of Lecture Series at UNM *200*
3. Asian Value and Growing Up Research Atmosphere *205*
4. Conclusions *212*

Chapter 16
Cultural Acculturation for One Asia United in Diversity *215*
1. The New World Order *215*
2. Cultural Exchange and Acculturation *216*
3. One Asia – Unity In Diversity *217*
4. Sinicization and De-Sinicization in Vietnam *222*
5. Hinduization and De-Hinduization *225*
6. Cham art, architecture and sculpture in Vietnam *227*
7. Westernization and De-Westernization *228*

Chapter 17
A Study of Japan's New Ocean View and Marine Education from *Coexistence with the Ocean* by Tomoya Akimichi *239*
1. Coexistence *240*
2. Japan's new ocean view *243*
3. Japan's future marine education *248*
4. Conclusion *250*

Section 6
Appendix
Number of Universities that received the Course Grant by Country/Region *255*
Introduction of Former Conventions *256*

Section 1
Proposal for Peace through Education

Chapter 1

The Politics of Peace through Education:

Classrooms, Streets and 'Dark Tourism' in Japan

Glenn D. Hook (University of Sheffield)

The topic of 'peace through education' (*kyōiku o tsujita heiwa*) brings into focus a number of issues related to the role, scope and significance of education for peace in postwar Japan. It not only suggests the need to address the contested philosophical question of 'what is peace,' but also to reflect on the role of different agents in educating the future generations about peace as well as inculcating attitudes and potentially taking action to promote peace. These tasks most crucially involve two agents, the postwar state and the school teacher. The first plays a critical, formal role through the Ministry of Education (now the Ministry of Education, Culture, Sports, Science and Technology, MEXT) as the ministry is charged with authorizing (or not) the school textbooks used by the teacher. Of particular concern in promoting peace through education are the history and social studies textbooks authorized for use in junior and senior high schools in Japan. The second acts as the main conduit through which information about issues of war and peace is passed on to future generations and attitudes as well as actions to promote peace are inculcated. The teacher, as the agent who shoulders the day-to-day responsibility for educating the next generation in the classroom, is both constrained by the content of the textbooks certified by the ministry as well as empowered through these daily interactions with the pupils.

While an investigation into the philosophical and other diverse meaning of peace is beyond the remit of our discussion (See Wiberg 1981), we can nevertheless draw on the field of peace research in order to alert us to the nature of the debate. One of the contributions made by peace research as a field has been to move the discussion on the meaning of peace forward through Johan Galtung's division between positive peace and negative peace (1964; 1969). 'Negative peace' essentially refers to the absence of direct violence, especially the absence of inter-state war at the international level. The importance of conceptualizing peace at the international level has been given further thought by Kenneth Boulding, who drew on Galtung's concept of peace to develop his own idea of 'stable peace' (Boulding 1991. Also see Boulding 1977). While from these perspectives a state of no-war internationally can be regarded as 'peace' the idea of positive peace takes the discussion further. It was initially viewed by Galtung in terms of the 'integration of human society' (1964: 2), but later came to be linked to the need to tackle issues of inequality, disparity and underdevelopment at the international level as seen in the call to address indirect or structural violence. In short, as the warless condition of negative peace may not be just, equal or even desirable, the concept of positive peace brings into purview the North South structural division between the developed and developing world, which would remain hidden under the rubric of peace as negative peace. This lack of development thus represents structural violence against the South leading to calls for the eradication of such inequality as a focus of concern for peace research (Galtung 1969). Herein lies one of the political implications of the emergence of the division between negative and positive peace.

These inter-related ideas of negative peace, stable peace and positive peace, which can be traced back to the evolution of the debates about the nature of the field in peace research during especially the 1960s and 1970s, have political implications in terms of the sites and agency for peace activities. As far as negative peace and stable peace at the international level is concerned, of central importance is the need to reduce the possibility of direct violence and inter-state war. To this end, the state becomes one of the main agents for reducing the possibility of war, at the same time as it remains the main agent in the prosecution of war. The point is illustrated by the well-worn adage of the late fourth century Roman writer Vegitius, 'if you want peace, prepare for war.' This dual role highlights the dilemma faced by state actors in maintaining arms to promote peace and reducing arms to prevent war. As the state's coercive means are in this way politically contested, individual and groups of citizen have taken to the streets as a way to constrain the state's behaviour, as seen in the rise and fall of peace movements over the decades (Gleditsch 1990). What this means is that, for teachers who view the role of promoting peace through education to include inculcating attitudes and potential action to support disarmament, constraining the role of Japan's Self-Defense Forces, and protecting Article 9 of the constitution, taking to the streets is to oppose the government taking a step along the road to war, not peace. In this way, peace through education brings into view the way the state and teachers as agents involved in the education of future generations diverge politically: building up the military and strengthening the alliance can be seen as for 'peace' or 'war.'

This point becomes particularly salient in cases where the legitimacy of the use of the coercive means of violence to achieve peace has been undermined, as in the case of the popular rejection of militarism in postwar Japan (Hook 1996). In the wake of Japan's defeat in the Asia Pacific war, the United States occupation forces at first set about the task of demilitarizing and democratizing both state and society. In the face of the perceived threat from communism, however, within a few years the self-same occupation authorities came to place greater priority on integrating Japan into the US-led anti-communist alliance, as evidenced by the creation of the National Police Reserve in 1950 (the precursor of the Self-Defense Forces established in 1954) and the signing of the US-Japan security treaty in 1951. But not before Article 9 of the postwar constitution, the famous 'peace clause,' had been promulgated a few years earlier and the delegitimization of military power had started to sink roots in Japanese society. Already in the early postwar years, then, demilitarization and Article 9 of the constitution as a way to promote inter-state peace at the international level, on the one hand, and the gradual build up of the military and the signing of an alliance treaty with the United States, on the other, made peace through education a politically divisive and contested issue, not one enjoying a consensus at the state and societal levels.

Looking back to the early postwar years, we can see how this contestation over peace through education led to the broadening of the scope of activities for peace carried out by Japanese teachers. The point is illustrated by the role of the Japan Teachers' Federation (*Nikkyōso*) from the late 1940s and early 1950s, should be when members of the union took to the streets in order to participate in the anti-security treaty protests and organized a range of conferences and workshops on issues of war and peace. To teachers, peace through education, as the slogan used at the time highlights, 'Don't send our pupils to war again!', meant action on the streets to oppose the security policy of the Yoshida Shigeru government, as well as education in the classroom to inculcate attitudes and potentially action to promote peace. As far as the agency of teachers is concerned, then, peace through education is intimately linked to peace through political action: the sites for activities to promote peace are both the streets and the classrooms.

As touched on above, this is especially important as official textbooks used at junior high and senior high school must be approved by the Ministry of Education following the institutionalization of the textbook certification system in 1946. As school textbooks act as an instrument for the state to promote a specific understanding and memory of the past among the next generation, a lack of political consensus on the past can be expected to lead to disputes over the content of the textbooks. Indeed, issues related to war and peace as dealt with in school textbooks have stirred controversy many times during the postwar era. The point is illustrated by the existence of competing views on Japan's role in the Asia Pacific war, with textbooks certified by the ministry over time coming to paint a more positive, nationalistic view of the nation, rather than the details of Japanese aggression and crimes. The case of Ienaga Saburo's history textbook and his detailed treatment of the Asia Pacific war as a war of aggression is the most salient case of the different political views of the war adopted by an historian and the ministry officials involved in the certification process (Selden and Nozaki 2009). Ienaga went on to fight a long court battle over calls to change some of the content of his history textbooks by the ministry's bureaucrats (For details, see Nozaki 2008).

But issues related to the treatment of the Asia Pacific war in school textbooks are not simply a domestic issue between the Japan Teachers' Federation and MEXT. As seen particularly from the 1980s onwards, the Asia Pacific war has become the source of a number of diplomatic disputes between the Japanese government and the governments of China and South Korea. During the era of the Nakasone Yasuhiro government, for instance, the revision of school textbooks through the certification system led to the expression the 'invasion' (*shinryaku*) of China being changed to 'advanced' (*shinshutsu*) into China. Clearly, 'advanced' is a euphemistic expression seeking to obfuscate Japan's aggressive war, rather than an expression evoking the clear sense of Japan as an aggressor against China, as in the case of 'invasion.' The Chinese government made a diplomatic protest in response to the usage of the expression in the newly certified textbooks. A range of other issues relating to peace and war have arisen in the intervening year, including disputes over the numbers killed in the 'Nanjing massacre,' reference to so-called the Korean and other 'comfort women' serving Japanese troops, and the role of Japan's Unit 731 in conducting biological experiments in China. In other words, as one of the key sites for promoting peace through education is the school classroom, and the instrument used to teach in the classroom is the school textbook, the content of especially history textbooks has become a deeply political question, reflecting the lack of consensus on the meaning and memory of the Asia Pacific war in Japan (Cave 2013).

In this way, peace through education has pitted the teachers in the classroom and on the streets with the bureaucrats of MEXT and the government more generally. Such politicization of school textbooks, culminating in the publication in

2002 of a revisionist history textbook by a neo-nationalist group, the Japanese Society for History Textbook Reform (*Atarashii rekishi kyōkasho o tsukurukai*), took the dispute over the memory of the war to a new level. The group published its own textbook, approved by MEXT, as part of the members' strong opposition to the way existing textbooks dealt with the Nanjing massacre, the 'comfort women' serving Japanese troops and other aspects of the war (Soh 2008). While the reform group's textbook has not been used by many schools (Szczepanska 2014: 64), its publication illustrates how textbooks continue to be an important site of political conflict over the memory of the Asia Pacific war to be instilled in the next generation. What we see here is how the teacher's role in promoting peace through education is constrained by the state as a result of the power of MEXT to authorize or, as some would argue, censor, school textbooks as part of a political project to remake Japan.

From the 1980s onwards, the continuing struggle within the classroom to promote peace through education was complemented by education for peace outside of the classroom, not as peace action on the streets, as touched on above, but as educational trips for school children (*shūgaku ryokō*). The sites visited on these school trips can be understand as educational 'dark tourism' (Lennon and Foley 2006), that is, educational visits to sites representing the manifestation of inhuman acts, as illustrated by tourists visiting Auschwitz in Poland, the Killing Fields in Cambodia and similar 'dark' sites. Within Japan, educational dark tourism for school children can be seen in visits to the atomic-bombed cities of Hiroshima and Nagasaki as well as to the site of the land war in mainland Japan, the Battle of Okinawa. While the original purpose of the Meiji institutionalization of educational trips for school children was to instil nationalism in the pupils (Selden and Nozaki 2009), these trips to the atom-bombed cities as well as to Okinawa offer a way for school teachers to inculcate attitudes and potentially action to promote peace. For such dark tourism is not simply about war in the past, but takes on political meaning in the present, too.

The political implications of dark tourism can be found in the link between these dark sites from the past and the present-day Japanese government's security policy. The decision of the Yoshida government to pursue a security policy based on signing the US-Japan security treaty and building up the defence forces was in essence a confirmation of Japan's acceptance of Vegitius's dictum, 'if you want peace, prepare for war.' For despite the existence of article 9 of the constitution, subsequent governments have gradually built up the military and increased security cooperation with the United States, as illustrated most recently by the passage of legislation by the Abe Shinzō administration to support Japan's participation in collective self-defense. With varying degrees of emphasis, this basic policy of maintaining the nuclear alliance with the United States and building up the Self-Defense Forces has continued as the security policy of Japan to this day. This security policy accepts the logic of peace through deterrence, premised on America's potential use of nuclear weapons to defend Japan, on the one hand, and the existence and operation of US military installations in Japan, overwhelmingly concentrated in Okinawa prefecture, on the other.

In this way, dark tourism about the past is deeply intertwined with the politics of the present, whether through visits to the sites of the atomic bombings or visits to the sites associated with the Battle of Okinawa. In the case of educational trips to Hiroshima and Nagasaki, the efforts made to promote peace by deepening the pupils' understanding of the effects of the atomic bombings in terms of the human costs and the destruction caused by the bombs can play a political role in the present. For visiting the atomic destruction of 1945 may serve as a catalyst for the pupils to question the present security policy of the Japanese government, which relies on nuclear weapons. While nuclear deterrence offers legitimacy for the existence but non-use of these weapons, it is precisely based on the latent potential for use that nuclear weapons exist. In this sense, the educational trips to Hiroshima and Nagasaki offer evidence of what could happen in the future, not simply in the past. Similarly, given the location of US military installations close to population centres in Okinawa, educational visits to the prefecture to learn about the Battle of Okinawa bring school children into face-to-face contact with the existence and operation of US bases in Japan. Such exposure to the 'dark' side of these outposts of American military power, as illustrated by the incidents of crimes committed by US military personnel, including violence and the rape of local women, as well as accidents arising from the operation of the bases, as seen in the case of the 2004 crash of a Sea Stallion helicopter into Okinawa International University, highlights how the alliance with the United States involves risks and costs to the Okinawans. In this sense, visits to Hiroshima and Nagasaki offer the opportunity for pupils to reflect on the politics of the nuclear element of the government's security policy, whereas visits to Okinawa offer the opportunity for them to reflect on the politics of the presence of US conventional forces in Japan.

Conclusion

The above discussion of peace through education in Japan has demonstrated how the lack of consensus on key issues of peace and war, as illustrated by the controversy over the treatment of the Asia Pacific war in school textbooks, is political in nature. This means that, in the face of the power of the state, the key agents for carrying out the day-to-day teaching about peace in the classroom, school teachers, are constrained in their role as educators due to the Ministry of Education's certification of textbooks for use in schools. This role is political as the ministry is seeking to promote a specific memory and understanding of the past, even though the past remains contested. We have seen how changes in the description of the war in textbooks and the certification of a nationalistic textbook have led to both domestic and international controversies. These controversies have arisen especially in relation to the treatment of the Asia Pacific War in history textbooks, such as the description of Japan's aggressive war in China as an 'advance,' the Nanjing massacre, the comfort women, and so on. At the same time, though, teachers from the very start have viewed the scope of peace through education to be not only teaching in the classroom, but protests in the streets, too, as symbolized in the early postwar era by the slogan, 'Don't send our pupils to war again!'. While the classrooms and the streets provide the two key sites for promoting peace through education, educational dark tourism to Hiroshima and Nagasaki as well as to Okinawa has come to offer another site for educational activity, potentially linking the history of the past to the politics of the present by encouraging pupils to ask: What are the political implications of a security treaty based on the potential use of nuclear weapons, on the one hand, and the deployment of American military forces posing risks and imposing costs on Okinawans, on the other? It is in the political contestation growing out of activities in all three sites of peace through education that we find the significance of learning about the past for generations of pupils looking towards the future.

References

Boulding, Kenneth (1977) "Twelve friendly quarrels with Johan Galtung," *Journal of Peace Research*, 14 (1): 75–86.

Boulding, Kenneth (1991) "Stable peace among nations: a learning process," in Elise Boulding, C. Brigagao and Keving Clements (eds.) *Peace, Culture and Society: transnational research and dialogue*, Boulder, CO: Westview Press, pp. 108–14.

Cave, Peter (2013) "Japanese colonialism and the Asia-Pacific War in Japan's history textbooks: changing representations and their causes," *Modern Asian Studies*, 47 (2): 542–80.

Galtung, Johan (1964) "An Editorial," *Journal of Peace Research*, 1 (1): 1–4.

Galtung, Johan (1969) "Violence, peace and peace research," *Journal of Peace Research*, 6 (3): 167–91.

Gleditsch, Nils Peter (1990) "The rise and decline of the new peace movement," in K. Kodma and U Vesa (eds.) *Towards a Comparative Analysis of Peace Movements*, Aldershot: Dartmouth Publishing.

Hook, Glenn D. (1996) *Militarization and Demilitarization in Japan*, London: Routledge.

Lennon, John and Malcolm Foley (2006) *Dark Tourism* (London: Thomson).

Nozaki, Yoshiko (2008) War Memory, Nationalism and Education in Postwar Japan, 1945–2007, London: Routledge.

Selden, Mark and Yoshiko Nozaki (2009) "Japanese textbook controversies, nationalism, and historical memory: intra- and inter-national conflicts," *The Asia-Pacific Journal. Japan Focus* 7 (24) 5. Available online at: http://apjjf.org/-Mark-Selden/3173/article.html. Accessed 8 July 2017.

Szczepanska, Kamila (2014) *The Politics of Memory in Japan: Progressive Civil Society*

Groups and Contestation of Memory of the Asia-Pacific War, Abingdon, Oxon: Routledge.

Soh, Sarah (2008) *The Comfort Women: sexual violence and postcolonial memory in Korea and Japan*, Chicago: University of Chicago Press.

Wiberg, Hakan (1981) "What have we learnt about peace?" *Journal of Peace Research*, 18 (2): 111–48.

Chapter 2

The Significance of Health among Human Conditions in Asian Communities:
Peace through Education

Eiji Makino (Hosei University, Japan)

Introduction

1. Purpose

The main purpose of this paper is to demonstrate that the health essential for Asian community development is a human condition that involves the integration of various cultural values.

2. Discussion

a. Clarification of the characteristics and limitations of common-sense/medical concepts of health

b. Philosophical and ethical examination of health based on the relationships linking nature, culture and people

c. Elucidation of the important roles played by peace, shelter, education, food, income, a stable eco-system, sustainable resources, social justice and equity as prerequisites for health

1. Ordinary Understanding of Health

1. Definition of health

a. "Health is a state of complete physical, mental and social well-being and not merely the absence of disease or infirmity." (Constitution of the World Health Organization (WHO))

b. Primary set of criteria for health definition – for individuals: no disease, good appetite, regular bowel movements, sound sleep, physical strength, absence of fatigue issues, solid functioning of the immune system, good posture/balance, normal physical development

c. Secondary set of criteria for health definition – for groups: indicators such as average life expectancy, mortality, neonatal and infant mortality rates, perinatal mortality rate, maternal mortality rate, morbidity rate, prevalence rate

2. Further definition based on the WHO Constitution

a. "(Enjoyment of the highest attainable standard of) health is one of the fundamental rights of every human being without distinction of race, religion, political belief, economic or social condition."

b. Thus, health is a fundamental human right.

c. To enjoy health, people need to be free from discrimination based on race, religion, political belief and economic or social conditions.

▶ 2. Philosophical Examination of Health: Consideration of Hans-Georg Gadamer's *The Enigma of Health*

1. The essence of health lies in its inherent mystery ("*Verborgenheit der Gesundheit*").

a. Health does not actually present itself to us. One can attempt to establish standard values for health.

b. The attempt to impose these standard values on a healthy individual would only result in making that person ill.

2. The characteristics of health: Health is a condition of inner accord.

a. Health is the rhythm of life, a permanent process in which equilibrium re-establishes itself.

b. It is not merely the phenomenon of human health, which almost cries out to be understood in terms of the natural conditions of equilibrium.

3. Destruction of health and destruction of nature

a. The natural conditions of equilibrium irreversibly destroy natural, social and human environments.

b. Science and technology, which cause uncontrollable situations, destroy the health of all living beings.

4. Challenges facing philosophers

a. Philosophers should not excessively focus on individual health-related phenomena or be constrained by causality in natural science.

b. Philosophers should encourage the awareness of a hidden harmony (*"eine verborge Harmonie"*) to bring about a form of protected composure (*"Geborgenheit"*).

5. Issues with Gadamer's views on health

a. The natural world is beyond human control due to catastrophic events such as devastating earthquakes, massive tsunamis and other natural disasters as well as serious man-made incidents.

b. Questioning of Gadamer's views: The concept of natural balance does not hold.

c. Health and its sustainability are not limited to relations with nature.

3. Prerequisites for Health

1. Eight fundamental conditions and resources are necessary for good health.

2. These are: a. peace, b. shelter, c. education, d. food, e. income, f. a stable eco-system, (g) sustainable resources, and h. social justice and equity.

a. Peace is the most important prerequisite for health.

b. Shelter is the smallest unit of social organization – the home – and offers physical and psychological comfort.

c. Education should satisfy the basic requirements for personal development, and includes moral, intellectual and physical types. To become educated, people must be healthy or have the capacity to be healthy.

d. Food is a fundamental prerequisite not only for survival but also for the achievement and maintenance of healthy growth as desirable for humans.

e. Income is an indispensable part of meeting the aforementioned prerequisites, and is a fundamental condition for economic self-sufficiency.

f. A stable eco-system is essential for the protection of humans against living, social and natural environments that threaten health.

g. Resource sustainability also requires the securement and supply of natural, material and human resources. To maintain health, a background of secure, stable day-to-day living and vibrant corporate activity is essential.

h. Social justice and equity serve as guiding principles in meeting the health prerequisites outlined in a. to g. above on a variety of levels ranging from individual to community considerations, and further to national and international levels.

4. Conclusions

(1) Health as a prerequisite for regular social function is a universal value that underlies various other values.

(2) Health as part of the human condition is inseparable from nature, culture and day-to-day living.

(3) Asian community development requires maintenance of the health conditions that underlie various ethnic/racial groups and cultures.

References

Anderson-Gold, Sharon, Progress and Prophecy. The Case for a Cosmopolitan History. In: J Rohbeck und H. Nagel-Docekal (Hersg.), *Geschichtsphilosophie und Kulturkritik*.Darmstadt 2003.

Beck, Ulrich, *Der kosmopolitische Blick oder: Krieg ist Frieden*. Frankfurt a. M. 2004.

Daniels, N., Kennedy, Bruce P. and Kawachi, Ichiro, *Is Inequality Bad for Our Health?*

Beacon Press, 2000.
Eagleton, Terry, *Idea of Culture*, Blackwell, 2000.
Ekardt, Felix, *Das Prinzip Nachhaltigkeit. Generationengerechtigkeit und globale Gerechtigkeit*, München 2005, 2. Aufl.
_____, *Theorie der Nachhaltigkeit. Rechtliche, ethische und polotische Zugänge – am Beispiel von Klimawandel, Ressourcenknappheit und Welthandel*. Baden-Baden 2011.
Evanoff, Richard, *Bioregionalism and Global Ethics*. Routledge, New York, 2011.
Featherstone, Mike, *Undoing Culture: Globalization, Postmodernism and Identity*, London 1995.
Gadamer, H.-G., *Über die Verborgenheit der Gesundheit*, Frankfurt a. M. 1993.
Held , David and McGrew, Anthony, *Globalization / Anti-Globalization*, Oxford 2002.
Koskenniemi, M., 'International Law and Hegemony: A Reconfiguration,' 17 *Cambridge Review of International Affairs* 2004.
Makino, Eiji, *Philosophy of Sustainability*, Housei U. P. 2013.
_____, Weltbürgertum und die Kritik an der postkolonialen Vernunft. In: Bacin, S., Ferrarin, A., Ra Rocca, C., Ruffing, M., (Hrsg.) *Kant und die Philosophie in weltbürgerlicher Absicht*, Bd.1. De Gruyter, Berlin/ Boston, 2013.
Nagel, Thomas, The Problem of Global Justice, in: *Philosopy and Public Affairs*, 33. 2005.
Scanlon, T., *What We Owe to Each Other*, Harvard U.P.1998.
Spivak, Gayatri Chakravorty, *A Critique of Postcolonial Reason*, Harvard U. P., 1999.
Vattimo, Gianni, *Vocazione e responsabilità del filosofo*, Genova 2000.
Welman, C., *The Language of Ethics*, H.U.P., 1961.

*Eiji Makino, Professor of Department of Philosophy, Hosei University, Tokyo, Japan

Section 2

Reports of the course on Asian Community

Chapter 3
Interculturalism in Communication and Education in the Courses of the One Asia Foundation

Asunción López-Varela (Universidad Complutense Madrid, Spain)

Abstract

This paper presents a paradigm for research on intercultural relations in education. In collaboration with the One Asia Foundation, Studies on Intermediality and Intercultural Mediation SIIM at Complutense University Madrid looks at 'cultural products' as fundamental connective links between all sectors of society. The program explores interculturalism at various levels: international, global, cosmopolitan, and cross-disciplinary. SIIM focuses on theory, method and application, looking at cultural expressions as connected to and dependent on other forms, situations, and activities of human expression.[1]

1. Introduction

The recognition of culture as a form of semiotic transference paves the way for the study of interculturalism in education. Each culture has its own semiotic traditions (from the Greek *sēmeiōsis,* i.e., observation of (burial) signs and (medical) symptoms). These include specific forms of social communication and representation (that preserve historical memory). Semiotics deals with the study and interpretation of signs (indexes, icons, symbols), both in artificially constructed languages (i.e. mathematical languages, computer codes, etc.) and in natural languages. In its more global dimension, semiotics implies the study of cross-cultural communication and representation.

Human culture is dependent on masses of signs and inherently social shared meanings. Communication requires the consciousness of more than one subject, that is, it is intersubjective.[2] The term 'culture' ('cultura' in other EU languages) comes from ancient Latin. Initially, it referred to the cultivation of land, indicating a system of shared codes and patterns that helped humans settle in particular environments during the Neolithic period. Although originally these patterns focused on land organization, the word 'cultivated' maintains a meaning that refers to a way of thinking and living in agreement with normative and (educational) instructional aspects. More recently, the concept of 'culture' has come add all other aspects shared by a group/community (i.e. background, civilization, custom, ethnicity, ethos, philosophy, society, tradition, values) and to the forms by means of which these aspects are represented (art, literature, music, architecture, scientific theories, and so on).[3]

Thus, intercultural or cross-cultural communication and representations point to the effort of crossing over and meeting other cultures. This effort becomes particularly significant when exploring the differences between Eastern and Western world views. Although this paper traces a possible route to explore cross-cultural meaning-making in the educational context, the study of intercultural relationships is also very relevant to communities of international professionals, migrant workers, international enterprises, and so on.

2. Theoretical Background

1. The impact of technology on cross-cultural communication

In traditional oral cultures, signs and meanings were less easily transported across space and time. During the latter half of the 20th-century, however, faster and cheaper international transportation, together with the growth of media technology, have expanded the stream of human signs and meanings. In the past, printed formats, in the form of manuscripts and books and their translations, contributed to move and re-locate cultural representations to other world locations. The advancement of technology has made information and communication cross-culturally accessible. First it was the telegraph and the telephone, later radio, television and radio. More recently, the Internet and digitalization.

Paradoxically, and perhaps also as a consequence, the mobility of information is not always accompanied by an increase in intersubjective, intercultural communication. Virtual communities such as blogs and social networks like Youtube, Twitter, Facebook, Instagram, etc. create, distribute and receive cultural meanings at the trans-territorial level of cyberspace. But many critical voices claim that the exchange of diverse meanings and varied sign systems across the World Wide Web or through the use of modern cell-phones has, in fact, contributed to the disentanglement of the bonds that have traditionally joined people together.[4]

Mobility can be considered a key semiotic feature in the new educational paradigm. Meanings are no longer simple categorisations. They are processes that occur in a variety of combinations that include cultural, ethnic, gender, and class aspects. Therefore, contemporary identities are made up of a repertoire of features which are mobilized and converted into speaking positions with performative (actional) power. A crucial question is whether or not cross-cultural education serves communities at all levels (local, national and international). The second question concerns the tools required to include this kind of education in the classrooms.

In order to answer the first question we need to look at how cross-cultural change can be organized in the following levels: (1) the microenvironment (private space: dwelling-place, work space, offices, private gardens, etc.); (2) the level of proximate environments (semi-public space, blocks of flats and their immediate surroundings, parks, green spaces, etc.); (3) the public environment level, involving built spaces (villages, towns, cities; for a study of urban environments and the natural environment (the countryside, landscape, etc.); (4) the level of the global environment (the environment in its totality, both built and natural) that also includes natural resources and, of course (5) the virtual level of a hypothetical 'webness' in cyberspace. The common denominator across the 5 levels is the fact that cross-cultural communication depends on the understanding of other people's set of values.[5]

The second question concerns the pragmatic aspects of the research presented; that is, what tools can help improve intercultural competences in educational environments.

2. Emotions and Values

Increasingly mobile and transient societies present the need for people to understand others who they may find, not only very different from themselves, but also holding attitudes and beliefs which may be difficult to accept. This kind of understanding across differences in value systems requires positive empathy. The sharing of emotionally charged information (values) encourages pro-active cooperative behaviours. How exactly does this complex process occur? How do emotions like love, joy, hatred, sadness, fear, shame and so on become charged with positive or negative connotations that can facilitate or prevent intercultural cooperation?

The significance of emotions and their impact upon daily life has engaged thinkers for millennia. The earliest medical theories (Egyptian and Mesopotamian) related affective changes to deficiencies in bodily substances that created emotional imbalances. The Greek physician Hippokrates of Kos (c.460–c.370 BCE) developed the theory of the humours, positing a relation between an excess or a lack of any of four distinct bodily fluids that would presumably influence human temperament. For Aristotle (384–322 BCE) emotions derive not just from the interactions of body substances but also from human actions and interactions with the surrounding world. Aristotle's notion of *eudaimonia* (*"eu"*="good" and *"daimōn"*="spirit") relates happiness and virtue. Aristotle understood virtues not just as essential dispositions to act in a certain way (i.e. honesty, compassion, generosity, etc.), but as complex mindsets that encompass individual and social desires, values, attitudes, interests, expectations and so on. Galen of Pergamon (c.129–200 CE) based his studies upon Aristotelian and Epicurean sources. Also inspired by Aristotle, the Persian doctor Ibn Sinā (Avicenna 980-1037) related the four elements of cosmos (earth, water, air, fire) to sensible qualities (hot, cold, wet, and dry) and to his theory of 'four temperaments,' which also included the mental aspects of self-awareness and action as well as emotional and ethical attitudes.

In ancient China, the so-called 'five elements or agents' (*WŭXíng*) a conceptual scheme found for instance in the *Mawangdui Silk Texts* (c.168 BCE) is still used to explain a wide array of phenomena (cosmic cycles, the interaction between internal organs, or changes in political regimes). Unlike the Greek concern with substances, *WŭXíng* refers to natural processes that relate temporary states in nature and associated patterns of behaviour: Wood (Spring/growth), Fire (Summer/flowering), Earth (late-Summer/fruition), metal (Fall/harversting), and Water (Winter/retreat & storage). Each phase feeds the next and, based on a particular directional energy flow between phases, interactions can be expansive, destructive, or exhaustive.

The fundamental reason for the importance of emotions in all areas of research is the fact that they are at the chore of human experience. Discerning emotions engages an interdisciplinary discussion that has preoccupied philosophers, political theorists, ethical thinkers, psychologists or scientists.[6] In Western cultures, the dominant social patterns view them as 'substances', place emphasis on positive emotions and minimize negative ones. Grounded on Taoism and Buddhism, the Asian cultures of China, Japan or India view emotions as 'processes' seeking a balance between positive and negative.

Emotions are experienced mentally as discrete, consistent and coordinated sets of responses to internal or external events with a particular significance for the organism (values). These responses range from the physical (facial, verbal, gestures and so on) to unconscious physiological expressions (sweat, pupil dilation etc.). Persistent emotions might induce particular behavioural patterns and action tendencies (shyness, fury...). The mental representations of emotions after they occur are termed 'feelings'. Moods are less intense and diffuse affective states.[7]

Emotions are the substance of values. Values are human qualities which attribute relative importance to what we think, what we say and what we do. They can be individual as well as culturally shared, and they are experienced as emotional energy that finds expression in the priorities we set, and the choices we make. Partly genetically inherited, values are mostly culturally developed in our lifetime, whether consciously or unconsciously. In order to make them evident to us and to others, they need to be transformed into conscious awareness so that, in socialization, we can align them with those of other people's. In the case of multicultural groups, these alignment requires specific strategies and skills that need to be learnt.

3. Research Methods: Intercultural Values and Education

The process of analysing one's own values is a prerequisite for understanding others. Intercultural relations are dependent on culture, age, sex, social class, etc., all of which condition our perspective or point of view. Intercultural relations also proceed in contexts marked by ever evolving socio-economic conditions.

Intercultural awareness may be defined as the tuning of one's own behaviour according to the comprehension and communication with other cultures. It needs to be developed through adequate educational programs which emphasize learning in a climate of cross-cultural acceptance, trust and care for others. By analysing their own cultural perspective in an active way, students become more intercultural aware. One example is the blog created by students from different nationalities and cultures who discuss varied intercultural aspects in relation to living in Madrid city.[8]

Another approach used in SIIM to make students more culturally aware is 'intercultural shock', based on contact with students from diverse cultural backgrounds. As the global educational context is increasing multinational, it is not difficult to find students from diverse ethnic groups and cultures taking the same course. One example is the course on Asian Studies funded by the One Asia Foundation.[9] A shock is a kind of miscommunication or 'clash' resulting from cultural differences; in particular, with regards to the stranger aspects. It functions as a mirror, making students aware of self-differences. SIIM classroom uses intercultural conflict movies Bend it Like Beckham (2002) Syriana (2005), Crash (2004), Mississippi Masala (1991) or Persepolis (2007) to trigger awareness, as well as contextualizing lectures.

Although observing and listening help students to understand, they are not sufficient for the development of empathy. Here training is directed to asking questions that go beyond passive forms of learning. Group work discussion and negotiation in a multicultural classroom is an efficient method to help different cultural values emerge to the surface. In SIIM we use a 'Design Thinking' methodology in the following steps: 1: Teaching students to look at the own cultural background using the own culture as the point of reference. 2: Teaching students to be aware of how their own culture is seen by classmates from different cultural backgrounds. 3: Teaching students to see other classmates' values various perspectives (not just their own point of view). 4: Teaching students to be aware of how people from other cultures are seen.

While 'Design Thinking' methodology is good in the first stages of the process, SIIM also relies on the use of visual organizers to help get beyond the more abstract symbolic forms of language. Visual organizers rely on icons and indexes (pointers), that is, signs that have a closer resemblance to the reality they represent (i.e. maps, pictures, gestures and non-verbal language). With roots in schema theory, visual organizers allow the processing of information meaningfully across the following categories: cyclical, hierarchical, sequential and conceptual. For instance, concept diagrams can describe a concept/value and its relationships; story maps assist in integrating previous and existing knowledge, make predictions and summarize key points, helping manage data quickly and easily; Venn diagrams are a wonderful tool to compare concepts and values. They use two joined bubbles with different concepts/values and converge in the middle showing some characteristics in common. A network tree is composed by several bubbles growing from the top to the bottom, making clear the difference between super-ordinate and subordinate concepts; spider maps also serve to establish relationships in terms of priorities, rather than hierarchies. Problem-solving visual organizers facilitate the organization of information according to dimensions such as high/low or less/more, etc.

Using visual organizers, participant-students in SIIM intercultural-classroom are envisioned as trees. The branches of the tree are the visible appearance of values. They are shown in the differences and similarities between ourselves and others (skin, hair, body built, eye colour, tastes, everyday habits, etc.): the trunk the observed attitudes (i.e. the way people move, their greetings, the way the talk, how the show emotions, etc.); the roots are ingrained cultural values that can be inferred from the appearance and from the observed attitudes and reactions. This can be seen in the video student created with the tree-symbol.[10]

Attention to the communicative context involves physical (i.e. the degree of proximity when people engage in conversation), psychological (i.e. how pre-established conceptions about different cultures influence our attitudes to others), and social aspects (i.e. interrelations between participants). In this part, SIIM employs "Learning by Doing" and "Experiential Learning" based on real practice (Living UniLab Project) with NGOs.[11]

Finally, the class focuses on the frame of reference of each participant, that is, the power position from which they observe and act. This is built in socialization processes within the family and different reference groups such as educational environments. It is based on sex differences, urban-rural background, education, culture, etc. The building of understanding and empathy requires that student learn to shift their frame of reference and place themselves in other people's place. Students learn this through the use of storytelling techniques and problem solving activities in experiential learning.

4. The Results

The above methods for the instruction of intercultural awareness are tested by a) a pre-survey b) the implementation of the described methods enhancing intercultural awareness; c) a post-survey. N° of students attending the Asian Studies course in Spring 2017 was 31

Limitations include: 1) the fact that understanding cultural codes that vary substantially from one's own codes can be very difficult; 2) the teacher needs to be a trained professional mediator-facilitator to be able to conduct the process; 3) sometimes, there are insufficient structural capacities at the institutional level (i.e. 'Design Thinking' requires longer temporal frameworks than ordinary

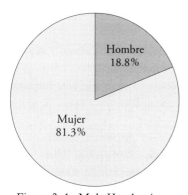

Figure 3-1 Male Hombre/ Female Mujer ratio

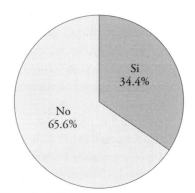

Figure 3-2 Importance of Intercultural Aspects (pre-survey)

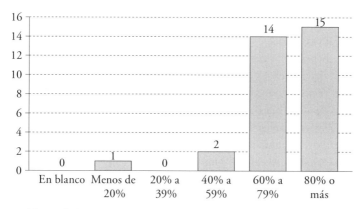

Figure 3-3 Importance of Intercultural Aspects (post-survey)

classes, and it also needs open classrooms with mobile furniture so that participants can move around freely).

Notes

1. http://www.ucm.es/siim
   K. Robins. (Ed.). *The Challenge of Transcultural Diversities: Cultural Policy and Cultural Diversity*. Strasbourg: Council of Europe Publishing, 2006.
2. A. López-Varela. "Exploring Intercultural Relations from the Intersubjective Perspectives through Creative Art in Multimodal Formats". *Lexia. Revista di Simiotica 5–6*, 2010, 125–147.
3. G. Hofstede *Culture's Consequences, Comparing Values, Behaviours, Institutions, and Organisations across Nations*. Thousand Oaks CA: Sage Publications, 2001
   G. Kress."Thinking about the notion of 'cross-culture' from a social semiotic perspective." *Language and Intercultural Communication* 12. 4, 2012, 369–385.
4. A. López-Varela Webness Revisted. *A Pleasure of Life in Words: A Festschrift for Angela Downing*. Ed.Carretero *et al*. Madrid: Universidad Complutense. Vol.2, 2006, 513–33.
5. A. López-Varela (Ed.) Cityscapes and Semio-Cultural Industries. International Journal of the Humanities. Commonground Publishing. University of Illinois Research Park, 2014.
6. M. C.Nussbaum, *Upheavals of Thought: The Intelligence of Emotions*. Cambridge Univ. Press, 2001.
7. K. R. Scherer "What are emotions? And how can they be measured?" *Social Science Information* 44, 2005, 693–727.
8. https://oneasiafoundationmadrid.wordpress.com/
9. https://www.ucm.es/siim/one-asia-foundation-cross-cultural-partnerships
   https://www.ucm.es/siim/one-asia-foundation-2017-webinars-and-lectures
10. https://www.youtube.com/watch?v=7Cee9p1RaN0
11. https://iyfspain.wordpress.com/

Chapter 4

Practice of "Asian Community Theory"

Xu Shoutong (Sanya University)

University of Sanya is a comprehensive university with more than 20, 000 students, located in Sanya on Hainan Island, the southernmost tip of China. The "Asian Community Theory" course at University of Sanya is sponsored by School of Law and Sociology where I belong (which was named as "School of Social Development" at the time of application for course). It is the first time that the "Asian Community Theory" course was held in Hainan Island and it is also the ninth university who has offered this course in China.

1. History of the "Asian Community Theory" course at University of Sanya

The "Asian Community Theory" course was started in October 2012. Originally scheduled in September one month before, unfortunately it was encountered that the Japanese government announced to nationalize Diaoyudao Islands (Japan: Senkaku Islands). Then the Chinese government took quick response and led to limited exchange activities with Japan in various fields. As a result, we could not proceed as planned. The lecturers who were supposed to attend this course from outside the island could not make it and we had to cancel the air tickets. Although it was reopened in October, since the course was unable to hold it public in campus, it was still a challenge to invite students and teachers to the hotel conference room near the university where the lecturers stay.

However, since it was impossible for us to hold the lecture in the hotel forever, it was suspended after we gained understanding from foundation side. Fortunately, we were able to obtain permission from the university side at the end of April of the following year and began full-scale courses from May. In the meantime, it is believed that the faculty never gave up the negotiation with the relevant departments has make an achievement.

2. Current results and problems

In University of Sanya, "Asian Community Theory" lecture was initiated in the fall of 2012 and has been carried out five times continuously up to 2017. Up to date, there are only four universities that have offered this course more than five times in China, and University of Sanya belongs to one of them. The lecture theme is "Asian Community Theory - from the past and present perspective of East Asia" for the first year, "Asian Community and Asian Social Development" from the second to fourth year, "Asian Community Theory - Aiming for Reconciliation and Symbiosis" for the fifth year. It became a regular subject (elective subject) of the university from the third year, when all the students in the university were able to take this course. On the other hand, due to the limited number of elective courses compared to general subjects in the university, separate courses were set up to compensate for at least 15 times aligning with the foundation wishes. At first, when the number of students exceeded 100, multiple classes has been adopted. After it became a regular subject of the university, the number of students who attended the course remains between 60 and 80.

In the course, we were able to invite a few unnamed scholars as lecturers from Taiwan, Japan, Korea etc. besides the mainland China. In Japan alone, Yoji Sato, Foundation President; Zheng Jun-bong, Chief Researcher; Hiroshi Tanaka, professor emeritus of Hitotsubashi University; Tetsuro Kato, visiting professor of Waseda University; Toshihiko Matsuda, professor of International Research Center for Japanese Studies, etc. had made this trip. With the success by the participation of the excellent lecturers, this course has been highly recognized by the students. What's more, some students even wanted to have more similar courses. It was the first time that so many scholars gathered from the outside within such a short time in University of Sanya. The students are very happy to be able to listen to lectures from both domestic and abroad.

Besides, one time when I issued a scholarship certificate from the foundation, I mistook a student's name. Then the student asked for rewriting his name and asked the foundation to reissue it, which also proved that this course is highly valued by all the students.

It is the greatest achievement that I have built up an Asian Community and have deepened the concept for the students. Various themes have been discussed in the lectures such as Asian community and politics, economy, society and history. However, we also realized some problems. One of the problem is that the real fact has not been recognized yet sometimes. For example, part of the students believed that Japan never apologized for the history. However, I taught what was really going on, such as Japan had apologized once. Since then such subversion happened frequently.

In the third year, I posted the notification before the lecture and summary after the lecture on the website of School of Law and Sociology. An article with a photograph which shows the real-time status of the course was mainly written by students who participated and posted after checked by the writer. It was believed that this action can not only spread the content of the course widely inside and outside the campus, but can also raise the autonomous awareness of the students and help them acquire the expertise related to the "Asian Community Theory". And since the 4th year, we mainly wrote and posted the articles for lecturers outside the university.

As for current problems, the first one is that there are some students who hold doubts about whether the Asian Community can be achieved and when it will be achieved. This is probably because the Asian Community has no realities like EU and its vision has not been clearly shown up. In addition, the poor system of "Asian Community Theory" or "Asian Community" hindered students' learning. In particular, the lack of systematic professional books for

Asian Community Theory was not able to encourage the students. Such problem should be solved with the efforts of all the experts involved in this course as well as myself. At the same time, maybe it is also necessary for these experts to have a research program.

3. Participation in conventions and visiting other universities

Since I was responsible for the Asian Community Theory Course, I have participated in related conventions in Asia and sponsored by the Foundation every year, not only in domestic, but also in other countries such as Japan and Korea.

In August 2012, I went to Incheon, Korea to participate in the convention organized by One Asia Foundation for the first time. There were more than 350 scholars from more than 10 countries in the convention, like United Nations Conference. Before that, I had only participated in various symposiums organized by three countries of Japan, China and South Korea. This conference was the start for me to attend the event where many cross-nation experts gathered. Ever since then, I have participated in the convention held in Jeju, Shanghai and Phnom Penh, the number of participants both from domestic and outside the host country increased continuously. Expect for Asia, there were also several scholars from remote America and Europe. Every year at the convention, in addition to academic exchanges, we shared the updates and consolidate the personal relationship as well. Every year, new blood can be acquainted, which made the convention a place of "Gaining New Insights through Reviewing"

Meanwhile, we have received invitations to attend courses as many as we received requests to host courses from domestic and overseas universities that set up grant lectures, including domestic universities such as Zhongshan University, Zhejiang Gongshang University, Minzu University of China, Hainan University, Dalian University, Changsha University, and dozens of oversea universities such as Dankook University from Korea and Kanto Gakuin University from Japan. So that I was able to deepen the "Asian Community Theory" with local professors and auditors. Every time, various questions from local college students and graduate students were gathered, which makes me excited. Once in one university of Japan, when talked about the Kwantung Army Unit 731 who had done terrible human experiments near Harbin in China, I was surprised that there were several students with zero knowledge about this history. Although I was able to experience the actual condition of Japanese history education at that moment, I still felt that it was still very difficult to solve history problems in East Asia.

If there was no such grant lecture, I would never have had such meaningful exchanges and valuable experiences. From now on, we will continue to broaden our boundaries with these exchanges opportunities and deepen our understanding of "Community". Besides, we will also continue to work together with fellows who share the same will of achieving "Asian Community".

Finally, from the perspective of School of Law and Sociology, we will continue to utilize the Foundation's subsidies to enrich the "Asian Community Theory" class, foster rich atmosphere of "Asian Community" in university, and evoke the interests of teachers and students as many as possible. I would like to disseminate and deepen "Asian Community Theory" as further as possible and pay back to the great support from One Asia Foundation.

2017.8

Section 3

Perspectives towards an Asian Community – Part 1
Politics, Economics, Environment and Social Matters

Chapter 5

The Idea of Community and the Transformation of World Politics:

Perspectives from IR Theory

Bahadir Pehlivanturk (TOBB University of Economics and Technology)

In the last few years we witnessed many discussions about the future of the liberal world order. There seem to be a rare concurrence of ideas that it is coming to an end. Compared to a decade ago or even a few years ago this is a surprising conclusion, as the idea of the *End of History* seemed to be the dominant perception.

[1]After all, the last half of the 20th Century was marked by the rise of a liberal political world order based on market capitalism. Even though some argue that globalization is not a phenomenon of the 20th century and the world has been getting smaller since centuries, new developments in transportation and information technologies undoubtedly made the world much more connected. Sime might also argue that, end of the Cold War removed the last vestiges of serious political resistance to economic, institutional, and cultural integration of the world, thus creating a world community on neoliberal principles. The trend seems to be further accelerated by the establishment of new networks of connections that span the world thanks to social networks technology, deepening connections between people to people, people to institutions, and institutions to institutions. All these transformations were eased by the development of a large variety of global and regional international institutions, a vibrant civil society, an active media and business world, and the evolution of international law.

Then why is the liberal world order is being questioned? Developments such as the rise of nativist and populist politics in Europe and USA, the Brexit, or the emergence of regimes with authoritarian character in various countries around the world can be given as the main culprit leading way to the questioning of the liberal world order. Most analysis extensively focus on the role of USA as the creator and sustainer of the neoliberal world order. For instance, prominent scholar Joseph S. Jr. Nye argues that it was USA who saw value in devoting resources and attention to providing global public goods such as an open economy and international security, as well as maintenance of international institutions that form the base of the open world system.[2] The ideas that led to this system did not emerge suddenly. Many world events such as the conflagration of the 1930s which led to the Second World War that were preceded by the economic collapse of Great Depression gave rise to calls for a more open world system. All these experiences led the Western leaders and elite to work on the construction of a different world, which would try to see economic and security issues not as solely national concerns, but as issues needing large scale cooperation of all state and non-state actors. More importantly they have also sought to devise what we can call the seeds of a rule-based international system, hoping that this would lead to both peace and prosperity for all. Thus, the liberal international order emerged after the Second World War as a loose array of international institutions working on the principles of free trade. This system has led to the development of different types of regional communities of states. These communities such as EU and ASEAN, ostensibly had economic integration as their main mission. However, in many cases they have gone beyond economic rationalism and developed a sense of identity, transforming themselves into political and cultural communities as well, with varying levels of integration. EU, as the most successful of such community of states, has become not only a common market but a political community with a supranational character and developed a European identity as well. ASEAN, arguably a much more diverse grouping, unexpectedly developed some level of a Southeast Asian identity as well, besides its successful economic integration. There are many such community of states around the world with various levels of economic and political integration, fostering different levels of cultural sense of belongings. The relations between such regional groupings have also deepened towards what could someday be called a world community.

In almost all of the studies on integration a heavy emphasis is given to the role of United States as the main public goods provider. Thus, as the US power is challenged, as US domestic politics gives a picture of disarray, as its actions become more unpredictable and questioned, more and more it will be questioned whether these regional and global communities will survive or the idealistic conception of a world community can ever be a reality.

However one would be wrong to think that the globalization phenomenon is solely a result of a visionary conceptualization of a small number of US or Western elite. It would be a too narrow conceptualization and a too much of an actor driven approach to solely take a Western group of elite's ideologies or interests as the main drive for globalization. The world community idea and globalization are more than a USA or Western interest. There are very real and practical reasons that compel sate and non-state actors to be a part of this system, or at least cooperate with this vision.

First and foremost, it is the increase in economic, technological, and physical connectivity among actors in international relations, that made it necessary for the actors to cooperate against the reality of the global problems and threats that humanity collectively faced, such as environmental threats, large-scale migration, growing income gap, terrorism, and global financial crises, international crime, etc. Solution to these problems requires a new way of perceiving the world that can go beyond the traditional nation-state framework that we instinctively harbor, in such a way that we can expand our understanding that there is one world community spanning the globe, encompassing all national, ethnic, religious, political, and gender differences. In other words, increased connectivity creates common problems, which in turn necessitates common and coordinated policies, and which further necessitates a common conception of humankind as well.

Accompanied with technological connectivity and its results, a new way of understanding about the way that order is instituted in the world is also evolving, reflecting the necessities of cooperation. In the traditional way of thinking, it was more or less accepted and taken as a norm that disagreements could be solved by resorting to power politics. With the end-of the cold war, the expansion of international law, the strengthening of legal international structures, and the growing acceptance that world society had the obligation to protect other populations in other geographies from gross human rights abuses resulted in a new way of thinking that the world is evolving towards a rules and justice based order, rather than a power-based order.

The power-based perspective is best covered in what is called the Realist approach to international relations.[3] The starting point of Realism is that, international system has an anarchical structure. It accepts states as the major actors, and what is meant by anarchy is that there is no authority above the states to impose rules. This character of the system compels states to act as units that deem selfish calculations of national interest above anything else. According to Realists sustainable cooperation in such an environment is very difficult because survival becomes the major goal for the states, influencing their behavior. In such a world, excellence in calculated power politics becomes the major asset, pushing states towards an incessant struggle for power and influence where conflict is unavoidable and cooperation an exception. Together with these, the concept of power is also understood mostly in military terms or in terms of capacities such as population, territory, economic and technological progress, etc., which again reflect themselves as the basis of military prowess.[4] In harsher approaches in Realism it is argued that the elusive nature of power and the unresolvable insecurities of great powers would further create heightened conflicts and a perpetual series of crisis between great powers that makes the idea of perpetual peace among nations all but an utopia.[5] In Realism there is not much room for the idea of a community of states beyond temporary arrangements required by the necessities of balance of power politics, which are doomed to failure as the power balance in the world changes.

However not all international relations approaches have such a bleak outlook on the possibility of cooperation. Liberal theories, especially the Neoliberal variant, while acknowledging that the anarchical character of the international system makes cooperation among states difficult, argues that it can still be achieved. First of all, Neoliberals see a multitude of actors in the international system. While states are still the major actor, international organizations, multinational companies, transnational civil societies, and even individuals have an impact on the system. Public opinion as well as different bureaucracies and domestic actors also carry certain weight. Most importantly Neoliberals believe that the increased interconnectivity through international trade makes states interdependent on each other making conflict difficult.[6] They argue that democracy and spread of democratic regimes around the world would also have an effect of increasing cooperation, as these regimes are more sensitive to their domestic constituencies and the interests of business world.[7] Thus, according to Neoliberals, spread of democracy around the world can be taken as another aspect that can increase the chances of peace and foster cooperation. Neoliberals also allow a much larger role and agency for the international organizations and international regimes. They argue that these structures reduce transaction costs by regulating behavior of states, allow the development of procedures and rule-based behavior by creating transparency, allow fostering of cooperation by facilitating information exchange, and act as multilateral platforms that can aid the resolution of conflicts.[8]

While Neoliberalism allows more room for cooperation to exist in the world and a better explanation of why cooperation exists in an anarchical system, its explanation is mostly through rational material interests such as interdependency and the functioning of international institutions. The idea of a community would necessitate an explanation beyond material interests, probing on identities and common global or regional cultural conceptualizations. Such a perspective is provided by Social Constructivism. Social Constructivism focuses on nonmaterial aspects of international relations such as ideas, values, and identities. In other words, they see ideational and normative elements of social interaction as a major element of the social world.⁹ According to them, ideas and norms are shaped inter-subjectively. That is to say, these emerge as a result of continuing interactions among the actors that make up the society and it is something that is constructed. Social Constructivists reject the Realist idea that as a result of anarchy conflict is inevitable. In contrast, they argue that whether the relations between states or other members of the society can be constructed as conflictual or cooperative depend on the inter-subjective meanings and identities that these actors attribute to themselves and others within the society. A good example of this can be ASEAN where, despite serious cultural, administrative, religious, economic, and racial differences as well as some unresolved border issues, a Southeast Asian identity could still be fostered and expressed with a certain level of success.¹⁰ Among the traditional approaches to international relations, it can be argued that Social Constructivism allows the biggest room for the idea of "community" and explanation of its formation in various world regions.

Thus, from a Neoliberal and Social Constructivist perspective the development of a liberal world system can be taken as a positive development (though Social Constructivism is much more ambivalent about the prospects of a positive outcome). The development of international trade, transnational civil society, international law, and effectiveness of international institutions should facilitate the development of common norms, patterns of behavior, cooperation, and an understanding of a global community covering regional identities. At the onset of 21st century the common reaction to global environmental problems, immigration, non-traditional security problems, and reduction of the barriers to trade should have led to increased interaction among the states and individuals, allowing the idea of community to grow and encompass large swaths of world population.

However, in the recent few years we see reactionary tendencies in many countries against the unifying global forces and a resort back to violence, power politics, populism and nativism instead. The last few years witnessed a growing terror threat emanating from civil wars in failed states, which in turn created a wave of migration problem at epic proportions. While most countries in the world tried to respond to this problem by generously accepting and aiding these refugees, unfortunately this has also gave rise to xenophobic reactions in some part of the society, strengthening populist and nativist domestic policies. These reactionary phenomena can be observed in any country in the world, where fear rather than trust, bigotry rather than tolerance, and Machiavellian power politics rather than superiority of law seem to be gaining the upper hand. Rather than moving towards a world community, a move towards a dialectical construction of "other" seems to be the expanding norm for many societies in the world, further inflamed by hungry politicians.

While these problems are certainly not new, their almost concurrent emergence and wide spread implications after an almost uncontested era of liberalism and expanded interconnectedness mean that despite globalism and all the arguments for the shrinkage of the modern world, many world societies still continue approach the rest of the globe from an exclusionary perspective. The identities and feelings of connectedness among humans stop at the borders of the nation-state. So, it might be these narrow understandings of identity and limitations to the sense of belongingness that has to be transcended, so that enduring and inclusive global or regional communities can be established. The academic approach to this problem has been brought by Andrew Linklater. Linklater is characterized as a scholar among critical theorists within international relations studies, and Critical Theory had a distinct history of development then the traditional paradigms mentioned above. Here, I would like to evaluate the idea of the development of a "world community" in the studies of international relations, mainly focusing on the ideas of Andrew Linklater, specifically through his study "The Transformation of Political Community".[11] In order to make the discussions accessible for ones outside of the IR discipline, effort will be spent to be as little technical as possible with as little detail as possible. Yet, since this volume participants compose of a group that puts effort into the development of an "Asian Community", it will be useful and beneficiary to actually talk about the theory of global communities.

In order to understand what the global community and its transformation means we might have to revisit the above theoretical discussions with some additions. We have explained that the international system has an anarchical nature. It is also possible to say that it has what is called a Westphalian nature. The modern world system emerged after the peace of Westphalia in Europe at 1648, and it later expanded to the rest of the world by European colonization and later by decolonization.[12] In the past ages human populations politically organized themselves in many different forms such as hunter-gatherer bands, city states, and empires, where sense of belonging and identities were complex and overlapped. The Westphalian peace made nation-state as the major form of political organization in the the world. The human populations started to feel obligations mainly to their nations, or the state that ruled that nation, and fellow citizens. Since there is no overarching political structure to unify these distinct and competing nation states, the modern world system has an anarchical character, meaning that there is no central supreme authority in the world that can institute order to international politics, use coercive power to resolve disputes, or enforce law. This is in contrast to a domestic order where states assume such an authority. They can make and enforce laws through an apparatus and bring order to domestic societies. The fact that world system is anarchical does not mean that it is chaotic. Order is still instituted through power politics, interdependence, or by normative means, some of which are explained above. Anarchy simply means that the order of the international system is composed of independent states with no central authority above them, as opposed to the hierarchical nature of a domestic political system.

The 1648 Westphalia Treaty in Europe established the legal basis of modern statehood and marks the beginning of the modern international system. It brought a number of constitutive principles to the world politics. First it introduced the principle of territoriality in a modern sense. The human kind has started to be principally organized into exclusive political territorial communities with fixed borders. People live in these fixed borders under one specific state authority. In this sense, humanity is politically divided. Second principle is the principle of sovereignty. This is the most important constitutive principle of the modern world system. Sovereignty means that only the state has the supreme, exclusive political and legal authority within a set territory and people living in that territory No other state or force can interfere to the domestic issues under the authority of the sovereign state, thus comes the principle of non-interference in domestic affairs. The basic documents of international law carry this principal. In international law all other actors can have presence through their association to a nation-state. The principles of Westphalia had their way into the UN Charter and UN General Assembly as well, which now has 193 members, all accepted as sovereign states by other members.

Yet, as the time progressed the Westphalian principles increasingly got subjected to some challenges. For instance, the R2P (Responsibility to Protect) principle, which is an expanding new norm in international relations, argues that the world community holds the responsibility to protect other people in the world against gross human rights violations by their own states, challenging the principal of sovereignty. The spread of social media, deepening of international economic exchanges, especially finance, and the expansion of transcendent civil movements such as those for environment, gender, human rights, etc., and international migration have started to make borders more transparent, porous, and the Westphalian state system more problematic. In other words, as the challenges in the world assume a more global character, a coordinated effort to counter these challenges also require a concerted effort that should go beyond the confines of Westphalian nation-states. The understanding here is that; the nation-state division of the world that lacks a vision of a global community does not have the capacity to counter the troubles that humanity collectively faces, such as global warming, non-traditional security threats, global economy that shakes the world with systemic financial crises, large scale migration, and etc.

It could be argued that this is the starting point of Linklater's ideas, and he approaches to the Westphalian nature of the world system not only from a legal perspective but also from a normative perspective. He views our traditional understanding of the nation-state which takes it as the base of political organization in the world, as the cause of the world problems rather than the solution to them. Sovereign nation states were formed in the context of major wars. As Charles Tilly puts, "War made the state, and the state made war".[13] In order to consolidate their existence and power over populations, states chose to be deeply exclusionary in their dealings with minority cultures and alien outsiders, in effect creating a dialectical understanding between "us" and "them" among the society. Conflict was a means for achieving this goal.

Linklater argues that new forms of political community and ideas of citizenship are necessary to resolve global challenges. In his study "The Transformation of Political Community" he argues for new forms of political community that are cosmopolitan, sensitive to cultural differences as well as material inequalities.[14] Linklater is quite realistic in his understanding that having loyalties or identity bonds beyond predefined political boundaries are difficult to achieve. He argues that communities will not survive unless their members are prepared to define their interests in the light of a more general good, however its application necessitates clearly defined limits. He understands that the survival of political community owes much to the fact that the social bond between citizens and the state does not extend to aliens. The "[p]olitical communities endure because they are exclusive, and most establish their peculiar identities by accentuating the differences between insiders and aliens."[15] In other words, there has to be systems of inclusion and exclusion so that communities will be tied to each other. This fact unfortunately creates the effect that the union between the members of a community may clash with obligations to the rest of the human race.[16] Than how can it be possible to create universalistic or at least more expansive and inclusive loyalties that are in accord with strong emotional attachments to specific communities?

To facilitate the emergence of such a community, Linklater advocates that the political community must be transformed in certain ways. First of all, he makes an argument for a cosmopolitan understanding that there should be a greater respect for cultural differences. To put more broadly, he argues that there must be a "cosmopolitan ethic which questions the precise moral significance of national boundaries".[17] Class, ethnicity, gender, race and alien status must become unimportant with regard to citizens' duties and rights. In other words, our sense of community must not stop at the border of the nation-state but expand to the rest of the world. He argues that a moral deficit arise when citizens attach more moral significance than is justified to differences between fellow nationals and aliens.

As citizens of a certain country, people feel responsibility to -or feeling solidarity with- only fellow citizens. Moreover, there is a "recurring practice of establishing collective identities by demeaning cultures elsewhere".[18] Therefore in order to overcome this, an understanding of a "global citizenship" is necessary so that we can face global problems collectively. Linklater's ideas are built on philosophies of Kant and Marx. Kant has argued that legal rights must cover not only the rising bourgeoisie, but the members of other societies as well, which is a necessity of liberal societies. Marx similarly argues that moral deficits can only be eradicated by enlarging the sphere in which human beings treat one another as equals. In order to achieve a political transformation towards a "world community", dialogue must be made central to social life and international relations, with an eye for ethical development. The most effective means for achieving this is to create institutional frameworks. Establishment of civil societies and organizations with the goal of creating communities and establishing international linkages is necessary. For example, conferences that have "community" as their theme with the aim of increasing interaction across border is one humble way of establishing and expanding dialogue. By such methods, it can be hoped that, a solidarist international order can be built in time in which states might feel more obligation to cooperate in order to protect agreed moral principles such as basic human rights, or take collective action against global problems. What is necessary is the emergence of a "transnational civil society" to create the conditions in which "individuals could unlearn their perceptions of estrangement from other peoples and learn how to associate with them in more humane arrangements [sic]", in order to enlarge the sphere in which human beings treat one another as equals.[19] Some call this idea a post-Westphalian political community.

As mentioned above, Linklater's ideas emanate from the Critical Thinking in the discipline of international relations. The major principles of his ideas are developed from the Frankfurt School of thought especially from Jurgen Habermas.[20] In their work the Frankfurt School critical thinkers try to find emancipatory forces that will aid humanity for a better future. Andrew Linklater used the key principals developed by Habermas to argue that emancipation in the realm of international relations should be understood in terms of the expansion of the moral boundaries of a political community. From this perspective, emancipation of humanity is understood as a process in which states lose their ethical and moral significance, in turn to be replaced by enlarged understandings of community that transcends borders. In today's world in most cases state borders mark the furthest extent of our sense of duty and obligation. For critical theorists, from an ethical stand point, this is indefensible, and it necessary to move towards a situation in which citizens share the same duties and obligations towards non-citizens as they do towards their fellow citizens.[21]

This approach also has its critics, as nation-state still is the basis of international law, and it is still unavoidable to solve global problems without going through nation-state structures, thus further establishing ideational limitations they impose. Furthermore, the ability to create the desired transcendent understanding is no doubt a very difficult task as humans have very strong psychological attachments to their current demarcated identities. After all, the modern history is written as the history of nation-states. Thus, such a normative leap needs the wholesale transformation of the present institutions of world governance. What critical theory hopes to achieve is to first identify, and then nurture, the present circumstance that might lead towards the direction of emancipation.

Linklater is optimist in this sense that structures such as EU (or possibly ASEAN as a basis for an Asian community) represent progressive tendency in contemporary world politics.

Furthermore, it can also be argued that the nurturing of a global norm where the identity and feelings of solidarity and responsibility do not stop at the borders of the nation-state and expand to other parts of the globe to cover the whole humanity, might actually be unavoidable in future, as the sustainability of development and prosperity, daunting environmental challenges, as well as the security of humanity necessitates such a leap. The technological advance, increased connectivity among humanity, and the resulting global problems create serious collective action problems, and addressing these problems requires a sense of community that transcends our petty differences and embraces the larger humanity that shares this earth.

Notes
1 Fukuyama, F. (1989). The end of history?. *The national interest*, (16), 3-18.
2 Nye Jr, J. S. (2017). Will the liberal order survive: The history of an idea. *Foreign Aff.*, *96*, 10.
3 Morgenthau, H. J. (1985). Politics Among Nations, revised by Kenneth W. Thompson. *New York: Knopf*, 4–15.
4 Waltz, K. N. (2010). *Theory of international politics*. Waveland Press.
5 Mearsheimer, J. J. (2001). *The tragedy of great power politics*. WW Norton & Company.
6 Keohane, R. O., & Nye, J. S. (1977). *Power and interdependence* (pp. 8–9).
7 Doyle, M. W. (1983). Kant, liberal legacies, and foreign affairs. *Philosophy & Public Affairs*, 205–235.
8 Keohane, R. O. (2008). *International Institutions and State Power: Essays in International Relations Theory*. Boulder: Westview Press.
9 Wendt, A. E. (1987). The agent-structure problem in international relations theory. *International organization*, *41* (3), 335–370.
10 Acharya, A. (2014). *Constructing a security community in Southeast Asia: ASEAN and the problem of regional order*. Routledge.
11 Linklater, Andrew, *The Transformation of Political Community*. Polity Press, 1998.
12 Jackson, R.H.; P. Owens (2005) "The Evolution of World Society" in: John

Baylis; Steve Smith (eds.). *The Globalization of World Politics: An Introduction to International Relations*. Oxford: Oxford University Press

13 Tilly, Charles, and Gabriel Ardant. *The formation of national states in Western Europe*. Vol. 8. Princeton Univ Pr, 1975.

14 Linklater, A. (1998). *The transformation of political community: ethical foundations of the post-Westphalian era*. Univ. of South Carolina Press.

15 Ibid. p.1.

16 Linklater, A. (1990). *Beyond realism and marxism: Critical theory and international relations*. Springer.

17 Linklater, A. (1998). *The transformation of political community: ethical foundations of the post-Westphalian era*. Univ of South Carolina Press. p. 2

18 Ibid. p. 3

19 Ibid. p. 4.

20 Hobden, Stephen and Jones, Richard Wyn: Marxist theories of international relations. In: Baylis, John and Smith, Steve: The Globalization of World Politics. Oxford 2006

21 Baylis, J., Smith, S., & Owens, P. (Eds.). (2017). *The globalization of world politics: an introduction to international relations*. Oxford University Press. p. 141–142.

Bibliography

Acharya, A. (2014). *Constructing a security community in Southeast Asia: ASEAN and the problem of regional order*. Routledge.

Baylis, J., Smith, S., & Owens, P. (Eds.). (2017). *The globalization of world politics: an introduction to international relations*. Oxford University Press.

Doyle, M. W. (1983). Kant, liberal legacies, and foreign affairs. *Philosophy & Public Affairs*, 205–235.

Fukuyama, F. (1989). The end of history?. *The national interest*, (16), 3–18.

Hobden, Stephen and Jones, Richard Wyn: Marxist theories of international relations. In: Baylis, John and Smith, Steve: The Globalization of World Politics. Oxford 2006.

Jackson, R. H.; P. Owens (2005) "The Evolution of World Society" in: John Baylis; Steve Smith (eds.). *The Globalization of World Politics: An Introduction to International Relations*. Oxford: Oxford University Press.

Keohane, R. O., & Nye, J. S. (1977). *Power and interdependence* (pp. 8–9).

Keohane, R. O. (2008). *International Institutions and State Power: Essays in International Relations Theory*. Boulder: Westview Press.

Linklater, A. (1998). *The transformation of political community: ethical foundations of the post-Westphalian era*. Univ. of South Carolina Press.

Linklater, A. (1990). *Beyond realism and marxism: Critical theory and international relations*. Springer.

Mearsheimer, J. J. (2001). *The tragedy of great power politics*. WW Norton & Company.

Morgenthau, H. J. (1985). *Politics Among Nations*, revised by Kenneth W. Thompson. New York: Knopf, 4–15.

Nye Jr, J. S. (2017). Will the liberal order survive: The history of an idea. *Foreign Aff.*, *96*, 10.

Tilly, Charles, and Gabriel Ardant. *The formation of national states in Western Europe*. Vol. 8. Princeton Univ Pr, 1975.

Waltz, K. N. (2010). *Theory of international politics*. Waveland Press.

Wendt, A. E. (1987). The agent-structure problem in international relations theory. *International organization*, *41* (3), 335–370.

Chapter 6

Multi-level Governance and Regional Economic Cooperation:
Case of Northeast Asia

TSAI Tung-Chieh (Professor, Graduate Institute of International Politics, National Chung-Hsing University)

Abstract

Since its emergence near the end of the Cold War, the new wave of regionalism has captured the attention of observers. The phenomenon so called "new regionalism" not only exudes the characteristic of "spill over", as described by functionalist theory, but has also created discussions about the appearance of new styles of cooperation on the regional level such as sub-regionalism or multi-level governance. In the beginning of the new century, the world seems to be reorganizing its mode of social interaction. This paper addresses the development of multi-level governance and regional economic cooperation in Northeast Asia.

Keywords: multi-level governance, new regionalism, sub-regionalism, Northeast Asia

1. Rethinking New Regionalism and Its Influence

1. From Nation-State to Region

Generally speaking, although the nation-state remains the most important actor in global stage, new variables has already brought about clear "structural shocks." As early as the mid-1960s, Alberto Melucci has called attention to the development of "supra-national" organizations by explaining how these new institutions are diluting the control and influence of nation-states.[1] Today, capital globalization eats away the scope of government control. In turn, the demise of the nation-state becomes more than just a fairy tale, despite the fact that nation-state remains the only legitimate source for the budget management and political governance.[2] Of course, we also cannot ignore the nation-state and its response towards the wave of globalization. However, from an alternative angle, influence from regionalism or so-called "regionalizing movement" may be greater than reflex actions by the nation-state amidst a wave of change. While globalization garnered academic spotlight in the 1980s, discussions on regionalism and regional regimes grew as well. The transformation and continued expansion of the EU can be said to occupy the center of attention. Some observers describe this development as "new regionalism" which exudes bottom-up character of functionalism, [3] and developed amidst the shift towards multipolarity in the late Cold War Era. First to emerge from the trend is a new concept of the region or often denoted as "sub-regionalism" or "sub-regional economic zones" (SREZs).[4] Since then, other terms such as "growth triangle", [5] "natural economic territories,"[6] and "extended metropolitan regions"[7] appeared. Issues related to so called "micro-regionalism" was the latest addition to the vibrant discussion on regionalism. Table 1 shows the characteristics of different levels of regionalism.

Table 6-1 Types of Different Regionalism

	Regionalism	Sub-regionalism	Micro-regionalism
Geographical conception	traditional ex. Asia	divisional ex. Northeast Asia	Sub-state ex. growth triangle
Main actors	Major power	Middle power	Local government
Action aims	Trade framework Non-discrimination	Anti-globalization Anti-regionalism	Economic growth Comparative interest
Advantage	Scale economics	Distribution of interests	Policy flexibility
Limitation	Geo-political cleavage Power struggle	Blurred definition Lack of consensus	Challenge from state system Limited market scale

Since 1980s, accompanying its economic growth, a new wave of regional cooperation swept across East Asia.[8] Not only did institutions that exude characteristics of open regionalism and new regionalism, such as APEC, began to appear, proposals such as the Pacific Community (proposed by U.S. President Bill Clinton) and the East Asia Economic Community (proposed by Malaysian Prime Minister Mahathir) emerged as well. At the same time, the development of cooperation on the sub and micro-regional level is also worth of our attention. Clearly, in the beginning of the twenty-first century, we can see that the world is re-organizing the interaction of human societies through multi-level governance. Besides international organizations at the highest level (represented by the WTO), regional regimes that represent traditional state interests (such as the EU and NAFTA) sub and micro-regional cooperation models all influence the way humans interact. This article seeks to examine the development of regional cooperation in Northeast Asia from the global, regional and sub-regional levels.

2. From Anarchy to Community

Whether realism or liberal institutionalism, "anarchy" remains the main focus in daily life of international relations. In response, many proposals for cooperation have emerged, including the idea of "community." Just as Charles Morrision et al point out, "community is a group of citizens or nations bonded by close interdependence and share a sense of identity through interactions."[9] Identity and institution are the two pillars of community making. The rationale for community building emanates from two sources: the general feeling of insecurity from anarchy and the expectation of (security) guarantees through interest sharing and establishment of norms.[10] Regardless of other concerns, the term "identity" alone remains a topic of debate. As the individual can have many different sources of identity at the same time, it's impossible to identify the individual with only one identity.[11] Moreover, even though identity often serves as the foundation of "we group," the existence of "others" is oftentimes a more important precondition.[12] Others provide the "we group" with legitimacy to protect the interests of its members.

In spite of its continued use by social scientists, Terri Mannarini and Angela Fedi acknowledge that "community" is an ambiguous concept.[13] In the realm of international relations, the concept of "security community" is particularly relevant.[14] For Amitav Acharya, "the core concept of a security community views international relationships as a course of learning from each other and forming a common identity driven by bargaining, interaction and socialization."[15] In the terms of constructivism and inter-subjectivity, Wendt notes that through social processes, states learn to construct their identities and interests in interaction, and then cooperating states can form a collective identity based on interdependence, common fate, homogenization and self-restraint.[16]

The community building process concentrates on the issue of identity. The existence of common values is the main driving force for community building. Geographic proximity is often the precondition for the development of shared values. The current wave of regional integration rests on common values as its psychological foundation.[17] It is worth noting that common values alone cannot serve as the driving force for integration. The existence of a certain level of solidarity is also critical. In other words, members to the region must share a consensus to translate shared values into common policy.[18] In terms of "institutions," according to neo-institutionalist scholar Douglass North, institutions are the "rules of the game" or "the humanly devised constraints that structure human interaction."[19] Institutions form from the incentive structure of a society and serve as the underlying determinants of economic performance.[20] James March and Johan Olsen argue that once created, institutions become political actors that take on a life of their own, affecting the flow of history and shaping the environment in ways unintended by their creators.[21]

The community can be regarded as an overarching framework that provides benefits to its members at all levels. As such, the community building process cannot the response of institutional design towards challenges from the environment. As Tang points out, "for the community to survive and sustain itself, it needs to be functional and serve the needs of its members; this calls for the institutionalizing of norms and code of conduct." [22] Musing over the formation of community in Northeast Asia, Vinod Aggarwal and Min Gyo Koo point out that the external shocks, goods, countries' individual bargaining situations and the existing institutional context are factors that community building in the region cannot neglect.[23] The end of the Cold War, the Asian financial crisis and the 9/11 attacks --- the triple shock --- generated many critical external variables that would have important consequences for regional relations and the development of multilateral institutions.[24] Finally, not only are "identity" and "institution" both critical factors for community building, they are also indispensable in adding to our understanding of the community. In terms of community building in East Asia, Hadi Soesastro discusses regional development under the concept of "institutional identity", which demonstrates that the institution can take on life on its own just like the community.[25] On the other hand, Emanuel Adler and Patricia Greve argue that a security community based on collective identity and the so called "balance of power" order based on institutions, are distinct but coexisting and often overlapping approaches at understanding regional security governance.[26] In general, although development of the community or institutionalization may not be the only or best approach to resolving the security dilemma, in an anarchic world of limited policy choices, they beg our greater acknowledgment.

2. Sub-regional Community Building and Its Challenges

1. Emerging China-Japan-Korea Cooperation

As table 1 suggests, sub-regionalism is the main driving force behind new regionalism. One difference between sub-regionalism and traditional regionalism is that the actors involved are not necessarily major powers but middle powers.[27] In addition, compared to protectionist sentiments implied in regional projects driven by major powers, sub-regionalism is often "open" in nature. For the latter, the ultimate goal of integration does not necessarily entail the coalescence of regional blocs, but rather aim at increasing the level of economic development among states through the deepening of cooperation. In turn, sub-regionalism seeks to increase the level of resistance among regional members against globalization or regional projects driven by major powers. In case of

East Asia, despite ASEAN's aspiration to serve as a bridge between Southeast and Northeast Asia through multilateral channels of negotiation (ASEAN +1 and ASEAN+3), it may not enough to hold back integration by the respective sub-regions in the short term. In 2003, ASEAN passed the Second Bali Accord and set its eyes on establishing the ASEAN Economic Community before 2020. On the same day, China, Japan and Korea passed the Joint Declaration on the Promotion of Tripartite Cooperation. These attempts at cooperation suggest a shifting of power in the East Asian economy.

Compared to Southeast Asia, Northeast Asia's languid development in sub-regionalism is a fact. The complicated political environment is the main reason for its sluggishness. However, political détente near the end of the last century, especially since the end of the 1997 Financial Crisis, helped to facilitate close cooperation between China, Japan and South Korea (the core countries of Northeast Asia). Besides the frequent summits after 1999, the Development Research Center of the State Council (DRC, China), the National Institute for Research Advancement (NIRA, Japan), and the Korea Institute for International Economic Policy (KIEP) were assigned the track-two research for the feasible establishment of a tripartite FTA. In 2004, above joint research committee began research into "Sectoral Implications of a China-Japan-Korea FTA." In the same year, CJK adopted the "Progress Report of Trilateral Cooperation" and the "Action Strategy on Trilateral Cooperation" in the tripartite summit meeting.

In 2008, the joint committee released a final report to conclude six years of research that trilateral cooperation should lead to win-win boosts in GDP to all partners. In 2009, the CJK Summit confirmed the completion of joint studies by the private sector and announced the initiation of a further round of joint research by business, academia and government in the following year. According to several studies, the CJK-FTA will have an estimated market size of 1.5 billion people, USD 7 trillion in GDP and USD 2 trillion in total trade. Economic interactions among CJK alone contribute to 80% of total trade and 70% of total investment in East Asia. It's clear that their cooperation will have a major impact on regional cooperation in East Asia.

Currently, as a result of differences in the level of development between CJK, experts expect China to have the least gains from a regional FTA. Such grim economic outlook has prompted China to move beyond trilateral cooperation and actively push for integration of the entire region (which includes China, Russia, Mongolia, Japan, and the Koreas). Proposals include the establishment of the Northeast Asia Economic Cooperation Council (NEAECC), following in the footsteps of the Pacific Economic Cooperation Council (PECC), and the establishment of the Northeast Asia Development Bank (NEADB), as a regional mechanism for liquidity. As China's economic development continued into the twenty-first century and East Asia became ever dependent on trade with China, Beijing pursued closer economic relations with its neighbors. Since the establishment of the Closer Economic Partnership Agreement (CEPA) between China and Hong Kong in 2003, Beijing signed a similar agreement with Macau in 2004 and completed free trade area with both in 2007. Since 2003, China has actively promoted the establishment of the CJK-FTA while making claims that the timing may also be right for the establishment of a Northeast Asia Free Trade Area.

2. Political Dialogue in Northeast Asia

Nevertheless, proposals continue to exceed result in terms of sub-regional cooperation in Northeast Asia. CJK has initiated a series of proposals near the turn of the millennium. In 1999, the CJK leaders used the ASEAN Summit as an occasion to host an informal meeting, which officially sparked trilateral cooperation. In the second meeting in 2000, CJK leaders agreed to hold summit annually. In 2002, CJK further confirmed trade, info technology, environment, human resource development and culture as the key sectors for cooperation. After eight informal meetings, CJK decided to host a trilateral summit outside the ASEAN framework in 2008. In the Joint Declaration released after the summit, CJK support the expansion of the regional currency swap mechanism and promise not to introduce new trade barriers in the region. CJK also confirmed the Joint Announcement on Disaster Management Cooperation and agreed to hold bilateral talks regarding important issues such as North Korea's development of nuclear weapons, natural disasters and global warming. In 2010, CJK agreed to establish a permanent secretariat which to be located in Korea and jointly supported by CJK next year.

However, it is worthy to note that history and territorial disputes remain major issues in China-Japan and Japan-Korea relations. A complete trilateral framework may be difficult to emerge in the short term. This has caused some observers to envision the future of Northeast Asia to be an interconnected, open cooperation system based on various forms of institutional binding and embedded or complementary institutions. Nevertheless, political deadlocks were not enough for states to ignore the remnant pressures from the global financial crisis. In the 2012 summit, CJK agreed to initiate FTA negotiations en route to a regional economy that exceeds the size of the European Union. As both Japan and Korea are heavily dependent on the Chinese market, China seems to hold the most bargaining chips among the three powers.[28] On the other hand, as the initiator of regional integration, China seems to have more opportunities to induce domestic economic change as well. While China has an opportunity to orient economic integration in Northeast Asia, progress remains to be observed.

3. Development of Micro-regional Economic Circles

Micro-regionalism is sometimes known as "sub-sub-regionalism."[29] Although most progress in integration originate from economic factors, micro-regionalism emphasizes the re-shaping of political space through pragmatism and generates discussions on "cross-border regions."[30] Kenichi Ohmae calls these new units the "region state" and points out that "the definition of these units do not originate from their geopolitical status; the key is whether these units have the right scale and scope to become a natural business unit in global economy."[31] Compared to the active role of states in the globalization and regionalization movement, sub-state actors are the main driving force in sub-regionalization movements. Local or regional government replaces the central government as the main actor.[32] Micro-regionalism may be described as an economic strategy to increase global competitiveness through mutual cooperation based on the principle of comparative advantage which pulls together units that are geographically proximate but do not necessarily share common political values.[33] Micro-regionalism implies that states are willing to allow localities to participate in the international division of labor despite political differences.

1. Cross-Border Economic Cooperation

In terms of cross-border cooperation, bilateral approach remains important in Northeast Asia despite incessant calls for the establishment and expansion of regional cooperation. For example, since the collapse of the Soviet Union, Beijing and Moscow initiated a new period of cooperation in the immediate aftermath of the Cold War. Moscow adjusted its foreign policy focus from politics to economics in the post-Cold War period and proposed the Great Vladivostok Free Trade Area project in 1992. After the signing of the Treaty of Good Neighborliness and Friendly Cooperation between China and Russia, and latter's participation in the Shanghai Cooperation Organization in 2001, China-Russia relations began to move towards more active cooperation. Hunchun City (China) and Khasansky (Russia), located in the lower delta region of the Tumen River, became important experimental sites for that. Since 2002, both countries have begun to invest efforts towards the establishment of a transnational economic zone between the two regions.

Besides cross border development in Hunchun and Khasansky, China and North Korea sought cooperation as well. After Pyongyang's entry into multilateral meetings for the joint development of the Tumen River valley, China and N. Korea established the Rajin-Sonbong (Rason) Special Economic Zone. North Korea opened the ports of Chongjin and Rajin to increase trade and exchange with China. Although Pyongyang enjoyed a taste of liberalization through the Rason Economic Zone, imited progress encouraged Pyongyang to announce the establishment of the Sinuiju Special Administrative Region in 2002, with the hope of following in the footsteps of China's development experience and break through economic stagnation. After confirming the guidelines of "government guidance, business participation and market operation" in 2005, China and North Korea invested in the development of 16 frontier ports. Development revolves around three frontiers: Dandong – Sinuiju, Tonghua – Hyesan and Hunchun – Rason. In 2011, Pyongyang officially initiated the Rason Economic Zone and the Hwanggumpyong – Wihwa Islands Economic Zone. Kim Jong-il's sudden death curtailed progress in the economic zones.

Finally, with CJK filling in the regional power vacuum left open by the Soviet's collapse, for Mongolia, its immediate concern was to improve relations with CJK and eventually participate in the establishment of the regional system. In 1991, Mongolia passed a number of basic regulations including the foreign business investment act and economic zone act. In 1995, Mongolia entered the Tumen River Area Development Programme (TRADP) and along with China, Russia and the two Koreas, jointly agreed to the formal agreement to establish the TRADP Consultative Commission. At the same time, Mongolia and China established a transnational economic zone between Zamyn-Uud and Erenhot. In 2002, Mongolia passed the free trade area act and decided to establish the country's first free trade area in the border city of Altanbulag. Since the turn of the millennium, Mongolia has invested much effort towards upgrading the Zamyn-Uud and Erenhot economic zone to FTA status.

2. Sea Rim Areas in Northwest Pacific

Besides cross-national economic zones centered on land based interactions, many proposals for cooperation in proximate seas in the Western Pacific such as the Japan Sea, the Yellow Sea and the East Sea have been raised as well.

The so-called Pan Japan Sea Economic Zone (PJSEZ) is perhaps one of the most well-known and discussed micro-regional projects in the list of sea rim area cooperation in the Western Pacific to date. According to Nishikawa Jun's article and a report released by the Japanese government in 1992, the proposed zone spans coastal regions along the Japanese Sea, including the prefectures of Tottori, Aoyama, Niigata and Hokkaido, the Russian Far East, the eastern coast of the Korean Peninsula and China's northeastern regions. The purpose of the economic zone is to combine the abundance of Russia's natural resources, China's labor power, North Korea's resource and sea port, South Korea's industrial capability and Japan's capital and technology into a regional formula for development. In 1994, the local governments of Jilin (China), Tottori(Japan), Kangwangdo (S. Korea) and Primorsky (Russia) established the Pan Japan Sea Local Summit Meeting, which hailed the subsequent participation of Mongolia's Central Province (Tov Aimag). In the sixth meeting (1999), proposals and suggestions including the establishment of a Pan Japan Sea economic cooperation system and economic exchange sites were raised.

The PJSEZ provided the initial spark to a series of micro-regional projects in Northeast Asia. Aside from Nishikawa, Japanese economist Okawa Yuhei raised the concepts of East Asia Mediterranean Sea and Pan Yellow Sea Economic Zone in last 1980s. South Korean academics also had their own conception of regional cooperation as well, which hoped to absorb an opened China and geographically proximate regions such as Japan's Kyushu region into the Korean economic belt. Through above cooperation, Korean academics envisioned an increased role for Seoul in a re-organized regional economic structure. Scholarly ambitions went as far as projecting (and imagining) Korea to become the "new growth center" in the world. For example, President Roh Tae-woo has proposed the West Coast Development Plan in 1988 as an effort to reverse the trend of Korea's long term industrial imbalance towards the East.

In terms of the Pan Yellow Sea Economic Circle, two exchange mechanisms exist for the project. First, based on conclusions reached at 1999 ASEAN+3 meeting, CJK established the Yellow Sea Rim Economic and Technology Conference (YSRETC). Based on the joint participation of the government, economic groups, business, academia and research institutes, the YSRETC aims to reinforce exchange and cooperation in trade, investment, technology and personnel in this micro-region. Another mechanism that merits attention is Organization for East Asia Economic Development (OEAED), initiated in 2004. The OEAED has its roots in the East Asian Pan-Yellow Sea City Conference held in Kyushu in 1991, and is a joint economic initiative on the metropolitan level that seeks to strengthen inter-city cooperation. In 2006, OEAED adopted the Tianjin Declaration on East Asian Economic Cooperation and agreed to consolidate economic cooperation among cities on all aspects. The Declaration represents a determination among OEAED cities to promote policy negotiations on the state level through cooperation between the regional economic and tax free zones of CJK. Furthermore, the Declaration also presents a consensus on issues including the promotion of financial cooperation, establishment of a regional exchange fund, environmental protection and the expansion of cooperation in various fields.

In contrast with the development of initiatives based on waters, the Tumen River Project demonstrates an alternative type of cooperation. The TRADP originated in China's call for joint development in Northeast Asia in the late 1980s. Beijing's proposal subsequently gave rise to a related study by the United Nation's Development Programme (UNDP) in 1990 and two years later (1992), the TRADP Programme Management Committee was officially established. In 1995, China, Russia, the Koreas and Mongolia agreed to the establishment of the TRADP Coordination Committee and the Consultative Commission and a Memorandum of Understanding on Environmental Principles, which symbolizes a new stage in international cooperation in the Tumen River area. It is worth noting that despite the realization of TRADP, progress stagnated due to conflicting opinions among member states and pressures generated by the Asian Financial Crisis. Investment in the TRADP was not stepped up again until the 2000s. Meanwhile, China also included the TRADP as a focus in its official long term plans for 2010. The progress in the TRADP remains to be observed.

4. The Prospect of Great East Asian Integration

Due to the expansion of imperialism since the late 19th and global economic progress in the second half of the 20th century, East Asia seems to boast a high degree of economic connectivity and interdependence for a long time.[34] Such development contributed to the emergence of a rich wave of regionalist conceptions. However, most proposals remain verbal or in the study stage. It seems that East Asian leaders are relatively quiet in terms of the development of regionalism; working institutions remain far and few.

1. From ASEAN plus to East Asian Summit

In contrast with the quick pace of regionalist movements in Europe and North America, East Asia continues to fall short of any clear consensus and goal for regional cooperation. The fact that APEC includes too many extra-regional entities hinders the organization from playing a dominant role in East Asia integration. On the other hand, despite the fact that ASEAN serves as the most developed sub-regional institution in East Asia, "power" may prove to be a more important factor than "consensus" in the development from sub-regional to regional cooperation. Power is not something the chronically impotent Southeast Asian states are known to provide. Even if Southeast Asia can participate in integration through ASEAN, the helm of East Asia regionalism may nevertheless be reserved for CJK. At the annual 10+3 meeting in 2000, South Korean President Kim Dae-jung proposed the East Asian Community (EAC), an initiative the East Asian Vision Group (EAVG) 2001 report supports as the goal of East Asia integration. In 2002, the EAVG further proposed the establishment of the East Asia Free Trade Area, the East Asia Investment Zone and the East Asia Summit as middle and long term goals for progress towards EAC.

2004 was a turning point for the development of regional integration in East Asia. In the annual 10+3 meeting, member states decided to expand the original framework into the EAS. Despite the seeming progress towards multilateralism, several conflicts remain in terms of expansion. Above all, a leadership problem emerged as ASEAN began to worry about CJK's growing voice in regional integration. Second, expansion led to the question of membership. Before the EAS commenced in 2005, the foreign ministers of ASEAN laid down the preconditions for entering the EAS: the state must be a complete dialogue partner of ASEAN, have actual relations with ASEAN and recognize the Treaty of Amity and Cooperation (TAC) in Southeast Asia. Regardless of potential barriers to dialogue, the first EAS in 2005 produced the Kuala Lumpur Declaration. Dialogue states agreed to adopt the stance of ASEAN and China, which confirms ASEAN as the dominant force in the EAS in the current stage. Despite the fact that the 10+3 did not expand to 10+6 (the addition of India, Australia and

New Zealand) in the 2005 EAS, it is worth noting that the EAS has developed into a regional forum that is only superseded by APEC in size. Participating states of the EAS encompass more than half of the world population and harbor a GDP value of 9.2 trillion USD --- something not to be ignored.

2. Between East Asianism and Asia-Pacificism

While EAS seems to demonstrate the rising influence of East-Asianism, such influence did not provide reasons for the U.S.-led Asia-Pacificism to back down. The 2004 APEC Business Advisory Council (ABAC) meeting saw the introduction of a proposal to establish a Free Trade Area of the Asia Pacific (FTAAP). Under U.S. President George W. Bush's support and oversight, FTAAP was deemed a long term goal in the 2006 APEC summit declaration.

However, several regional developments disrupted progress in the FTAAP proposal. ASEAN's adoption of the ASEAN Charter in 2007 and its re-proclamation to complete the ASEAN Economic Community by 2015 once again put Southeast Asia in the spotlight. Realization of the China-ASEAN Free Trade Area (CAFTA) in 2010 significantly challenged the viability of the FTAAP. On the other hand, the Obama administration's Return to Asia strategy provided the basis for U.S. participation in the Transnational Strategic Economic Partnership (TPP), a multilateral regional project formed in 2005 by New Zealand, Singapore, Brunei and Chile. By inviting Australia, Vietnam, Malaysia, Peru and Japan to join the initiative, Washington hoped to replace a stagnant FTAAP with the TPP. In this case, the APEC framework may become increasingly negligible while countries in the Asia-Pacific are put in difficult shoes.

Meanwhile, in August 2006, ASEAN countries and Japan agreed to a joint study for the establishment of a grand FTA scheme involving all sixteen countries in Asia (the 10+6 framework). Despite great ambition, Japan and ASEAN continue to be trapped in limited progress over the establishment of a Japan-ASEAN FTA. A bright light amidst stagnation is that the ASEAN Economic Minister Meeting has agreed to Tokyo's proposal for a joint study on the potential establishment of an East Asian free trade area to be carried out by experts from the sixteen countries in Asia. In addition, ASEAN welcomes Japan's proposal to invest 86 million USD for the establishment of a regional think tank. Cooperation between Japan and ASEAN provided the context for the quick adoption of the ASEAN Framework on Regional Comprehensive Economic Partnership (RCEP) by the EAS. The RCEP has achieved a status that rivals the TPP, with its potential members coming from the 10+6. In a sense, East Asianism fought back.

5. Conclusion

It is clear that Northeast Asia is located in the midst of a complex multi-level network that consists of regional, sub-regional and micro-regional cooperation. Moreover, each level has its independent driving force and goal for development. Regionalism seeks to establish a more competitive economy of scale through supra-national interactions while sub-regionalism seeks a balance between increasing competitiveness and maintaining national identity. Micro-regionalism is a form of top-down supra-national interaction that seeks to rediscover the relationship between geography and real human activities, and redefine the international distribution of labor based on classical economics. Whether the goal of regionalism on each level is fully understood or not is beside the point. As Etel Solingen points out, the characters of East Asia's current integration movement are informality, consensus building and open regionalism.[35]

Nonetheless, the open character of East Asia integration is not inflexible.[36] The reason for possible variation lies with the past. The adoption of open regionalism in East Asia was a combined result of a specific time period (Cold War), geopolitics (the region being located at the frontline of U.S. containment strategy), conditions for development (many countries were in the start off stage in the post-colonial period) and member attribute (high variation). As these preconditions change over time, at least since the 1990s, signs of increasing regional autonomy and decreasing openness can be seen in the EAEG, ASEAN plus N, East Asia Community and many other bilateral and multilateral FTAs. The

East Asian miracle of the 1980s contributed to the development as well. East Asia's development in regional integration begs three questions: Is East Asia following a specific path towards integration? How do past changes and the current integration network influence regional development? Finally and most importantly, how can East Asia achieve a breakthrough in regional integration?

Clearly, both East Asia and Northeast Asia are dominated by the phenomenon of "more proposals than actual integration." In terms of multilateral and bilateral proposals that seek assistance from the international community, CJK can be deemed to possess an abundance of imagination. Yet most projects fail to materialize and remain in the stage of conflicting opinions. On the other hand, it is also clear that East Asia is moving towards micro-regional cooperation. Although countries have invested great amounts of resource and personnel towards research while signing many agreements and meeting frequently, perhaps differences among states remain too steep to overcome. As states are unable to reach consensus in a short period of time, yet remain unwilling to abandon the hope for further integration, micro-regionalism --- consensus building among geographically proximate and politically less sensitive local bodies --- became a viable temporary option. Looking towards the future, in terms of short and mid-range development, the complex integration network that includes sub- and micro-regional cooperation can be expected to provide more flexibility for policy discussions. However, supra-national interfaces and non-governmental networks may influence or even reshape regional identity and contribute to political implications for East Asia.

Finally, for some academics, U.S. intervention is the main reason that integration has yet to take shape in East or Northeast Asia.[37] In addition, we should pay attention to the lack of a regional consensus for integration in East Asia. As the previous discussion suggests, not only does the competition between East Asianism and Asia Pacificism continue to flare in East Asia, proposals not limited to Neo-Asianism, Pacific Way and Asian View continue to complicate discussions on regional integration.[38] Different conceptions about the future of integration among vested interests in the region do not simplify the situation any further. In other words, deepening or upgrading the level of state interactions becomes a hurdle when the issue of "identity" cannot be overcome to establish consensus. This is the raison d'etre for this author to commence with a discussion on communal identity. If the idea of "community" cannot be promoted as a fundamental principle that undergirds regional cooperation and confidence building, the institutionalization of integration in Northeast Asia will continue to be just a castle in the sky.

Notes

1. Alberto Melucci, *Challenging Codes: Collective Action in the Information Age* (Cambridge: Cambridge University Press, 1966), p. 150.
2. see Vincent Cable, *The World's New Fissures: Identities in Crisis* (London: Demos, 1996), pp. 20–22; Susan Strange, *The Retreat of the State: The Diffusion of Power in the World Economy* (Cambridge: Cambridge University Press, 1996); Georg Henrik von Wright, "The Crisis of Social Science and the Withering Away of the Nation-state," *Associations*, 1 (1997), pp. 49–52.
3. Bjorn Hettne, *The New Regionalism: Implications for Global Development and International Security* (Helsinki: UNU Wider, 1994), p. 4.
4. Chia Show Yue and Lee Taso Yuan, "Sub-regional Economic Zones: A New Motive Force in Asia-Pacific Development," in C. Fred Bergsten and Marcus Noland, eds. *Pacific Dynamism and the International Economic System* (Washington: Institute of International Economics, 1993).
5. Thant, Myo and Min Tang, eds. *Growth Triangle: Theory to Practice* (Manila: Asian Development Bank, 1996).
6. Robert A. Scalapino, "The United States and Asia: Future Prospects," *Foreign Affairs*, Winter91/92, pp. 19–40.
7. T. G. McGee and Scott Macleod, "Emerging Extended Metropolitan Regions in Asia-Pacific Urban System: A Case Study od the Singapore-Johor-Riau Growth Triangle," paper presented at the Workshop on Asia-Pacific Urban System, The Chinese University of Hong Kong, 1992.
8. Norman Palmer, *New Regionalism in Asia and Pacific* (Lexington: Lexington Books, 1991), p. 5.
9. Charles Morrison, Akira Kojima, and Hanns W. Maull "Community Building with Pacific Asia," The Triangle Papers, No. 51 (New York: Trilateral Commission, 1997), p. 2. http://www.gbv.de/dms/sub-hamburg/229966055.pdf
10. Zygmunt Bauman, *Community: Seeking Safety in an Insecure World* (London: Polity, 2001).

11 Kristina Jonsson, "Unity-in-Diversity? Regional Identity Building in Southeast Asia,"Working Paper in Contemporary Asian Studies Working Paper, No. 29 (2008), p. 3; James Tully, "Identity Politics," in Terence Ball and Richard Bellamy eds., *The Cambridge History of Twentieth Century Political Thought* (Cambridge: Cambridge University Press, 2003), pp. 518–519; Anthony Burke, "Questions of Community: Australian Identity and Asian Change," *Australian Journal of Political Science*, Vol. 45, No. 1 (2010), pp. 78–79.

12 Zhang Xiaoming, "Regional Identity and Northeast Asian Community Building," *East Asian Review*, Vol. 9 (March 2005), pp. 117–123; Andrej Tusicisny, "Security Communities and Their Values: Taking Masses Seriously," *International Political Science Review*, 28: 4 (2007), p. 427; Ted Hopf, "The Promise of Constructivism in International Relations Theory," *International Security*, 23: 1 (1998), pp. 171–200; Richard Ned Lebow, "Identity and International Relations," *International Relations*, 22: 4 (2008), pp. 473–492.

13 Terri Mannarini and Angela Fedi, "Multiple Senses of Community: The Experience and Meaning of Community," *Journal of Community Psychology*, 37: 2 (2009), pp. 211–227.

14 Raymund Jose G. Quilop, "Building a Security Community in Northeast Asia: Options and Challenges," *International Journal of Korean Unification Studies*, 18: 2 (2009), p. 127; Jiangli Wang, "Security Community in the Context of Non-traditional Security," *World Economics and Politics*, 343: 3, http://www.rsis-ntsasia.org/activities/fellowship/2007/wjl%27s%20paper.pdf

15 Emanuel Adler and Michael Barnett eds., *Security Communities* (Cambridge: Cambridge University Press, 1998).

16 Alexander Wendt, *Social Theory of International Politics* (Peking: Peking University Press, 1999), pp. 308–317.

17 "No Community without Cooperation: Regional Institutions and Asia's Security Order," Report of the Sentosa Roundtable on Asian Security 2007–2008, p. 6; Torsten Weber, "Remembering or Overcoming the Past?: 'History Politics', Asian Identity and Visions of an East Asian Community," *Asian Regional Integration Review*, Vol. 3 (2011), p. 40; Rawl Abdela et. al. eds., *Measuring Identity: A Guide for Social Scientists* (Cambridge: Cambridge University Press, 2009); Klaus Eder and Bernhard Giesen eds., *European Citizenship: National Legacies and Colonial Projects* (Oxford: Oxford University Press, 2000).

18 Sunhyuk Kim and Hans Schattle, "Solidarity as a Unifying Idea in Building an East Asian Community: Toward an Ethos of Collective Responsibility," *The Pacific Review*, 25: 4 (2012), p. 476.

19 Douglass North, "The New Institutional Economics and Development," in John Harriss et al. eds., *The New Institutional Economics and Third World Development* (London: Sage, 1997), p. 23.
20 Douglass North, "Economic Performance through Time," *The American Economic Review*, Vol. 84, No. 3 (1994), p. 359.
21 James March and Johan Olsen, "The New Institutionalism: Organizational Factors in Political Life," *American Political Science Review*, 78: 3 (1984), pp. 734–749.
22 Tang Siew Mun, "No Community Sans Concert? The Role of Great Powers in Institutionalizing an Asian Security Community," in See Seng Tan ed., *Do Institutions Matter? Regional Institutions and Regionalism in East Asia* (Singapore: S. Rajaratnam School of International Studies, 2008), p. 64.
23 Vinod Aggarwal and Min Gyo Koo, "An Institutional Path: Community Building in Northeast Asia," in G. John Ikenberry and Chung-in Moon eds., *The United States and Northeast Asia: Debates, Issues and New Order* (New York: Rowman and Littlefield, 2008), p. 288.
24 Andrew Yeo, "Bilateralism, Multilateralism and Institutional Change in Northeast Asia's Regional Security Architecture," EAI Fellows Program Working Paper Series No. 30 (Seoul: The East Asia Institute, 2011), p. 16; Byung-Woon Lyou, "Building the Northeast Asian Community," *Indiana Journal of Global Legal Studies*, 11: 2 (2004), pp. 257–310.
25 Hadi Soesastro, "East Asia Economic Integration: The Search for an Institutional Identity," http://cloud2.gdnet.org/cms.php?id=research_paper_abstract&research_paper_id=11205
26 Emanuel Adler and Patricia Greve, "When Security Community Meets Balance of Power: Overlapping Regional Mechanisms of Security Governance," *Review of International Studies*, Vol. 35 (2009), pp. 59–84.
27 Glenn Hook and Ian Kearns, eds. *Sub-regionalism and World Order* (London: MacMillan Press, 1999), p. 6.
28 Ka Zeng, "Multilateral versus Bilateral and Regional Trade Liberalization: Explaining China's Pursuit of Free Trade Agreements," *Journal of Contemporary China*, 19: 6 (2010), pp. 647–9.
29 James Rousseau, "Governance in the Twenty-first Century," *Global Governance*, 1 (1995), p. 26.
30 James Rousseau, "Governance in the Twenty-first Century," *Global Governance*, 1 (1995), p. 26.
31 Kenichi Ohmae, *The End of the Nation States* (London: HarperCollins, 1995), p. 6.

32 Chia Siow Yue and Lee Tsao Yuan, "Sub-regional Economic Zones: A New Motive Force in Asia-Pacific Development," in Fred Bergstein and Marcus Noland, eds. *Pacific Dynamism and the International Economic System* (Washington: Institute for International Economics, 1993), p. 236.

33 Mitchell Bernard and John Ravenhill, "Beyond Produce Cycles and Flying Geese: Regionalization, Hierarchy, and the Industrialization of East Asia," World Politics, 47: 2 (1995), pp. 171–209.

34 Wei Kiat Yip, "Prospects for Closer Economic Integration in East Asia," *Stanford Journal of East Asian Affairs*, 1 (2001), p. 106; Joshua Kurlatzick, "Is East Asia Integrating?" *The Washington Quarterly*, 24: 4 (2001), p. 21.

35 Etel Solingen, "East Asian Regional Institutions: Characteristics, Resources, and Distinctiveness," in T. J. Pempel, ed. *Remapping East Asia: the Construction of a Region* (Ithaca: Cornell University Press, 2005), pp. 32–38.

36 Richard A. Higgott, "The Political Economy of Globalization in East Asia: the Salience of Region Building," in Kris Olds et al. eds. *Globalization and the Asia-Pacific: Contested Territories* (New York: Routledge, 1999), pp. 91–106.

37 Ted G. Carpenter, "From Intervenor of First Resort to Balancer of Last Resort," in Selig Harrison ad Clyde Prestowitz, eds. *Asia after the Miracle* (Washington: Brookings Institute Press, 1998), pp. 294.

38 see K. Mahbubani, "The Pacific Way," *Foreign Affairs*, 74(1995), pp. 100–111, and L. Low, "The East Asian Economic Grouping," *The Pacific Review*, 4(1995), pp. 375–382.

Chapter 7

'East Asian Safe Community' Drawn in 'Nagoya':
War, Disaste, Calamity

Song, Whanbhum (Seoul Women's University, Korea)

This year is the 7th anniversary of the Great East Japan Earthquake and Tsunami (referred to as the 3.11 Great East Japan Earthquake in Korea) that happened at 2:26 p.m. on March 11, 2011. The Global Institute for Japanese Studies of Korea University (renamed from the Institute for Japanese Studies) swiftly formed and started to operate a dedicated research team from March 14, 2011, three days after the occurrence of the great earthquake. This served as a momentum to observe devastating damage that Japan faced, though on the screen of the television, and to predict that Japan would show passive or introverted reactions in one form or another. Since these changes in Japan were expected to continue to have a significant impact on its neighboring countries in East Asia, including Korea, in unexpected areas until now, we thought that disasters in Japan could not be approached separately from Korea.

Before long, the research team was expanded and reorganized under its new name – 「Post-3.11 and Humans: Disaster・Security・East Asia」. The performances and detailed activities of the research team have been reported on several occasions, and the following reports can be referred to: Song, Whanbhum, 「'The Great East Japan Earthquake' in History seen from '3.11'」, 『Japan Review 2012-The 3.11 Great East Japan Earthquake and Japan-』, Moon Publishing, 2012; 「'East Sea Rim Studies' Seen from the Aspects of Disaster and Safety in the 'East Sea Rim Region'」, 『Asia Pacific Journal』 Vol.

19-3, 2012; and 「'Historical Seismic Studies' as Converged Japanese Studies-Comments on 'Disaster Studies'-」, 「The Korean Journal of Japanology」 Vol. 100, 2014.

From now on, I will look back on the achievements that I have made so far and take this as a starting point for new studies. I have had about 20 opportunities to deliver presentations, join discussions and preside over seminars or symposiums over the last 5 years. By year, there were four occasions in 2012 (Presentation titled [Disaster and Safety of the East Sea Rim] in the International Conference of the Institute of Global Affairs of Kyunghee University (Dynamics and Multilayers of the East Sea Rim) held in Kyunghee University on April 26; Presentation titled [the '3.11 Great Earthquake' seen from Calamities of Ancient Times] in the International Conference of the Society for Cultural Interaction in East Asia held in Korea University on May 11-12; Presentation titled [Studies Conducted in Korea on Disasters in Japan after '3.11'] in the International Academic Forum of the Institute for the Research of Disaster Areas Reconstruction of Kwansei Gakuin University held on May 18; Presiding over the 1st Session of the International Joint Conference of Kwansei Gakuin University and the Global Institute for Japanese Studies titled [The Great East Japan Earthquake and Japan-Projections on Japanese Society and Korea from the Perspective of Disasters-] held in the Global Institute for Japanese Studies on September 18); 6 occasions in 2013 (Presentation titled [Disaster Studies Based on the Humanities in Korea-Focusing on Publishing Translated Books on Disaster Studies in Japan-] in the Research Exchange Forum of the Department of International Cultural Exchange of Gakushuin Women's College held under the theme of [Promotion of Disaster Studies and Seeking for International Cooperation] in Gakushuin Women's College, Japan, on January 17; Presiding over the 3rd Session titled [The Great East Japan Earthquake and Environment, International Cooperation] of the International Conference of the Global Institute for Japanese Studies held under the theme of [Promotion of Disaster Studies in East Asia and Seeking for International Cooperation] in Korea University, Korea on March 9; Presentation titled 「the Great Earthquake as Visible History」 in the 2012 Symposium on Frontier of Humanities held by the

Department of Literature of Okayama University under the theme of [Japan seen from Korea] in Okayama University, Japan on March 13; Presentation titled [Seeking for Revival after the Great East Japan Earthquake from the Perspective of Humanities-For the Views and Convergence of Humanities] in the 2nd Session and presiding over General Discussion in the 3rd Session of the Academic Seminar of the Global Institute for Japanese Studies held under the theme of (the 3.11 Great East Japan Earthquake and Disaster Studies-Beyond Translation) in the Global Institute for Japanese Studies on August 29; Presentation titled 「Natural Disasters and Reversal of Policy in Ritsuryo State」 in the Korea-Japan Joint Symposium held under the theme of [Humans and Society after 3.11] in the Graduate School of Kagoshima University, Japan on October 23; Presentation titled [the 3.11 Great East Japan Earthquake and Disaster Studies in Korea] in the International Symposium hosted by the Office of Assemblyman Choi, Jae-cheon under the theme of (the Effects of 3.11 Fukushima Nuclear Disaster on Korean Society) in the National Assembly Building, Korea on November 6); 5 occasions in 2014 (Presiding over the Morning Session titled (Japan's Complex Ideology and Culture, and Education) and Invited Presentation in the Afternoon Session titled (Converged Discussion on Cultural Research Methods-'About the 3.11 Great East Japan Earthquake'-) of the 88th International Symposium of the Korea Associate of Japanology held by the Society of Japanese History and Culture under the theme of (Convergence of Japan Studies From the perspective of Humanities and Social Sciences) in Chungang University, Korea on February 28; Presiding over General Discussion of the Symposium for the 3th Anniversary of the 3.11 Great East Japan Earthquake Symposium held by the Global Institute for Japanese Studies under the theme of [the 3.11 Great East Japan Earthquake Seen On-site and Symbiosis] in the Global Institute for Japanese Studies, Korea on March 3; Presentation titled [East Asia Seen from the Aspects of Disaster and Safety] in the East Asia Institute of Zhejiang Gongshang University, China on October 15; Presentation titled (News Articles on Disasters Seen in Libraries in Japan) and presiding over the International Symposium jointly hosted by Kagoshima University and the Global Institute for Japan Studies under the theme of [Disasters and

Cross-boundary Knowledge (越境知): From Globalized East Asia] in the Global Institute for Japan Studies, Korea on November 14; Presentation titled (Seeking for Japanese Values from the Perspective of Korea-in Relation to the 3.11 Great East Japan Earthquake-) in the Symposium of the Korea Association for Japanese Thought held under the theme of [Is Co-existence and Symbiosis Possible in East Asia?] in Kyunghee University, Korea on November 15); 3 occasions in 2015 (Presentation titled ['Safety of Humans' Seen through 'Disasters'] in the 2015 Joint Symposium of Humanities Korea (HK) held under the theme of ["Korean Society Asks, and Humanities Answers"] in Konkuk University, Korea on March 28; Presiding over the International Symposium for the 4th Anniversary of the 3.11 Great East Japan Earthquake jointly held with the Korea Occupational Safety Research Institute under the theme of [Seeking for 'East Asia Safety Community' against Disasters and Industrial Accidents] in Korea University, Korea on April 17; Lecture titled ['Safety of East Asia' against 'Wars' and 'Disasters'] in the Seminar held by the Graduate School of Korea National Defense University, Korea on December 9); and 2 occasions in January, 2016 (Presentation titled [Introduction to the Theory of East Asia Safety Community: Wars·Disasters] in the Department of International Cultural Exchange of Gakushuin Women's College, Japan on January 12; and Presentation titled [Beyond the Region: Seeking for the Theory of East Asia Safety Community] in Kagoshima University, Japan on January 23). The number of papers that were publicly issued and contributions to the media for the same period was also approximately 20. By year, there were 2 articles in 2011 (March 21, [Historicity Found in the 'Sense of Order' of the Public], 「Korea University Newspaper」 Vol. 1665; and May, 「Post-3.11 Japan, and East Asia」, 「East Asia History Issues」 Vol. 50); 6 articles in 2012 (March, (co-authored), 「The Great East Japan Earthquake in History seen from 3.11」, 「Japan Review 2012-3.11 Great East Japan Earthquake and Japan-」, Moon Publishing; May, (jointly-translated), 「The Meaning of the Darvish Fever in Japan after the 3.11 Great East Japan Earthquake」, 「Platform」 Vol. 33 (May·June), the Incheon Foundation for Arts & Culture; May, 「Verification of the 3.11 Great East Japan Earthquake」, the Post-3.11 and Humanity Research

Team of Korea University, Moon Publishing; May, 『The Faith and Disasters of Japan's Ritsuryo State-'Faith in Four Heavenly Gods (四天王)' and 'Zhenguan (貞觀) Great Earthquake'-』, 『The Journal of Japanology』 Vol. 34, the Institute of Japanese Studies of Dongguk University; December, (co-authored), 『The Faith and Disasters of Japan's Ritsuryo State-'Faith in Four Heavenly Gods (四天王)' and 'Zhenguan (貞觀) Great Earthquake'-』, 『Religion and Culture of East Asia』, the Association of East Asia Ancient Studies, Kyungin Publishing; and December, 『'East Sea Rim Studies' Seen from the Aspects of Disaster and Safety in the 'East Sea Rim Region'』, 『Asia Pacific Journal』 Vol. 19-3); 5 articles in 2013 (March, (translated book), 『Philosophy of the Conservation and Revival of Cultural Heritages-Regeneration of the Creative Relationship with Nature』, Korea University Press; March, (jointly translated), 『The Great East Japan Earthquake-Seeking for Revival from the Perspective of Humanities-』, Korea University Press; May, (co-authored), 『The Great East Japan Earthquake in History Seen from 3.11』, 『The Great East Japan Earthquake and Japan-3.11 Seen from Korea-』, Kwansei Gakuin University Press; May, (jointly translated), 『Comment on the Great East Japan Earthquake-For Sustainable Revival-』, Korea University Press; and December, 『Natural Disasters and Reversal of Policy in Japan's Ritsuryo State』, 『Journal of Japanese Thought』 Vol. 25); 5 articles in 2014 (May 10, 『For the 3rd Anniversary of the Great East Japan Earthquake』, 『Korea University Newspaper』 Vol. 1744; March, (co-authored), 『Great Earthquake as Visible History』, Research Report 21 Project 『Symbolic Concepts and Culture of Disaster・War・Epidemic』, the Department of Literature of Okayama University; April, (co-authored), 『Prologue: The Effects of the 3.11 Great East Japan Earthquake on Korea』, 『Japan's Revival from Disasters-The 3.11 Great East Japan Earthquake and Humans -』, Inmunsa; May, (co-authored), 『'The 3.11 Great East Asia Earthquake' and 'Historical Seismic Studies' as a New Category of Studies』, 『Japan Review 2014-Transformed Japan-』, Interbooks; and August, 『Historical Seismic Studies' as Converged Japanese Studies-Comments on 'Disaster Studies'-』, 『The Korean Journal of Japanology』 Vol. 100); and 2 articles in 2015 (January, 『The Great East Japan Earthquake and Cooperation between Korea and Japan in the

Starting Point of Disaster Studies in Korea」, 「Korea-Japan Cooperation」 Issue of Spring, Korea-Japan Cooperation Committee; and July, 「Diversity of Korea-Japan Relationship: 'Security Acts' and 'the 3.11 Great East Japan Earthquake'」, 「Analysis of Security Affairs」, the Research Institute for National Security Affairs of Korea National Defense University). The 20 presentations and 20 documents listed above may not be exactly identical in terms of wordings. However, they are enough to read changes in the overall interest and several keywords can be extracted from them. The keywords set initially include 「Disaster・Safety・East Asia」, and they have been used as central keywords until now. The next important implication is that the focus of studies on disasters in Japan has been shifted to how to interpret them from the perspective of Korea, which shows the self-reflection on the fact that the results of the studies of our research team have been focused on translating studies on disasters that were published in Japan (refer to the Academic Seminar held under the theme of 「「3.11 Great East Japan Earthquake」 and Disaster Studies-Beyond Translation」 in the Global Institute for Japanese Studies, Korea on August 29, 2013). In line with the self-reflection, the current focus of my studies is laid on 「safety of humans」 and 「safe community」, putting 「humans」 and 「symbiosis」 before anything else.

Meanwhile, the flow of interest can be captured from the directions of the symposium that has been held by the Global Institute for Japanese Studies in around March, every year. The symposium was held on the 1st anniversary of the 3.11 Great East Japan Earthquake in 2012 under the theme of 「Lessons from the 3.11 Great East Japan Earthquake–About Complex Crisis and Crisis Management–」; on the 2nd anniversary, 「Promotion of Disaster Studies in East Asia and Seeking for International Cooperation」; and on the 3rd anniversary, 「the 3.11 Great East Japan Earthquake Seen On-site and Symbiosis」. On the 4th anniversary, the symposium was jointly held with the Korea Occupational Safety Research Institute under the theme of 「Seeking for 'East Asian Safe Community' against Disasters and Industrial Accidents」. To sum up, the key ideas of the symposium include 「lessons from disasters」, 「cooperation in disaster studies」, 「symbiosis on site」 and 「seeking for safe community」.

These efforts took a turning point when 「the Sinking of the Sewol Ferry (referred to as the Capsized Ferry Accident in Korea in 2014 in Japan)」 happened on April 16, 2014. 「The Sinking of the Sewol Ferry」 brought an unforgettable shock to Korean society and called for serious reflection for a while. After the accident, our research team accepted the Hankyoreh's request for an overseas interview, and the interview was covered in the articles titled 「Post-disaster Korea Put to the Test」 (『Hankyoreh 21』 Vol. 1009, May 5, 2014) and 「the Beginning of Korean Disaster Studies」 (『Hankyoreh 21』 Vol. 1014, June 9, 2014). The focus of my studies since April, 2014 has settled down to 「safety of humans」 (the Joint Symposium of Humanities Korea (HK) held in Konkuk University on March 28, 2015) and 「East Asian Safe Community」 (the International Symposium for the 4th Anniversary of the 3.11 Great East Japan Earthquake held in Korea University on April 17, 2015). Meanwhile, 「the Sewol Ferry」, 「MERS, an infectious disease」 and 「state-written history textbooks」 were selected as the most important events in Korean society in the end of 2015 (Yonhap News, December 13, 2015), which indicates that our work is still a 'living and breathing' ongoing task. Moreover, seeking for 「East Asian Safe Community」 is not a problem that Korea must solve alone. It must not end as an attempt to seek for solutions only, but it is nothing but a grand plan to secure safety across East Asia.

Efforts to design the 「safe community」 based on this basic recognition were made once again in the 2017 Nagoya Convention of the One Asia Foundation, which was all the more meaningful. Plans for the safe community so far have been focused on politics, economy and security, cherishing the interest of members only.

Why haven't we highlighted plans for the 「safe community」 that puts the 「safety of humans」 before anything else so far? In particular, efforts to establish 「East Asian safe community」 must be made based on bold but flexible ideas that go beyond the border and nationality of a country. 「Safety」 in human society is not just against 「disasters」 or 「calamities」. 「Safety」 should be secured also against 「wars」.

By doing so, the key theme of the existing theory of East Asian Community can be shifted to 「safety」, which is expected to serve as an opportunity to step forward to establish a materialized safe community in East Asia, not an imaginary community.

Section 4

Perspectives towards an Asian Community – Part 2
History, Education, Thought, Philosophy and Religion

Chapter 8
Sharing and Accumulating Understanding of Neighbor Countries and Their People:
A Foundation for Asian Community

Seok-won Song (Kyung Hee University, Republic of Korea)

1. Asian Community and Understanding of Neighbor Countries and Their People

Through the history, there have been numerous attempts to pursue reconciliation and cooperation among countries beyond past conflict and confrontation in forms of unions. However, practically, only meager number of meaningful unions has made. As we all assume, a union among disparate nations is an ideal, and the path to make an ideal into reality is paved with abundant obstacles. A case in point is the European Union. The European Union aims at a united Europe in political, economic, and sociocultural fields. Still, the EU allows its members to selectively participate in its regional policies, not forcing them to cooperate with the Union as a whole. This directly shows the difficulty of forming a full-scale union among countries. As we know, the Association of South East Asian Nations (ASEAN) proclaimed its identity as an economic union, setting aside politics and security. This proclamation may show that an economic union is the best result the countries can come up with in the regional circumstances. At the same time, the proclamation is based on the premise that a political or a security union in South East Asia is impossible.

In the meantime, Asia comes into the spotlight once again in the global stage. In the past, some scholars used a term the *four little dragons of Asia*[1] with a sense of awe. However, that awe also included a sense of contempt toward the stasis of Asian countries other than the four little dragons. Even in debates over *Asian values*,[2] Asia was a connotation of political backwardness distorting universal democratic values. In contrast, in recent debates concerning Asia, there has been a meaningful change. Asia became an *alternative* for current civilization in ecology and in the environmental issue. In the current debates, some foresaw that Asian civilization or at least Asian values would replace European ones, which has deemed as the mainstream.[3] Can Asia be the mainstream, as they predicted? If so, what conditions should be met to make that into reality? To make the foresight into reality, relationships among Asian countries need to be cooperative, and a cooperative relationship tends to be based on trivial understanding of neighbors. Only when understanding of neighbor countries and their people is accumulated and expanded enough, any cooperation would be available. Under this premise, this article will deal with a few themes regarding the understanding.

However, in any region, understanding of neighbor countries and their people is hard to be accumulated. Especially, in Asia, there are a great number of obstacles on the path to true understanding. As a *region*, Asia is the most disparate region in the globe; disparate ethnicities, religion, and culture. The political and economic circumstances differ from each other. Maybe that is the reason for the attempt seems unachievable to consider Asia, which comprises numerous and disparate population, as 'one region.' Thus, accumulating the understanding in Asian region is a tough sell, without a doubt. In fact, although there have been plenty debates over Asian community among academics, ordinary people in Asia still hardly consider themselves as same Asians. Meanwhile, it is worthy to pay attention to the self-categorization of Asian population in multicultural countries like the US, Canada, and Australia. In those countries, Asians mostly categorize themselves with their nationalities such as Korean American, Japanese American, and Chinese American. At the same time, they also use the regional categorization, Asian American.[4] For instance, an interpellation is taking place in American society categorizing Asians immigrants as Asian Americans dividing them from other racial groups such as African Americans, and Hispanic Americans.

Albeit Asian American group has same American citizenship as other groups do, in their daily lives, they end up realizing a stone wall regarding their nationalities is before them. Nevertheless, when it comes to other regional categories, they call themselves as the same Asian Americans. In addition, it is also worthwhile to pay attention to the term Asian literature is in use along with other national categories such as Korean literature, Japanese literature, Chinese literature, and Thai literature in Western academics. Still, there hasn't been a clear definition for Asian literature. Although terms like Asian immigrants and Asian literature is generally in use, it is hard to say that each terminology is integral. However, we should pay attention to that the view considering Asia as one group is a significant change. To labor the point, the prerequisite for a united *community* in Asia is a clear self-identification as an *Asian* among whole populace in the region. And this naturally leads us to the importance of accumulating understanding of neighbor countries and their people from a very base.

2. Various forms of the Understanding of Asian Neighbors

Then, how the understanding of neighbor countries and their people can be accumulated? In the basics of unification theory, regional unification should be tactically implemented in the perspective of spillover from low politics to high politics, no matter its form. Therefore, what we need is a clear boundary of Asia set by reinforced low politics in the region. In this regards, we need to come up with a possibility for the understanding by exploring Asia from diverse perspectives of low politics including culture, literature, art, design, and so forth. In fact, there has been abundant volume of Asian community studies. Still, most of them are simply focused on politics and economics. This tendency is the result of the past goal and strategy of Asian community. Nevertheless, true Asian community should be grounded on low politics—accumulating and sharing the understanding. Under this basis, this article will focus on primary six themes, setting aside the fact that there are more themes.

First of all, Asia must free itself from the roots of geopolitical *conflicts*, since this region is where diverse geopolitical conflicts and cooperation converge.

Geopolitics has evolved and changed from A.T. Mahan's Theory of Insular Dominance[5] to H.J. Mackinder's Heartland Theory,[6] to N.J. Spykman's Rimland Theory.[7] This change shows that geopolitics was an excuse for the expansion of sphere of influence by superpowers during the WWI and WWII.[8] The Japanese Empire's so-called the Greater East Asia Co-Prosperity Sphere was also rooted in such a geopolitical idea. To be specific, the Japanese Empire set up its theory for the Greater East Asia Co-Prosperity Sphere based on K. Haushofer's Lenbensraum (living space) theory, and the empire used it to justify its invasion on Asia.[9] The Greater East Asia Co-Prosperity Sphere meant every ethnic groups of East Asia prospering pivoting around Japan and habitats of them. And the political ideology, or the catchphrase was "Asian economy for Asians." In reality, however, the catchphrase was nothing but a political slogan to justify the empire's invasion on China and South East Asia at the time, and an excuse for Japan's reign on South and East Asia. The empire's geopolitical strategy based on the Sphere failed at last, and numerous East Asians including Japanese were lost. And the consequences are still taking effect on relationships between East Asian countries and Japan. This painful past is still one of the biggest obstacles hindering mutual understanding among East Asians, and blocking building Asian community. Like so, East Asian *past* is the quintessential case which shows how geopolitical strategy of one country can exacerbate conflicts and confrontations between countries. Furthermore, this *past* is making a tough sell tougher. In other words, what happened in the past is one of the biggest hurdles for regional integration in the present and the future, because of the fact that a country exploited the union of Asia to justify its invasion and conquests rather than common benefits of the region. So, henceforward, Asia needs to build geopolitical cooperation apart from its past roots of geopolitical conflicts.[10] A joint development on border area would be a meaningful start point for that kind of cooperation. In fact, multiple joint investments and joint developments are being planned —and some of them are even taking place; for instance, development projects on Chinese-North Korean-Russian border, Korea East Sea Rim area, the Mekong River area. These joint projects, though slowly proceeding, are very important signs in terms of accumulating cooperative experience in Asia. Such experiences are the first step for accumulating, and sharing multifaceted understanding.

Second, reinforcing and expanding mutual understanding through literature. Literature contains peculiar sentiments of each nation or ethnicity. Hence there are always literary categories named after each nations' or each ethnicities' identity. Therefore, it is hard to say that *regional literature* or *world literature* exceeding borders or ethnicity has specifically formed. Although most of us have read world literary collections in our childhood, the collection in this context is nothing but a mere a set of texts from globally famous authors, rather than collection from each country's literature. Moreover, Korean literature, Japanese literature, and Chinese literature is specific per se, but Asian literature is opaque so far. Nevertheless, when we narrow the scope to East Asia, specifically to Korea, China, and Japan, there was East Asian literature tradition. In fact, the three East Asian literature shared Chinese letter system, government official recruitment system—though Japan wasn't—, religion, and common written form of literature. At the same time, the three also developed their own literature such as *Hanshi /Baihuashi* (漢詩/白話詩, Chinese traditional Poetry), *Hyang-ga* (鄉歌, Korean traditional poetry), and *Waka* (和歌, Japanese traditional poetry). Especially, short poetic forms of these three countries—*Jueju* (Pentarains with 20 letters, Heptarains with 28 letters), *Waka* (5/7/5/7/7 letters for five lines making 31 syllables), and *Haiku* (5/7/5 letters for three lines making 17 syllables)— are surprisingly similar in their forms. Despite these short poems have a limitation because only a certain group of people—the ruling class and the intellectual can enjoy them, these people could understand other neighbor countries' poems as well, and they probably could grasp emotions in the poems. It's because the poems were written in Chinse Character, which was a touchstone of cultivation at that time. Without a doubt, defining the whole Asian literature clearly in a sentence or dividing it from other regional literature is not an easy task. Classifying one single country's literature objectively is a hefty task per se, so it is a waste of time to say how massive it is when it comes to Asian literature. Anyway, aforementioned three East Asian countries actually could understand each other's emotion in the past. And it has a lot of meaning—albeit that understanding was limited to certain group of people, rather than the whole populace. In addition, we can even see various Asian nations' literature, not only the three East Asian countries, is being introduced to each other nowadays. And the public is the main consumer of Asian literature. In this respect, we may say accumulating and sharing of understanding of Asian neighbors through literature is only a step ahead.

Third, more information about Asia needs to be spread through various media—though, knowingly, it's a part of Asian literature. Not only audiovisual contents such as television series and films, written texts dealing with Asia are scarce in general. Only in a handful of countries, there are a small number of books generally or specifically explaining about various cultures of Asia. Admittedly, there are a few prerequisites for a book to exist in the market; an author with an expertise, a publisher who can willingly take all risks of publication, and readers who are curious of Asian countries. And these prerequisites need to be met all at the same time. Among the prerequisites, the most important one is readership. Only when there are readers, any book can be written and published. In modern times, each and every country focused on making *reading masses* on the way to building nation-state.[11] Reading bases on literacy, and literacy leads to comprehensison of the ideal of the country. Naturally, literacy was the most important priority for governments at the time. And in early modern days, written texts such as newspapers, magazines, and books greatly contributed to creating *reading masses*.[12] Today, we are on the way to postmodern times from modern one. Still, when it comes to building regional community, we need *reader's communities*[13] similar to reading communities in the modern times. Members of those communities would be people who willingly read Asian texts and who learn how to live with their neighbors cooperatively.

Fourth, we need to explore Asian beauty in art and design, and expand the understanding. Recently, one Korean cosmetics company came up with the results of its research on experiences and perceptions of Asian beauty. The first result was *the Water and Asian Beauty*.[14] The result was published in a book, and the followings are the contents of the book: '*Asian Beauty Flows with Waterways,*' '*Flowing Water, the Best Natural and Aesthetic Beauty,*' '*East Asian Aesthetics of*

Water Depicted in Modern Design,' 'Shapes of Water: Water in Asian Films,' 'How did Neurosis, Destruction, and Curse of Water Became a Symbol of Life,' 'Subak and Ecologic Beauty: A Case Report on Balinese Agriculture and Water,' and 'Korean Culture on Water and its Sensual Beauty.' What is interesting is that the book is trying to explore Asian beauty connecting water to design and films. The book is a journey to find the ultimate Asian beauty through exploring connotations, symbols, and aesthetics of water in Asian culture. And this journey would be a way to the understanding of Asian neighbors per se. The next theme of the following book expected to be Beautiful People, and it's thrilling to see how they depicted beautiful Asian people.

Fifth, mutual understanding of Asian medicine should be deepen, and the understanding would include traditional medicinal herbs, recuperations, and folk remedies that have been accumulated since the past. Considering the fact that the author currently works at a university famous of Korean medicine, the author would like to emphasize the importance of this theme. Oriental medicines have different names; Korean medicine, Chinese medicine, *Kampo medicine or Kokan medicine* in Japan, Traditional Mongolian medicine, Tibetan medicine, and Ayurveda in India. The treatment in those Oriental medicines is eradicating the root of the disease and readjusting the balance between yin and yang, and recuperating functions of intestines. In this regards, each traditional medicines are all complementary. Therefore, what needed are more connections, and creating Asian medicine as the understanding of Asian neighbors.

Sixth, we need to focus on the dynamic movement of interregional immigrants. In these days, there are colossal number of immigrants and emigrants.[15] And Asia is not an exception from this phenomenon. Especially, there is a spike increase in the number of interregional migrants in Asia. In most cases, immigrants tend to be the minority in countries of residence. Meanwhile, they play an important role as a bridge to their mother countries, and as a creator of hybrid culture, though they experience discrimination from the majority. Despite most of them face hardship in countries of residence, when we realize their possibility as a bond for East Asian solidarity, we could understand them in a way. The understanding brokered by migrants will be one of the most meaningful foundations for Asian community. To make the true understanding of neighbors possible, each and all governments need to educate both their citizens and immigrants to make them Homo Empaticuses.[16]

3. Expanding the understanding of Asian Neighbor Countries and Their People

Without a doubt, there are more themes of the understanding of Asian neighbors, not only aforementioned six themes. The task before us is to find, debate, and share about other types of understanding of Asian neighbors. I look for possibility to include more themes in this debate. The understanding of neighbor countries and their people is not a meta-discourse, and no need to be. Rather, this understanding is an inevitable prerequisite to build Asian community, since it includes the process of sharing Asian identities through trivial, but diverse understanding on neighbor Asians. In this process to be sympathetic to our neighbors, and to become Homo Empaticus, the understanding and recognition among Asian countries and their people can expand. Furthermore, Asian community can be real through this expansion of this understanding.

Notes

1 Ezra F. Vogel, *The Four Little Dragons*, Harvard University Press, 1991.
2 Daejung Kim et al., *Asian value*, Tradition and Mordern, 1999.; Hwan Lee, *Modernity, Asian Value, Globalization*, Moonji Publishing, 1999.; Daniel Bell, *East Meets West: Human Rights and Democracy in East Asia*, Princeton University Press, 2000
3 Refer to 梅原猛,『人類哲学序説』, 岩波書店, 2013, as an archetype.
4 武者小路公秀・浜邦彦・早尾貴紀編,『ディアスポラと社會變容：アジア系.アフリカ系移住者と多文化共生の課題, 國際書院, 2008, pp.61–68.
5 A. T. Mahan, *The Influence of Sea Power Upon History, 1660–1783*, Little, Brown and Co, 1890.
6 H. J. Mackinder, *Our Own Islands: An Elementary Study in Geography*, G. Philips, 1907.
7 N. J. Spykman, *America's Strategy in World Politics: The United States and the Balance of Power*, Harcourt, Brace and Company, 1942.
8 Younghyoung Lee, *Geopolitics*, M-add, 2006.

9 Karl Haushofer, *Das Japanische Reich in seiner geographischen Entwicklung*, L.W. Seidel & sohn, 1921.
10 Seun Kwon et al., Dynamics in Korean East Sea Rim Network, Kyung Hee University Press, 2016.
11 永嶺重敏,『〈読書国民〉の誕生：明治30年代の活字メディアと読書文化』, 日本エディタースクール出版部, 2004.
12 Seok Won Song, "Power and Newspaper of Japanese Empire: Concering from late 1920s to 1935,"『日本研究』16 (2011): 373–394.
13 龍澤武, "On Reading Community in East Asia," *Source book: The East Asia Publishers Conference*, 2006.
14 Asian Beauty Expedition, *Water and Asian Beauty*, Minimum, 2017.
15 An Increase in migration and its following appearance of multicultural society certainly is a megatrend in 21st century. For additional explanation of megatrend, refer to John Naisbitt, Megatrends: The New Directions Transforming our Lives, Warner Books, 1982.
16 Yong-Chan Kim, "An Increase in migration and its following appearance of multicultural society certainly is a megatrend in 21st century," *Research in Social Studies Education* 23, no.1 (2016): 1–13.

References

Asian Beauty Expedition, *Water and Asian Beauty*, Minimum, 2017.
Bell, Daniel, *East Meets West: Human Rights and Democracy in East Asia*, Princeton University Press, 2000.
Haushofer, Karl, *Das Japanische Reich in seiner geographischen Entwicklung*, L.W. Seidel & sohn, 1921.
Hwan Lee, *Modernity, Asian Value, Globalization*, Moonji Publishing, 1999.
Kwon, Seun et al., *Dynamics in Korean East Sea Rim Network*, Kyung Hee University Press, 2016.
Kim, Daejung et al., *Asian value*, Tradition and Mordern, 1999.
Kim, Yong-Chan, "Trend of the 21st Century and the Direction and the Task of Democratic Citizenship Education in the Multicultural Society," *Research in Social Studies Education* 23, no.1 (2016): 1–13.
Lee, Younghyoung, *Geopolitics*, M-add, 2006.
Mackinder, H. J. *Our Own Islands: An Elementary Study in Geography*, G. Philips, 1907.
Mahan, A. T. *The Influence of Sea Power Upon History, 1660–1783*, Little, Brown and Co, 1890.
Naisbitt, John, Megatrends: *The New Directions Transforming our Lives*, Warner Books,

1982.

Spykman, N. J. *America's Strategy in World Politics: The United States and the Balance of Power*, Harcourt, Brace and Company, 1942.

Seok Won Song, "Power and Newspaper of Japanese Empire: Concering from late 1920s to 1935," 『日本研究』 16 (2011): 373–394.

Vogel, Ezra F. *The Four Little Dragons*, Harvard University Press, 1991.

梅原 猛,『人類哲学序説』, 岩波書店, 2013.

永嶺重敏,『〈読書国民〉の誕生：明治30年代の活字メディアと読書文化』, 日本エディタースクール出版部, 2004.

武者小路公秀・浜邦彦・早尾貴紀編,『ディアスポラと社會變容：アジア系・アフリカ系移住者と多文化共生の課題』, 國際書院, 2008.

龍澤武, "On Reading Community in East Asia," S*ource book: The East Asia Publishers Conference*, 2006.

Chapter 9

Interreligious Dialogue between North and South Korea to Build a Peace Community

Professor Kwangsoo Park (Department of Won-Buddhism, Dean of the Graduate School of Asian Studies, Director of the Research Center of Religions, Wonkwang University, Republic of Korea)

1. Introduction

We currently live in a multicultural and multi-religious society. With the rise of globalization, religious communities are confronting a transformation from a closed exclusivist society to an opened pluralist society. The first public dialogue and cooperation among religions began with the historical meeting of the Parliament of the World's Religions in Chicago, in 1893. Although the 'Parliament of World's Religions in 1893' was not held again until its centennial anniversary both in Bangalore and Chicago in 1993, several international religious associations actively sought dialogue, understanding, and cooperation among religions and actively pursued a change of how religions could interact with each other. When I was a graduate student at the University of Wisconsin-Madison, I attended the centennial anniversary of the Parliament of the World's Religions in Bangalore, India (1993) without knowing much about international religious organizations. After that, I participated in dialogues of various religious organizations such as the Korean Conference on Religion and Peace(KCRP), the Asian Conference on Religion and Peace(ACRP), the World Conference on Religion and Peace(WCRP), the World Fellowship of

Buddhists(WFB), the International Association for Religious Freedom(IARF), the Millennium World Peace Summit, World Parliament of Religions and others. Also, it was an excellent opportunity for me to open dialogue between North and South Korean religious leaders since 1997.

Korea has been divided into North and South Koreas for more than 70 years. And, the relation between them has been at a standstill and getting worse in mixed political and military situations with a strong conservative government policy of South Korea and U.S.A., against the military threat with tests of nuclear weapons under the leadership of Kim Jeong-Un, the Chairman of the National Defense Commission of North Korea. In difficult political and military tensions, The 2018 inter-Korean summit took place on 27 April in 2018 at the South Korean side Panmunjeom of the Joint Security Area between Moon Jae-in, President of Republic of Korea(South Korea), and Kim Jong-un, Chairman of the Workers' Party of Democratic People's Republic of Korea(North Korea).

How can we try to bring both long-harbored hope and enmity toward the unification and reconciliation, security and peace to the Korean peninsula? In my essay, I would like to share my experience of inter-religious dialogue and cooperation among North and South Korean religious leaders.

2. Inter-religious dialogue and experience in traditional Buddhist Teachings and *Won*-Buddhism in Korea

1. Inter-religious experience in traditional Buddhist Teachings

The Buddha Gautama Siddharta had a deep experience of various religious traditions in his lifetime, and showed his broad and vast knowledge of other religious traditions. Buddhism is founded by the Buddha who was seeking for the truth before his enlightenment as a member of the Śramaṇa,[1] the mendicant practitioners. The term 'Śramaṇa' means "seeker, one who performs acts of austerity, ascetic." For this reason, Buddhism "originally belonged to the Śramaṇa movement, as did Jainism and other religious currents." [2]

The Śramaṇa tradition of India provided a diverse range of religious beliefs and practices. The Buddha Gautama visited leading masters such as Ārāda Kālāma and Udraka Rāmaputra,[3] and engaged in extreme ascetic practices.

Although the Buddha could not achieve his final enlightenment by following extreme acetic practices, he could find a righteous practice of the Middle Way such as The Eightfold Right Paths (ⓅÂ ariya-aṭṭhaṅgika-magga) to achieve nirvana in his teaching of the Four Noble Truths (ⓅÂ cattāro ariyasaccāni)

The Buddhist Scriptures frequently describe the Buddha Dharma as the righteous path to achieve nirvana, but the other teachings are not.[4] At the same time, when the Buddha was asked by Sakka the deva-king, he answered that "Those monks who are released through the total ending of craving are the ones who are utterly complete, utterly free from bonds, followers of the utterly holy life, utterly consummate. Therefore not all brahmans & contemplatives are utterly complete, utterly free from bonds, followers of the utterly holy life, utterly consummate."[5] Although all brahmans and contemplatives are entirely complete and utterly free from bonds, they could be utterly complete and free from bonds when they are released through the total ending of craving.

During King Ashoka's reign, although he believed in Buddhism, he kept his openness to other religious beliefs and traditions that all religions shared a common and positive essence to desire self-control and purity of heart. Therefore, he encouraged people to respect and understand other religions. In the Rock Edict Nb 12 and other Rock Edicts of King Ashoka, we find his emphasis on listening to and respecting the doctrines professed by others. Also, it is strongly recommended for people to be well-learned in the good doctrines of other religions.

1) All religions should reside everywhere, for all of them desire self-control and purity of heart. Rock Edict Nb7 (S. Dhammika)
2) Contact (between religions) is good. One should listen to and respect the doctrines professed by others. Beloved-Servant-of-the-Gods, King Piyadasi, desires that all should be well-learned in the good doctrines of other religions. Rock Edict Nb12 (S. Dhammika)
3) In the past there were no Dhamma Mahamatras but such officers were appointed by me thirteen years after my coronation. Now they work among all religions for the establishment of Dhamma, for the promotion of Dhamma, and for the welfare and happiness of all who are devoted to

Dhamma. They work among the Greeks, the Kambojas, the Gandharas, the Rastrikas, the Pitinikas and other peoples on the western borders. They work among soldiers, chiefs, Brahmans, householders, the poor, the aged and those devoted to Dhamma – for their welfare and happiness – so that they may be free from harassment. Rock Edict Nb5 (S. Dhammika)[6]

To implement his open policy of religions, as written in the Rock Edict Nb5, King Ashoka appointed Dhamma Mahamatras as the Officers of faith in order to work for the welfare and happiness of all who are devoted to Dhamma among the Greeks, the Kambojas, the Gandharas, the Rastrikas, the Pitinikas and other peoples on the western borders.

2. Inter-religious dialogue and experience in *Won*-Buddhism in Korea

Won-Buddhism, founded by Master Sot'aesan (Pak Chung-Bin 1891-1943) in Korea in 1916, helps individuals to achieve inner peace while actively working on global peace-building projects. While Koreans were suffering severe suppression under Japanese colonialism (1910-1945), Sot'aesan attained great spiritual enlightenment in 1916 and founded *Won*-Buddhism to lead "all sentient beings drowning in the sea of suffering to a vast and immeasurable paradise by expanding spiritual power and conquering material power through faith in a religion based on truth and training in morality based on facts".[7]

Before his enlightenment, Sot'aesan encountered people with various religious backgrounds and adopted several different religious approaches such as prayer, inquiry, and ascetic meditation. It was a time for him to randomly experience other religious traditions without relying on religious literature. He decided to give up the search for a spiritual guide, and practice meditation without any guidance from a teacher. And after four years of self-guided meditation that was very much ascetic in nature, Sot'aesan finally realized enlightenment on April 28, 1916.

Master Sot'aesan tried to establish the ideal type of model for a new religious order in the future. He considered that a new creative synthetic religion was necessary to guide people to act in concert and agreement and to rectify public morality which was daily declining.[8] He was very eager to learn about other religious teachings. One of the members of the Donghak religion came to see Sot'aesan and asked a question about how to broaden his knowledge. He answered that "When I meet you, I learn about Donghak; and when I meet a follower of another religion, I gain knowledge about that religion, too."[9] This attitude of Sot'aesan was also applied to Christianity. His previous Korean religious leaders, Suun and Chungsan, had a very negative view of Christianity, but Sotaesan claimed that Christianity and his teachings were not different, and both shared the same purpose. When he met with Cho Song-gwang, who had been an elder in the Presbyterian Church for decades, he said,

> A true disciple of Jesus in Christianity will know what I am doing, and a true and intimate disciple of mine in this Order will also know what Jesus did. One who does not see the truth feels like an apostate, estranged from each religion and being hostile to the other religion. Those who are enlightened to the truth know that all religions are of one household although they have different names in accordance with the different times and districts of their foundations.[10]

To explain the same original principle of religions, Sotaesan gave a parable: various religious teachings are the brothers of one family who have lived in different countries for a long time. He criticized the exclusive tendency of religions, and when he met a close-minded Christian minister, he insisted that the minister be liberated from the boundary of the Christian realm. Those who do not make wider observations, being used to their customs and insisting on what they are concerned with, slander others and reject other customs. In this way, they cannot slough off their rules (paradigms) and old customs, and consequently they fall into prejudice, erecting an impregnable fortress between themselves and others. This prejudice causes antagonism and conflicts between nations, churches, families, and individuals.

Sotaesan's knowledge of religions was experiential. His experience and conversation with people of other religions expanded his knowledge of religions. He looked forward to the maintenance of harmonious relationships between people and between religions, and awaited the destruction of the barricades that were separating them.

Among the teachings of the Buddha and Master Sot'aesan in relation to other religious traditions, we could find their core teachings to acknowledge other religions and learn the truthful teachings of other faiths. I consider this attitude as the basis of interreligious dialogue and cooperation. Panikkkar emphasized an important aspect of 'dialogue': "Dialogue—the exchange of views, the encounter of beliefs on equal grounds with mutual confidence, complete frankness and without ulterior motives—is today considered an indispensable element in the search for truth and the realization of justice."[11]

Concerning the cultural aspect, UNESCO developed the idea of 'Culture of Peace' and 'Cultural Diversity,' and the U.N. designated 2001 as the Year of Dialogue among Civilizations. In 2005, the General Assembly of UNESCO adopted the 'Protection and Promotion of the Diversity of Cultural Expressions,' which affirms "that cultural diversity is a defining characteristic of humanity"; and "that cultural diversity forms a common heritage of humanity and should be cherished and preserved for the benefit of all." Furthermore, the UNESCO declaration justifies a minority's defense of its cultural diversity as "an ethical imperative, inseparable from respect for human dignity." We comply with the adoption by the UN General Assembly of its resolution 62/90 entitled "Promotion of Interreligious and Intercultural Dialogue, Understanding and Cooperation for Peace", which declares 2010 as the International Year for the Rapprochements of Cultures.

In this regard, it is important for us to recognize and respect other cultures, faiths, and ethnic groups as our own by practicing the idea of 'Culture of Peace' and 'Diversity of Cultural Expressions' as a fundamental guideline to bring a harmonious peace in the world.

3. Inter-religious dialogue and cooperation among North and South Korean religious leaders

I would like to share my experience on the Korean Peninsula about how to understand and respect other religious or cultural heritages. The history of inter-religious cooperation has not had a long history in South Korea, but it has now developed into a real effort to overcome the division of the nation and to reconcile and unify the Korean people. In fact, the energy that religious organizations had devoted to the struggle for democracy in the 1970s and 1980s is now being re-directed into the movement for national reunification, and religions and NGOs are naturally playing a significant role in the efforts for peace and the reunification of the divided Korean Peninsula.

Security in the Korean Peninsula is still uncertain. After the 36-year colonial period under Japanese imperialism (1910-1945), Koreans experienced a grave war on the Korean peninsula between 1950 and 1953, dividing the country into South Korea (ROK) and North Korea (DPRK) for almost 70 years. Nowadays, although it is extremely limited, North Korea is growing tolerant of NGOs in their country because of the aid they bring during times of crisis, such as during the flood of 1994 and the drought of 1995. Religious leaders play a significant role in the establishment of peace and security. I would like to provide an example from the Korean Conference on Religion and Peace (KCRP) as to how we may reduce tensions and terrors on the Korean. The leaders of KCRP span the seven major religions in Korea: Buddhism, Cheondogyo, Confucianism, Catholicism, Won-Buddhism, Protestantism, and the Association of Korean Native Religions. In North Korea, there are four national-level associations of religions: Buddhism, Catholicism, Chŏndogyo, and Protestantism. The Korean Council of Religionists (KCR) is an umbrella group of these four organizations. Recently, North Korea publicized its decision to construct a Russian Orthodox Church.

In the summer of 1995, tremendous flooding caused grave damage to North Korea. The Communist North Korean Government officially asked the international community to send large-scale food aid, and the religious organizations in South Korea extended much assistance to the victims. The members of KCRP worked together with the civilian organizations to persuade the South Korean Government to send a large amount of food to North Korea by promoting the 'Signature Collecting Campaign of One Million People for Helping the North Korean Brethren and for Reconciliation' in 1997. The leaders of KCRP,

ACRP and WCRP deliberated over the best method to assist North Koreans with food and medical supplies. International organizations such as WFP, FAO, CARITAS, AMERICARES, and others also sent food and medicine to North Korea. This helped South Koreans better understand the need to help their former enemy. This aid led to some degree of North Korean trust for the NGOs. This trust reduced tension on the Korean peninsula and allowed for interaction between the two sides. Korea's divided nature is indicative of the role it must play in world peace as we stumble our way through the process of building 'one world.' Koreans have had both long-harbored hope and enmity toward the unification and reconciliation, security, and peace of their peninsula. While making every endeavor for dialogue and cooperation, the historical summit between South and North Korea on June 15, 2000, there have been enormous cooperative efforts to reduce tension and bring security to the Korean peninsula. The tension between the South and North regarding economics, political ideology, history, and geography provides a stage on which the drama of reconciliation is being played. This summit entailed positive actions such as frequently reuniting separated families. In addition, economic trade, humanitarian assistance, dialogue and cooperation in various fields rapidly grew in Korean peninsula to reduce political and military tensions.

However, despite all efforts to create a harmonious relationship between the South and North, a strong political and military tension in relation to North Korean nuclear weapon rapidly developed after the terrorist attack on the World Trade Center in New York(Sept. 2001). To compound the increasing tensions, George W. Bush made a statement against the North Korean regime as an "axis of evil."(Nov. 2001) Although the Korean peninsula has been in high tension, Korean religious leaders have continued interfaith dialogue and humanitarian support to North Korea until 2015 with the permission of the Korean government. The dialogue between North and South Korean religious leaders was almost completely blocked. After the impeachment of President Park Geun-hye on March 10, 2017, Koreans elected a new President of South Korea(Republic of Korea), Moon Jae-In. I hope the new President of South Korea opens dialogue between North and South Korea to reduce political and military tensions.

Now, President Moon Jae-In is extending the dialogues between North Korea and United States of America as well as South and North Korea.

When political talks have failed, although there are a lot of obstacles, humanitarian assistance from South Korea to North Korea as well as religious and academic exchanges between the two sides help to reduce political and military tensions on the Korean peninsula. Furthermore, mutual dialogue and cooperation in various civilian (NGOs) fields will contribute to overcome different cultural and religious heritages among Korean people through sharing cultural traditions and thoughts on both sides. Therefore, Korea may have a unique contribution to inter-religious dialogue and peace and security.

4. Conclusion

In a multicultural and multi-religious society, we are still confronting serious tensions in East Asia without resolving some political and territorial issues such as two Chinas, Tibet and China, South and North Koreas, and problems about the boundary between the two countries such as China and Japan as well as Korea and Japan. Particularly, there is still uncertain security in Korean peninsula. There are also more severe tensions between Western and Islamic countries after the terrorist attacks targeting such building as the World Trade Center in the US on September 11, 2001. After that incident, George Bush, then the President of the US called Afghanistan, Iraq, North Korea, and Iran as the "axis of evil." And, he began to engage in a war attacking Afghanistan and Iraq by using the most destructive weapons. Recently, the Trump government also bombed Syria and Afghanistan. Now, the world is entering an "age of terror" and "age of war against terror." In addition, there are increasing extremism of the Islamic State (IS) which is a radical Islamist group that has seized large swathes of territory in eastern Syria and across northern and western Iraq.[12] IS members' recent terrorism and mass killings and abductions in Europe such as *Charlie Hebdo* shooting (Jan. 7, 2015) in France and other recent threats have sparked fear and outrage across the world. Extremism of IS endangers to lose "Muslim hearts and minds."

Could we resolve confronting extremism against each other in and outside of Islamic Countries, Western Countries, or in Asia among the religionists? How could we cut the enemy relationship in hatred among different ethnic or religious groups?

Without changing our past paradigm in our life style and thinking, it might be difficult to bring peace in the world. Also, without action, we may not be able to actualize peace in our planet. Military power does not secure our common peace. The tremendous increase of mass destructive weapons such as nuclear weapons ended World War II, but took away human lives and caused a 'cold war' among super power countries. 'Terrorist attacks' and 'wars against terrorism' insisting 'infinite justice' will not end without changing our paradigm of thinking about justice and peace.

War was an instrument for solving conflicts in the past and in present. However, in the future, any war killing human lives should not be justified. Expansion of military power does not guarantee security but instead brings another serious tension in security among neighboring countries. By representing peace itself rather than looking out for one country's best interests, religious and political leaders may be able to offer more creative solutions in our pursuit of peace. Peace is not a simple state of ceasing fire and ending a battle. Peace could be easily realized by assisting other weak societies, helping disaster victims, or needy women and children in poor regions and countries rather than revenging against each other.

In my experience of inter-religious dialogue, I feel there are some weak aspects to be strengthened. It seems that it is essential for us to open and share our religious experiences of faith and practice based upon one's religious identity to enhance mutual dialogue and cooperation. Then, we may be able to build a more effective international network among international religious organizations to implement a theological pluralism into a 'practical pluralism'.

The increased contacts in the social network among different cultures and religions, together with the enhanced diversity in societies, could be perceived as significant opportunities to further enrich each culture and religion rather than as causes of tensions and conflicts. We have a common role to establish a peaceful world. Interreligious and intercultural dialogues among people from different religious backgrounds are part of the process of mutual understanding, mutual transformation, and mutual maturity to resolve the problems of poverty, terrorism, and antagonism in cooperation.

Interreligious dialogue is neither a monologue nor a driving force to evangelize one's faith to the other religious believers. Interreligious dialogue is a religious act of communication to enhance our spirituality. It is important to extend our boundary of belief and to enhance our spirituality as an expression of love and compassion.

Nores
1. Buddhism, Jainism, Ājīvika, Ajñana and Cārvāka were belong to the Śramaṇa tradition separate from the historical Vedic religion.
2. *ENCYCLOPEDIA OF BUDDHISM*, ed. Robert E Buswell Jr., New York: Macmillan Reference USA, 2004.
3. At the time of the Buddha Siddhartha, six heterodox teachers criticized the traditional Vedic teachings and challenged Brahman authority in the hierarchical order of the Indian society. The Buddhist Scripture describe the Buddha's experience of six major teachers as follows: Purana Kasyapa, Masharin Gosaliputra, Samjayin Vairatiputra, Kakuda Katyayana, Ajita Kesakambala, and Nirgrantba Jnatiputra, known as Mahavira, the founder of Jainism.
4. Thag 1 PTS: Thag 1-120 Single Verses: (selected passages) (excerpt) translated from the Pali by Thanissaro Bhikkhu © 2004(quoted from http://www.access-toinsight.org/tipitaka/kn/thag/thag.01.00x.than.html#passage-86) "Outside of this path, / the path of the many/ who teach other things/ doesn't go to Unbinding / as does this: Thus the Blessed One/ instructs the Community, / truly showing the palms of his hands. See other Scripthres addressed to Nagita: AN 5.30, AN 6.42, and AN 8.86.
5. DN 21 PTS: D ii 276 chapter 2 Sakka-pañha Sutta: Sakka's Questions (excerpt) translated from the Pali by Thanissaro Bhikkhu(quoted from http://www.access-toinsight.org/tipitaka/dn/dn.21.2x.than.html#goal)
6. Dhammika, S. (1993). "The Edicts of King Asoka: An English Rendering", The Wheel Publication No. 386/387, Kandy Sri Lanka: Buddhist Publication Society, ISBN 955-24-0104-6; Gombrich, Richard; Guruge, Ananda (1994). King Ashoka and Buddhism: Historical and Literary studies, Kandy: Sri Lanka; Buddhist Publication Society, 1st edition, ISBN 9552400651); Mookerji, Radhakumud

(1962). Aśoka (3rd ed.). Delhi: Motilal Banarsidas.
7 'The Founding Motive' in *The Scripture of Won Buddhism: A Translation of the Wŏnbulgyo Kyojeon with Introduction*. Translated by Bongkil Chung (Honolulu: University of Hawaii Press, 2003) p. 117. The history and doctrine of Won-Buddhism is mainly found in *Wonbulgyo Kyojeon* (圓佛教 教典, *The Scripture of Won-Buddhism*), Iksan: Wonbulgyo Press, 1962. After the death of Sot'aesan his disciples compiled the *Wonbulgyo Kyojeon*, which was first published in 1962. This scripture is divided into two sections, the *Chŏngjŏn* (The Righteous Canon) and the *Daejonggyeong* (The Great Canon of Sot'aesan Analects). Each section is divided into chapters and verses. From here on, I will simply state the section with the chapter and verse.
8 *The Scriptures of Won-Buddhism*, p.169. (*Daejonggyeong* in the *Kyojeon*, (1.8)) Master Sot'aesan mentioned the general features of his new religious order to his followers during his Embankment: "The order we are about to establish was unheard of in the past and there will rarely be anything like it in the future. The doctrine of such an order should be formulated with the following considerations. Morality and science should be improved side by side for the realization of a truly civilized world. One's moral cultivation should be carried out while one is busily engaged in daily work as well as at rest in order to improve moral cultivation and daily affairs together. Various religious doctrines should be synthesized for the realization of unity and harmony among them."
9 A follower of Donghak came to see the Master and said, "I have heard much of you and come to see you from afar. May you take good care of me!" The Master said, "If so, you must have something you are seeking. Tell me what it is." The visitor said, "How can I be an erudite person?" The Master said, "Your coming and asking questions is a good way of extending knowledge and my listening to what you say is another way of extending it. Let me illustrate the point. If one needs appliances and tools for maintaining one's household, one goes to a store to buy them. If you are in business with insufficient knowledge about business, you gain it in the world. Thus, my knowledge is not gained solely by my inquiry; I gain it from various people I meet. When I meet you, I learn about Donghak; and when I meet a follower of another religion, I gain knowledge about that religion, too." *The Scriptures of Won-Buddhism*, p. 208 (The *Daejonggyeong* in the *Kyojeon*, 161 (3.29))
10 *The Scriptures of Won-Buddhism*, pp. 339-340(*Daejonggyeong* in the *Kyojeon* (14.14))
11 R. Panikkkar, *Myth, Faith and Hermeneutics*, Paulist Press, 1983, p.232.
12 "What is Islamic State?" 26 September 2014, BBC News Middle East (http://

www.bbc.com/news/world-middle-east-29052144)

References

The Scripture of Won Buddhism: A Translation of the Wŏnbulgyo Kyojeon with Introduction. Translated by Bongkil Chung, Honolulu: University of Hawaii Press, 2003.

Dhammika, S., "The Edicts of King Asoka: An English Rendering", *The Wheel Publication* No. 386/387, Kandy Sri Lanka: Buddhist Publication Society, 1993.

Gombrich, Richard; Guruge, Ananda, *King Ashoka and Buddhism: Historical and Literary studies*, Kandy: Sri Lanka; Buddhist Publication Society, 1994.

Mookerji, Radhakumud, *Aśoka* (3rd ed.). Delhi: Motilal Banarsidas, 1962.

Thanissaro Bhikkhu© 2004 (quoted from http://www.accesstoinsight.org/tipitaka/kn/thag/thag.01.00x.than.html#passage-86)

Robert E Buswell Jr. ed., *ENCYCLOPEDIA OF BUDDHISM*, New York: Macmillan Reference USA, 2004.

R. Panikkkar, *Myth, Faith and Hermeneutics*, Paulist Press, 1983.

Chapter 10

Asia Seen from a Mongolian Perspective

Li Narangoa (The Australian National University)

Mongolia has undergone huge political and economic transformations in the last 28 years and has been emerging as an active player in international and regional affairs. Mongolia has learned lessons from the past of relying too much on its two neighbours and has actively been promoting trade and diplomatic relations beyond immediate neighbours, though these two neighbours are still the most important partners in Mongolia's economic development. In this new development of international relations, Mongolia's vision for and expectation from an Asian community has been evolving. This paper analyses Mongolia's changing perspective on Asia.

Mongolia's image of Asia and its own role in it are very complicated and complex due to its geographical location and historical memories of being dominated by its two immediate neighbours. Culturally and geographically, Mongolia is at the crossroad of Central Asia and East Asia and defines itself as being part of both Central and Northeast Asia today. Economically, Mongolia desires to become a part of the Asian and the Pacific community and increasingly politically wishes to be involved in regional and world affairs.

Historically, however, the Mongols had been resistant to any kind of Asian regionalism. First of all, regionalism was often initiated by big players like

China and Japan, such as the Pan-Asianism in the early 20th century. Mongols who were struggling to find and secure their identity as an independent nation separate from China were not part of the Pan-Asian regional idea. When China and Japan talked about Pan-Asianism, they implied that they would respect each other's sovereign and territorial rights and thus Mongols who wanted to be separate from China would be at odds with this. In other words, Mongols' aspiration for independence would not be recognized. Therefore, there were no words in Mongolian for Pan-Asianism in the 20th century, though the term Pan-Mongolism was very popular. Second, to form its own separate political identity, Mongolia was seeking assistance from Russia which is a non-Asian power.[1]

Why did Mongols aspire to become independent from China? The Mongols had not only a distinct pastoral identity different than the Chinese sedentary culture, but also a strong sense of historical identity referring to the Great Mongol Empire in the 13th and 14th century. After nearly a century of expansion across Eurasia, including what is today's Russia and China, the Mongol empire had fallen in the late 14th century and the Mongols were fragmented. Retreating to the north of the Great Wall, the Mongols hoped to come back and take over the lost territory. They traded with the Ming, who had replaced the Mongol Yuan dynasty south of the Great Wall. Attempts were made to unify all Mongols and retake the territory south of the Great Wall, but they were never fully successful. The expanding Russian and Manchu empires from the 17th century further fragmented the Mongols and the unification dream was gone for centuries. By the mid-18th century, the Qing dynasty (1636–1911) that replaced the Ming in ruling China occupied all the Mongol lands in Inner Asia, except the Buryats who came under Russian rule. On the eve of the Qing dynasty's fall in 1911, the Mongols north of the Gobi Desert declared independence under the leadership of the Buddhist religious leader Jebtsundamba Khutughtu. Towards the end of Qing rule, Chinese colonization had been advancing in Mongol lands. The Chinese had dominated business and trade while Chinese money lenders had been exploiting Mongolian herders and the nobility alike. Thus, the Mongols could not imagine being ruled by a Chinese controlled government. Moreover, according to their understanding, the Qing Dynasty was ruled by Manchus and when the Manchu emperors were gone there was no reason for them to be part of the fallen empire.

Therefore, despite the fragmentation for many centuries, the idea of building a Mongol state was inspiring. When Jebtsundamba Khutughtu as Bogd Khan called for all Mongols to join the newly proclaimed independent Mongolia to build a unified Mongol state in 1911, many Mongol leaders declared their willingness to follow Bogd Khan and hundreds of them migrated to Mongolia, including Inner Mongols from the south of the Gobi Desert and Buryats from the shore of Lake Baikal. Bogd Khan sent troops to liberate Inner Mongolia from the Chinese Republic by force after the Chinese Republic actively prevented Inner Mongols from joining the Mongolian cause in 1912. Fighting persisted throughout 1913, but Mongolian troops suffered greatly due to the lack of weapons and supply of munitions and withdrew. The tri-party agreement between China, Russia and Mongolia in Kyakhta was concluded in 1915; not only did it withhold recognition of Mongolia as an independent country, but it also limited her territorial extent. Inner Mongolia and Barga (in today's Hulunbuir region, Inner Mongolia) were not included in Mongolia's autonomy.[2] This treaty of 1915, sealed the division between Inner Mongolia and Outer Mongolia. After the death of the Bogd Khan, the revolutionaries abolished the constitutional monarchy and set up a Soviet style constitution, proclaiming the Mongolian People's Republic (MPR) in 1924. The new government received Soviet assistance in many fields, but was also able to carry out its own independent politics in the early years. From 1928 onwards, however, Mongolian politics more and more reflected Soviet dominance and the Soviet Union became Mongolia's sole trading partner.[3]

Thus, from the 1920s, Mongols on both sides of the Gobi desert took quite different historical trajectories. The MPR located in the north of the Gobi, which was referred as Outer Mongolia, was under Soviet domination with the broader idea of communism and Soviet socialist ideology and hence the idea of

Asia or Pan-Asianism initiated by Japanese and Chinese intellectuals were not attractive to say the least. For them the Asian regionalism was linked with imperialism. Moreover, the non-Asian Soviet assistance was the only way of avoiding the Chinese dominance. Mongols did not need Asian solidarity to achieve their independence as was the case for many Asia countries in the early 20th century. For the Mongols on the other side of the Gobi, the story was quite different. Failing to build a joint Mongol state with the north, they sought to find a path to autonomy if not independence within the Chinese Republican frame. When this hope was not materialized, they turned to the expanding Japan from the east. The eastern part of Inner Mongolia (including Barga) was incorporated into the new state Manchukuo in 1932. Inner Mongols west of Manchukuo declared for its autonomy in 1933 and started to build a quasi-state with Japanese assistance from mid 1930s.[4] These Mongols tried to utilize the approaching Japan for their movement of independence. Even the Inner Mongols who were under the Japanese occupation had a different idea of regionalism than that proposed by the Japanese. The greater East Asian Co-Prosperity Sphere was the Japanese slogan at the time. The Inner Mongols often referred it to as the Mongol empire. They implied that Asians and most regions of the globe peacefully co-existed under the Mongol empire with their own ruling principles. This also served to claim that Mongols had a great history of ruling the world and thus they deserved to have their own independent state. Only with their own Mongol independent state, could the Mongols contribute to greater Asia if not to the world.[5]

The Mongolian leaders both in the MPR and in Inner Mongolia shared the idea that the territory north of the Great Wall was traditional Mongolian territory. The MPR leader Marshal Choibalsan aspired for a post war world where the Mongolian nation state included Inner Mongolia, as the Bogd Khan had some thirty years earlier. The Mongolian army joined the Soviet army in the war against the Japanese and crossed the Japanese occupied Inner Mongolian border on 9 August 1945 to liberate the Inner Mongols and to unify the Mongolian national cultures. Many Mongols in Inner Mongolia, too, hoped for the unification. This unification dream was not materialized due to the interests of the Soviet Union and China, who secretly agreed that Mongolia (with a territory north of the Gobi) could be independent and China would acknowledge Russian special rights there; in return Russia would recognize China's territorial integrity over Inner Mongolia.[6]

After the Second World War, Mongolia gained its independence, but during the time of the Mongolian People's Republic, Mongols did not talk about Asian regional cooperation. Their attention was focused on the socialist brotherhood and the united socialist front which was supposed to be beyond ethnical, national and regional boundaries. From the 1960s, when China and the Soviet Union split, Mongolia aligned itself with the Soviet Union and concentrated on building a socialist system with Soviet help. Mongolia oriented itself towards the eastern European socialist bloc in all aspects of its diplomatic, political and economic relationships. This close affinity to the Soviet Union and other eastern European countries brought also a change in perspective about Asia and themselves. By emulating Soviet socialism and modernity, Mongolians not only tried hard to rid themselves of their nomadic 'feudal' past and culture, but also to 'escape' from Asia which was considered to be backwards by European orientalism and the Soviet idea of modernity. In terms of lifestyle, indeed Mongols had and have more in common with Central Asia which was then also part of the Soviet Union. They share the same kind of pastoral economy and a diet based more on meat and dairy products (like Europeans), while the rest of Asia is a more agrarian settled culture with rice, fish and vegetables as the main diet. Mongolia's most obvious cultural link to East Asia was religion, Shamanism and Buddhism. This religious link was abandoned by a purge of religion in several waves. Shamans went underground and Buddhist temples were destroyed. The traditional Mongolian scripts were replaced with Cyrillic alphabets. Even Chinggis Khan who had been the core of Mongol identity was condemned as a 'feudal lord' who oppressed the masses. Postage stamps which were issued to commemorate his 800 birthday were recalled by order of the Soviets in 1962.[7] The custom of celebrating Lunar New Year was abandoned for the sake of the

European calendar. Fine art also looked to the European style and techniques and often depicted urban lifestyle, workers and industrial achievement rather than nomadic herders. Mongols became more 'modern' and felt like part of 'Europe' rather than 'Asia' until a wave of new political idea came in the late 1980s which rang the bell for a new Mongolian identity.

When the Soviet Union collapsed, Mongolia introduced a democratic political system in 1990 and began to reassert its traditional culture, history and a new Mongolian identity which was mostly based on those aspects of Mongolian culture that had been rejected in the previous decades. Shamanism and Buddhism reemerged as part of the national culture, and the Lunar New Year celebration was reintroduced, Chinggis Khan was 'restored' as the national cult and even the traditional Uigurjin Mongolian script was reintroduced in schools, and shops and cafés put up the name in this script.[8] Not only did Mongolian traditional clothes become fashionable but also Mongolian calligraphy and traditional Mongolian art became very popular once again. Politically, Mongolia introduced a new constitution and set up a new set of foreign policy priorities which emphasized peaceful multilateral relationship with the West and East.

Since the political reform in 1990, Mongolia has been actively trying to be part of the Asian community. Asia emerged as a region that would boost Mongolia's economy and contribute to the construction of a new Mongolian identity and sovereignty. Strengthening Mongolia's position in Asia and securing a constructive participation in the political and economic process in the region is one of the most important directions for Mongolia's new concept of foreign policy which was set up in 1992. The concept of foreign policy emphasised the importance of the Asian and Pacific Region for Mongolia, in particular North-East Asia and Central Asia. The policy paper seems to suggest that Mongolia sees itself as part of Asian community before it sees itself as a global community. In addition after the Ukraine-Russian conflicts in 2014, Mongolia seemed to review its relationship with Western countries. The incident revealed that Mongolia would not be able to escape its geopolitical reality, even though it is able to create sound relations with its neighbours and the so-called 'third neighbours' in Europe and Americas.[9] Despite all the public concerns about the Chinese economic hegemony in Mongolia, the Mongolian government has been trying to maintain a good relationship with China. After all, China became Mongolia's biggest partner in trade and foreign investment. Mongolia supported the one China policy and hence rejected the independence of Taiwan which had been mapping Mongolia as part of China. Mongolia insisted that the Taiwan has to revise the map if Taiwan were to have any commercial and diplomatic relationship with Mongolia. Taiwan finally revised its map excluding Mongolia from the political boundary of the Republic of China. Japan and South Korea emerged as the biggest donors of foreign aid and importance in trade and investment partner.[10] Apart from Japan and Korea, India emerged as an important 'Third neighbour'.[11]

Asia also emerged as a region that consolidated Mongolia's political status in the world and at the same time where Mongolia could make a real contribution. The tension in the Korean Peninsula offered an opportunity for Mongolia to contribute to regional peace talks because Mongolia is the only country which had a good relationship with both Koreas and other countries in the region West.[12] Mongolia has been presenting itself as the Switzerland of Asia and offering itself as neutral ground for meetings concerning the Korean Peninsula. Mongolia is also ready to collaborate with China for its One Belt-One Road plan towards Central Asia via Mongolia.[13]

Central Asia is an important part of Asia that Mongolia had a common border with as well as sharing the same nomadic lifestyle and natural environment; it also shared the experience of having been dominated by the Soviets. The Mongolian public still consider themselves as part of Central Asia rather than Northeast Asia. In a sample survey that we have conducted in Ulaanbaatar in mid-2015, 48% of the answers were for Central Asia while only 21% for Northeast Asia (please see Figure 10–1)[14]. Culturally, most of the Mongolians consider their culture is unique (48% of the answers) while 24% of the answers referred to their culture as 'mixed'. Only 11% of the answers referred to Mongolian culture as 'Asian' while 7% as 'European' (Figure 10–2). The assertion that Mongolian culture is unique increases further to 70% when we separate the participants' answers according to their education level (Figure 10–3). That means that the more educated, the higher is their feeling for identifying Mongolian culture as unique. In other words, they are more conscious of their Mongolian identity.

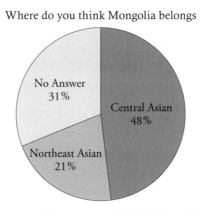

Figure 10–1 Survey conducted in mid-2015 (Participants 50 people).

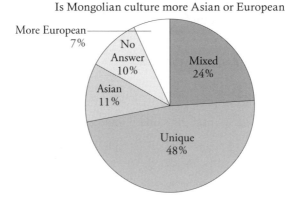

Figure 10–2 Survey conducted in mid-2015 (Participants 50 people).

Master's degree respondents on Mongolian culture

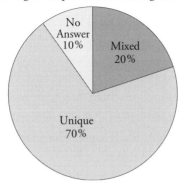

Figure 10–3 Survey conducted in mid-2015.

Though Mongolia recognizes the importance of both Central Asia and Northeast Asia, politically Mongolia identifies itself as a Northeast Asian country currently while popular identification still tends to be with Central Asia. In the definition of the government, Northeast Asia in general consists of China, Japan, the Korean Peninsula and Mongolia. Northeast Asia, though politically diverse, is very important for Mongolia's economic development and political status in the world. It is a region where the remnants of Cold War and cold-war thinking persist. The region hosts two of the largest economies in the world (China and Japan) and one permanent member of the UN Security Council. In addition, the issues of the South China Sea and the Korean Peninsula create difficulty in reaching common objectives for the region. Northeast Asia does not have common regional arrangements or mechanisms that can contribute to building confidence and resolving contentious issues. Here Mongolia seeks to play an important role as it has friendly relationship with all of the countries and does not have any existing territorial dispute with any of its neighbours.[15] Moreover, Mongolia is a small country and so countries do not feel threatened; it considers itself as an 'honest broker'[16] for promotion of peace and security in the region. As a Mongolian diplomat said referring to Mongolia's past history 'The Mongolian experience shows that today big states and small states could be in equal and helpful collaboration and it [i.e., the experience] even can become an important model for the advancement of the Northeast Asian unification process.'[17] Mongolia's interest is obviously to build a peaceful and stable regional political environment in which its own sovereignty would be protected.

To promote Mongolia's role as a mediator and broker of confident building and to make a contribution to reaching long term goals of regional peace in setting up 'consultative mechanism' of dialogue in Northeast East Asia (NEA), the former Present of Mongolia, Tsakhiagiin Elbegdorj proposed an 'Ulaanbaatar Dialogue on the Northeast Asian Security' in April 2013. Ulaanbaatar is suitable for the Dialogue on Northeast Asia because it 'can serve as a neutral meeting ground, literally and metaphorically, as Northeast Asia's Geneva and can be a multilateral venue for regional security dialogue.'[18] An international seminar with the same title was convened by the Mongolian Ministry of Foreign Affairs and Mongolia's Institute for Strategic Studies in June 2014. Apart from the Northeast Asian countries (including North Korea), some researchers and diplomats from the USA and European countries participated and had heated discussions. The second conference followed a year later. Some other events were also convened in this spirit: NEA's Cities Mayors' Forum (August 2014), NEA Energy Connectivity Workshop - Expert Level Meeting (March 2015) and Northeast Asian Youth Symposium (20 May, 2015). President Elbegdorj was an adamant promoter of the dialogue. He said at a conference in Tokyo: "… The Helsinki process took 10 years to be concluded. In Northeast Asia, the process might take more years. Nevertheless, we should work from now on to have a dialogue mechanism in the future."[19] In short, Mongolia is determined that it can make a positive contribution to the peace and stability of Northeast Asia.

The political interest of Mongolia politicians in Northeast Asia is partly because Mongolia is trying to shake of its past-communist identity after the reform in 1990 and actively seeking to become democratic nation. In addition, Russia's influence in the Central Asian Region is still strong and thus associating itself too close to Central Asia reminds many the 'old day'. To complicate things, both Russia and China share increasing interests in Central Asia and the

Sino-Russian relationship is getting closer. Mongolia has been an observer in the Shanghai Cooperation Organization (SCO) which includes the Central Asia States and Russia and China and aims to promote Eurasian political, economic and military collaboration. There is immense interest from China and Russia for Mongolia to join SCO as a full member. For Mongolia, Central Asia, both Russia and China have significant interest and influence and it does not want to be caught in between. Since SCO might create some tensions in Mongolia's foreign relations, Mongolia needs to be cautious in getting full membership.[20] As a result, Northeast Asia is much more safer for Mongolia to engage. Although there is China's influence, it is mitigated by the influence and interest of US, Japan and Korea. Some scholars, however, suggested that Mongolia needs to become part of the Eurasian transport and logistic routes (railway, highway) and connect Central Asia to East Asia to increase its importance in the region. It has also been suggested that Mongolia should use the SCO membership as a leverage to achieve a pledge from both neighbours to run the logistic routes of trade and energy transport between Russia and China through Mongolia.[21]

Mongolia's regional cooperation is not limited to Northeast Asia and Central Asia, but the entire Asia and Pacific region. Mongolia is also a member of the Conference on Interaction and Confidence-Building Measures in Asia (CICA), an inter-governmental forum for enhancing cooperation towards promoting peace, security and stability in Asia. Mongolia is seeking ASEAN and APEC cooperation. Since 1993, Mongolia has sought to become a member of APEC and to actively engage with ASEAN. Mongolia became a member of the ASEAN Regional Forum and the Asia Europe Meeting and assigned a permanent representative to ASEAN in June 2013. Mongolia has been lobbying for APEC membership. Becoming a member of APEC is an important step for Mongolia. 89.5 percent of Mongolia's trade and 50.6 percent of foreign direct inflows are from APEC states. Moreover, 96.4 percent of Mongolia's exports go to China, Canada and Russia. [22]

In order to convince ASEAN and APEC, Mongolia actively

participated in all types of informal and formal dialogues in Asia to strengthen its presence in Asia. Never before in Mongolian history have politicians talked so much about Asia and tried to be an integral part of Asia. Tsakhia Elbegdorj, the former President of Mongolia participated in the 21st International Conference on the Future of Asia "Asia Beyond 2015, the Quest for Lasting Peace and Prosperity" which was held in Tokyo in May 2015. In his speech, he emphasised the mutual trust and reginal integration among Asian countries:

- The 21st century is regarded as the Asian century. Asia's presence and role in global affairs has grown beyond expectations and it is predicted to further heighten.

- I believe that building mutual trust, promoting stronger ties and regional integration among all nations of Asia will enhance prospects for Asia's success. - Strengthening multilateral collaboration among Asian countries will fortify the foundation of prosperity of nations of Asia as a whole. This will also bring long-lasting peace and prosperity to the world.

He also highlighted the importance of Asia to Mongolia and Mongolian desire to be part of the Asian community. He also highlighted that Mongolia has great potential to add value to APEC. In addition, Mongolia is seeking to become a member of the Economic Research Institute for ASEAN and an East Asia member state. He stated in his speech that "For us to be an ERIA's member, it is necessary to be an official member of the East Asia Summit.[23] Currently Mongolia has observer status in APEC and has gained China and Russia's support in obtaining full membership for APEC.[24]

Mongolia's involvement in Asia has been mostly based on bilateral relationships. Mongolia is actively strengthening its bilateral relationship with Asian countries. It hopes that closer bilateral relationships with the Asian countries will help Mongolia become part of the Asian community. At the same time, Mongolia has been envisaging a forum that would include all Asian countries.

The former Mongolian President Elbegdorj called for establishing 'The Forum of Asia' which developed from the Ulaanbaatar Dialogue on NEA that he initiated in 2013. There is 'no single platform or mechanism of regional integration that is inclusive of all Asian states', he continued: 'In today's ever-changing environment, we need to establish a solid platform and inclusive mechanism to enable all Asian states to get engaged in regional dialogue and cope with its challenges and opportunities... Why should not we, our continent, have one regional platform of collaboration which includes all of our 48 UN member states? ... The Forum should focus on security, rule of law, environment, economic and social areas. More importantly, 'The Forum of Asia' should promote equal representation of interests of all sovereign nations in Asia, be it a small or big.' In his speech, he repeatedly used the words, 'we Asians' or 'our Asia' and emphasised the importance of guaranteeing each member state its independence, integrity, and way of development in the proposed Forum. In a way, this is an idea which by passing the current regional forums and creating a super forum of all Asians, not unsimilar to the European Union. And his vision of Asian region includes almost include the entire Eurasian land mass that was once ruled by the Mongol empire in the 13-14th century. In his own words: 'Our Asia is bounded by three oceans (Pacific, Indian and Arctic), five seas (Arabian, Red, Mediterranean, Caspian and Black), Ural River and the Ural and Caucasus mountains. And we are connected through the Suez Canal and the Bosphorus strait. These oceans, seas, mountains, river, canal and strait link us to the rest of the continents in the world.' The fourth Ulaanbaatar Dialogue on NEA was convened in June 2017.[25]

By way of conclusion, in the past, Mongolia was not interested in Asian regionalism or integration in the Asian community, but since 1990s it has been actively working towards a peaceful integration of the Asian community and trying to build up its international reputation. The promotion of regional integration is also based on a very strong newly obtained full sovereignty and reassertion of their own cultural identity. If in the past, the Mongolian had a minority complex towards their own culture (nomadic culture, not industrialized), now they have regained their confidence and claim to have unique culture, combining both Asian and European aspects. Mongolia has been actively carrying out soft power diplomacy to promote integration with Asia. Cultural exchanges in fine art, music, sport and more have been promoted in Asia and the Pacific.

Notes

1 Li Narangoa, 'Mongoru ga egaita higashi Ajia kyōdōtai' [East Asia in Mongol Imagination], in Matsuura Masataka eds., *Ajiashugi wa nani o kataru no ka: kioku, kenryoku, kachi*, Tokyo: Minerva shobō, 2013: 146–163.
2 Ewing, E. E. *Between the Hammer and the Anvil? Chinese and Russian Policies in Outer Mongolia 1911–21*. Bloomington, IN, Indiana University Press, 1980; Batbayar Tsedendambyn and Soni, Sharad K., Modern Mongolia. New Delhi: Pentagon Press, 2002; Lan Mei-hua, 'The Mongolian independence movement of 1911: A Pan-Mongolian endeavor' (Dissertation), Harvard University, 1996.
3 Alan Sanders, *The People's Republic of Mongolia*, New York: Oxford University Press, 1968.
4 The western most part of Inner Mongolia came under the control of the Chinese Nationalist Government. Li Narangoa, 'Educating Mongols and Making "Citizens" of Manchukuo', *Inner Asia*, Volume 3, Number 2, 2001: 101–126.
5 Li Narangoa, 'Mongoru ga egaita higashi Ajia kyōdōtai', 146–163.
6 Borujigin Fusure, *Chūgoku kyōsantō kokumintō no tai Uchimongoru seisaku 1945–49nen* [The Chinese Communist Party and Nationalist Party's Policies on Inner Mongolia 1945–49]. Tokyo: Fūkyūsha, 2011.
7 Kaplonski, Christopher. *Truth, History and Politics in Mongolia – The Memory of Heroes*. London and New York: RoutledgeCurzon, 2004.
8 Ole Bruun and Li Narangoa (Eds.). *Mongols from country to city: floating boundaries, pastoralism and city life in the Mongol lands*. Copenhagen : NIAS Press, 2006; Bruce M. Knauft and Richard Taupier (Eds.). *Mongolians After Socialism: Politics, Economy, Religion*. Ulaanbaatar, Admon, 2012.
9 Sergey Radchenko, 'Mongolia Hangs in the Balance: Political Choices and Economic Realities', *The Asia Forum*, March–April 2018, Vol. 6, No. 2 (http://www.theasanforum.org/mongolia-hangs-in-the-balance-political-choices-and-economic-realities/).
10 Bruce M. Knauft and Richard Taupier, (Eds.). *Mongolians After Socialism: Politics, Economy, Religion*. Ulaanbaatar, Admon, 2012.
11 Sharad K. Soni, 'The "Third Neighbour" Approach of Mongolia's Diplomacy

of External Relations Effects on Relations between India and Mongolia', in *India Quarterly: A Journal of International Affairs*, Vol. 71, Issue 1, 2015.
12 Batchimeg Migeddorj, 'Mongolia's DPRK Policy: Engaging North Korea,' *Asian Survey*, Vol. 46, No. 2 (March–April 2006): 275–297.
13 Sergey Radchenko, 'Mongolia Hangs in the Balance: Political Choices and Economic Realities', *The Asia Forum*, March-April 2018, Vol. 6, No. 2.
14 I would like to thank Itgel Chulunbaatar for helping to creat the Figures.
15 Jargalsaikhan Mendee, 'Mongolia's Dilemma: A Politically Linked, Economically Isolated Small Power', in *The Asan Forum*, Vol. 3. No. 5 (September–October 2015).
16 http://www.president.mn/eng/newsCenter/viewNews.php?newsId=1546. Accessed on 7 December 2015.
17 Zamba Batjargal, 'Hokutō Ajia Chi'iki Kyōryoku ni Okeru Mongoru no Yakuwari' [The Mongolian contribution to the Northeast Asian regional cooperation], NIRA Policy Research 18: 2 (February 2005): 74–75, cited in Li Narangoa, 'Mongolia and Preventive Diplomacy: Haunted by History and Becoming Cosmopolitan'. Asian Survey, Vol. 49, No. 2, March/April 2009: 358–379.
18 https://www.un.int/mongolia/mongolia/ulaanbaatar-dialogue. Accessed on 1 April 2018.
19 http://www.president.mn/eng/newsCenter/viewNews.php?newsId=1546.
20 Lkhamsuren Lkhagvasuren, "Evolution and Growth for Contemporary Mongolian Diplomacy: Consideration of Its Relations with the Shanghai Cooperation Organization," *Kan Nihonkai Kenkyū* [Japan Sea Rim Studies] 12 (Niigata, Japan) (June 2006): 6.
21 Alicia Campi, 'Transforming Mongolia-Russia-China Relations: The Dushanbe Trilateral Summit'. *The Asia-Pacific Journal*, Vol. 12, Issue. 45, No. 1 (November 10, 2014); Li Narangoa, 'Mongolia and Preventive Diplomacy: Haunted by History and Becoming Cosmopolitan'. Asian Survey, Vol. 49, No. 2, March/April 2009: 358–379.
22 Total trade between ASEAN and Mongolia in 2011 amounted to US$129.4 million, with Mongolia importing US$120.25 million worth of goods from ASEAN. http://www.aseanbriefing.com/news/2013/07/12/mongolia-attends-asean-regional-forum.html#sthash.w7s7fNah.dpuf.
23 http://www.president.mn/eng/newsCenter/viewNews.php?newsId=1546.
24 http://english.news.mn/content/194849.shtml.
25 http://montsame.mn/en/read/10517. Accessed on 1 April 2018.

References

Alan Sanders, *The People's Republic of Mongolia*, New York: Oxford University Press, 1968.

Batbayar, Tsedendambyn and Soni, Sharad K., *Modern Mongolia*. New Delhi: Pentagon Press, 2002.

Batchimeg Migeddorj, 'Mongolia's DPRK Policy: Engaging North Korea,' *Asian Survey*, Vol. 46, No. 2 (March-April 2006).

Borujigin Fusure, *Chūgoku kyōsantō kokumintō no tai Uchimongoru seisaku 1945–49nen* [The Chinese Communist Party and Nationalist Party's Policies on Inner Mongolia 1945–49]. Tokyo: Fūkyūsha, 2011.

Bruun, Ole and Li Narangoa (Eds.). *Mongols from country to city: floating boundaries, pastoralism and city life in the Mongol lands*. Copenhagen: NIAS Press, 2006.

Campi, Alicia. 'Transforming Mongolia-Russia-China Relations: The Dushanbe Trilateral Summit'. *The Asia-Pacific Journal*, Vol. 12, Issue. 45, No. 1 (November 10, 2014).

Ewing, E. E. *Between the Hammer and the Anvil? Chinese and Russian Policies in Outer Mongolia 1911–21*. Bloomington, IN, Indiana University Press, 1980.

Kaplonski, Christopher. *Truth, History and Politics in Mongolia–The Memory of Heroes*. London and New York: RoutledgeCurzon, 2004.

Knauft, Bruce M. and Taupier, Richard (Eds.). *Mongolians After Socialism: Politics, Economy, Religion*. Ulaanbaatar, Admon, 2012.

Mendee, Jargalsaikhan. 'Mongolia's Dilemma: A Politically Linked, Economically Isolated Small Power', in *The Asan Forum*, Vol. 3. No. 5 (September–October 2015).

Lan Mei-hua, 'The Mongolian independence movement of 1911: A Pan-Mongolian endeavor' (Dissertation), Harvard University, 1996.

Li Narangoa, 'Educating Mongols and Making "Citizens" of Manchukuo', *Inner Asia*, Volume 3, Number 2, 2001: 101–126.

Li Narangoa, 'Mongolia and Preventive Diplomacy: Haunted by History and Becoming Cosmopolitan'. *Asian Survey*, Vol. 49 No. 2, March/April 2009.

Li Narangoa, 'Mongoru ga egaita higashi Ajia kyōdōtai' [East Asia in Mongol Imagination], in Matsuura Masataka eds., *Ajiashugi wa nani o kataru no ka: kioku, kenryoku, kachi*, Tokyo: Minerva shobō, 2013: 146–163.

Lkhamsuren Lkhagvasuren, "Evolution and Growth for Contemporary Mongolian Diplomacy: Consideration of Its Relations with the Shanghai Cooperation Organization," *Kan Nihonkai Kenkyū* [Japan Sea Rim Studies] 12 (Niigata, Japan) (June 2006).

Radchenko, Sergey, 'Mongolia Hangs in the Balance: Political Choices and Economic Realities', *The Asia Forum*, March–April 2018, Vol. 6, No. 2.

Sharad K. Soni, 'The 'Third Neighbour' Approach of Mongolia's Diplomacy of External Relations Effects on Relations between India and Mongolia', in *India Quarterly: A Journal of International Affairs*, Vol. 71, Issue 1, 2015.

Zamba Batjargal, 'Hokutō Ajia Chi'iki Kyōryoku ni Okeru Mongoru no Yakuwari' [The Mongolian contribution to the Northeast Asian regional cooperation], NIRA Policy Research 18: 2 (February 2005).

Chapter 11

New Asian Youth Peace Education in the Fourth Industrial Revolution

Yang Young-chul (Professor, Dept. of Public Administration of Jeju National University in South Korea)

1. Introduction

1. The significance and purpose of the study

All humanity aspires to live in peace. Nevertheless, mankind is always exposed to a non-peaceful environment. It is difficult to list non peaceful types such as conflict between religion, nation, political and social class starting from the war between nations. This diversity of non-peace also refers to the diversity of its causes. Conflicts arising from physical warfare such as religion and territory, including war on resources, create conflicts, such as war. In addition, it is possible to find a lot of cases in which the emotions such as self-esteem have caused the non-peaceful situation.

Non-peaceful events, however, may be so predictable as this may be, but there are also many cases that occur in very improvised and irrational places. These cases come from a lack of understanding, misunderstanding, or ignorance of the other party. This, in turn, means that if the right understanding of the other party is preceded, the peace among them will be maintained. I think of the devastation that is the result of the non-peace conflicts. It brings a tremendous tragedy that can not be recovered in the present age.

It is 65 years after the end of the Korean War, but the aftermath of the separated families remains vivid. Though it has been 70 years since World War II ended, the families of victims and survivors of atomic bombs have been genetically linked to their offspring. The recent IS events in Syria and Iraq are destroying tens of thousands of ideas and the civilization origin sites of humanity. The fact that hundreds of thousands of refugees are standing in the midst of racial and religious conflicts also tells how important peace is.

There is no objection that mutual understanding among the ways of creating an environment of peace is most effective. It is a way to expand mutual human exchange on the basis of understanding the other's culture, system, and history. Although this method is a very simple method, it has rarely been fully implemented so far. There are also various factors such as the long history of long time score and ill-fated relationship as like between Korea and Japan, among Israel and Arab nations, etc. that the exchange with the other party is blocked from the source in various ways. However, the biggest cause is the mutual accessibility. It is difficult to access because of the physical distance, but language, culture, and financial difficulties did not allow access for mutual understanding and exchange. We can not overcome the gap between hope and reality.

Recently, however, technologies are emerging that can easily fill this gap. In particular, the technology and characteristics of the Fourth Industrial Revolution not only make physical distance meaningless, but also overcome temporal and verbal limitations. This characteristic of the fourth industrial revolution, such as super connectivity, super intelligence, super-convergence, shared economy, and on demand, and the technologies that operate on it, are dominating our lives. Within at least a decade, the Fourth Industrial Revolution predicts that it will be a central paradigm for our everyday lives.

Considering that peace education, especially youth peace education, is absolutely necessary, it is necessary to operate a platform for youth peace education applying the technology of the 4th Industrial Revolution. On this platform, it is necessary for Asian youth not only to promote mutual understanding, but also to provide an opportunity to experience local democracy by debating and resolving regional conflicts problems. This platform to create their own world by creating a field of mutual understanding in their perspective is needed. The starting point of this study is also here and its purpose is also here.

2. Methods and contents of research

As a research method, the research will proceed through the following process.

First, we will analyze basic literature on peace studies. In this process, the concept of peace, the purpose of peace education, and the methods and effects of peace education will be summarized on a conceptual level.

Second, we will look into the literature and cases related to peace education in many countries or region. In this study, we will compare and analyze the contents and methods of peace education in many countries or region.

Third, we will look at cases of youth peace education in peace education and why we need peace education for youth.

Fourth, we will look at ways of peace education for Asian youth by using the technology of the 4th Industrial Revolution. In this process, we will study the contents necessary for the youth peace education among the technologies and features of the 4th Industrial Revolution and describe its utilization plan.

Finally, I will look at the central subject of Asian youth peace education. In this study, the One- Asia Foundation will provide the reason why it should be the subject of peace education for Asian youth and how to use the technology of the 4th Industrial Revolution.

2. The necessity of peace education and the actual situation of youth peace education in Asia

1. Concept of Peace

The concept of peace is wildly defined. It is not easy to find a concept of peace that is consistent with philosophical and political as well as educational, religious, socio-cultural, and even economic terms. In general, however, peace researchers or peace scholars divide peace into two broad categories. In other words, the state without physical violence including war is called 'negative peace', and the state without structural violence and cultural violence is called 'positive peace'. In other words, the former could be called the peace of the concept of 'national security' and the latter could be called the 'peace of the human security' concept.¹

The concept definition of peace in this study will also be understood in this direction.

2. Necessity of Youth Peace Education

Let us first consider the concept and necessity of peace education before discussing the need for youth peace education. Peace education indirectly opposes various forms of violence that dominate society by teaching the causes of violence and providing alternative knowledge. Peace education is also aimed at transforming the present human conditions "by changing social structures and dominant modes of thought," as the well-known peace educator Betty Reardon pointed out. Peace education is taught in various courses from primary school to universities. Teach peace groups to community groups, adults and children.²

Peace education for them is about teaching peace, raising questions such as what peace is, why peace is not achieved, and how to achieve peace.³

What is the need to teach peace education to the youth in this study? Montessori shows that children are much more believing and open to others than adults and show love for others as the foundation of public opinion . Montessori believed that educators should develop their own mental side and prepare children for a way of life that supports peace. Educators tell us the direction of why we should educate children and youth about peace education.

Studies have shown that the concept of war and violence begins earlier than the concept of peace, usually beginning with the concept of war and peace from the age of six. By the age of 12, peace is understood as desirable human relations and the denial of war. From the age of 13, analytical and integration skills of human relations, hypothetical thinking, abstract thinking, and various information begin to develop. From this time on, I begin to understand the negative aspects of war, destructive consequences and emotions. Therefore, they are beginning to recognize structural violence and indirect violence.⁴ Therefore, it is absolutely necessary for them to have the correct peace education.

There is also a real case study. It is an example of peace education for the

Israeli and Palestinian youths who have been facing the extreme confrontation to this day. Israel-Palestine Research and Information Center ("Israel-Palestine") was established in 1988 as an independent civilian organization in order to cooperate with Palestine, Israelis, Arabs, Jews, Palestine Center for Research & Information, "a program that allows both Israeli and Palestinian youth to think about peace in one place. Among the programs that have achieved particular results are Israeli and Palestinian youths exploring the Northern Ireland conflict. It was not their own disputes, but the ability to see themselves through other disputes, and the participants brought about considerable cognitive changes. They were able to speak more frankly about their experiences and feelings than when they directly addressed the Palestinian issue, which led to the development of collective effects and the formation of intimate relationships. More than 90% of Israeli participants were able to write and submit to the Palestinians later, with only 25% of those without education. In addition, the language of the observers such as 'war', 'death' and 'obsession' decreased and the language of the will such as 'negotiation', 'compromise', 'resolution of conflict' There is a big change in linguistic sensitivity.[5]

In conclusion, overall education on peace and violence should be considered and strengthened as an infrastructure for lasting peace in the world, because it is most effective for youth with the most sensitivity.

3. Actual condition of youth peace education

Countries are conducting various kinds of peace education for youth. However, the contents are very different according to the history of each country, that is, experience and strength of war and violence. Among them, youth peace education will be briefly described as follows.[6]

1. Korea

In a short period, Korea is a country with a lot of historical facts to make peace, such as the Japanese colonial rule, US military government, oppression by the right wing government in the region, war between North and South Korea, repression of dictatorship regime. Therefore, peace education in Korea is very diverse. First, peace education in Korea has a long history of peace education related to reunification. Peace reunification education, which has been centered around religious organizations, has been studied mainly by government research institutes, research institutes of universities, and NGOs. However, the center themes of peace research has been diversified from peaceful reunification into conflict resolution education, violence prevention education, human rights education, ecological environment education, international understanding education, and other peace education Recently, multicultural peace education Is also added.

One of the programs in Korea is the 'Cross Cultural Awareness Program (CCAP)', which introduces unique youth peace education. This program is an intercultural comprehension training program launched by the UNESCO Commission with supported from the Korean Ministry of Education since 1998 to help the growing generation of to understand and respect other cultures. It is a program that invites foreign residents in Korea to elementary, middle, and high schools in Korea as a cultural classroom teacher and introduces the diverse cultures of their countries directly to students. This program not only provides students and teachers, Korean interpreter volunteers with opportunities for international understanding education in the era of globalization, but also gives foreigners who participate as cultural exchange volunteers an opportunity to experience and understand our society .

In particular, it is becoming a program that enables students to learn the values pursued by UNESCO, such as mutual benefit, peace, human rights and tolerance, and to cultivate global citizenship through cultural understanding, rather than simply introducing other cultures. It is a program to practice the concept of active peace.[7]

2. Japan

Peace studies in Japan, which had been bombed by atomic bombs, had been a demand for the times, as peace studies were being institutionalized steadily in the United States and Europe. Japan, defeated in the Second World War, became the historical responsibility of 'liquidation of the aggression war'.

Japan's peace study starts with a lost battle - the atomic bombing of Hiroshima and Nagasaki - war responsibility'. In 1973, with the founding of the Japan Peace Society, Japan's peace studies have been leapfrogged and settled. The Japan Peace Society, which started with 40 members at the time of its establishment, has now become a large organization with more than 800 members. The Japan Peace Society has been working on applying the theory of peace in Europe and North America to Japan since the publication of the Peace Studies in 1975.[8]

Today, peace education in Japan is changing in its approach. A new peace education program is being created by combining cultural expression activities and experiential learning. Among them, peace education for children and students is changing from war education to education of history, development, international , human rights, disarmament including nuclear dismantlement, and environmental education for 21st century. Peace Project in Hiroshima is a peace education program sponsored by the Miyagi High School Network. This program is designed to encourage students to express themselves in Hiroshima on August 6, a day when nuclear bombs fell on Hiroshima, through expressive activities such as band, sculpture, photography, and culture. The core of this PPIN is to create works related to peace, so-called 'peace and cultural activities'.[9]

3. Israel

Peace education in Israel is diverse. Outside, there are conflicts with Arab countries such as Palestine, which has been in war for a long time. Conflicts with the Arabs, 20% of the people within the country, and Muslim immigrants such as Sepharodik and European cultural immigrants, Ashkenazi "Conflicts between religions and conflicts between the" traditional Jews "and the" secular Jews "are extremely difficult. In order to resolve these social conflicts, Israel is raising various peace education efforts such as the establishment of an integrated education institution, the operation of the Jewish-Arab peace center, the local community movement, the life community operation, research activities and financial support.

Among them, the Peace Education Program for Youth is a face-to-face meeting with children's Teaching Children (CTC) educational activities. CTC helps students and teachers develop the skills needed to deal with conflict. The CTC runs for two years as part of the formal curriculum, and is conducted in pairs at the same time between the two neighboring schools. In the place where only one nation is gathered, the Jewish class and the Arab class are separated to discuss their national identity, hope and fear. When the two nations meet together, the theme of common citizenship is emphasized, which is a way to reach equality between the two groups in Israel.

The direct contact program arranges direct meetings for high school students and college students. The program has experience in which Jewish and Arab participants face prejudices against each other and deal with the difficulties of accommodating different people. In particular, there is also an independent program for Arab youth to use personal skills to treat the Palestinian-Arab minority's perceptions from a progressive point of view within the Jewish state.[10]

4. United States

Although the United States waged war with Japan during the Second World War, it was not a country that had relatively many wars or conflicts with other countries. This is because US basic diplomacy was isolationism.[11] Therefore, the peace movement and peace education in the United States began in earnest in the 1980s. In the United States, since the early 1980s, school teachers have been working to integrate conflict resolution education into school education. The development of conflict resolution programs in the United States is basically due to violence in society. In a situation where many people are resolving violent problems, the conflict resolution program has developed into an alternative way to pursue peaceful resolution of conflict and is now widely applied in American society.

Conflict resolution programs are now being adopted as one of school peace education in a variety of culturally and ethnically diverse American societies.

A representative case of the US conflict resolution program is the 'HIPP (Help Increase Peace Program)' of the American Friends Service Committee. This section explores alternative workshops that can help young people form a good perspective on social and economic inequalities that cause conflict and violence in American society. One of the goals of this program is to create a classroom that enables peace. Therefore, it can be said that peace education in the United States is centered on students and teachers.[12]

5. Germany

Germany was the country that caused both World War I and World War II. So there is no country that will not suffer from Germany. Therefore, the most active field of globalization education in Germany is peace education. In Germany, peace education first began with an emphasis on understanding neighbors, since most wars have been widespread among neighboring nations. Therefore, peace education in Germany begins with France. In 1963, President Adenauer of Germany and Degol President of France initiated the 'Youth Exchange Program'. Between 1870 and 1945, between Franceans and Germans who waged a third war, this exchange project is a concrete program peace.

This interchange project sets the goal of peace and more, the goal of reconciliation and friendship between the two countries. Therefore, it is a living experiment of peace education. This exchange project has received a lot of support from a lot of grants, such as sports exchanges among youth, exploration of historical sites, political debate, dancing, art and music, field practice, learning German and French on a cross-base basis.[13]

Germany's peace education has recently been focusing on education for peace in the country due to the increase of multiculturalism. Currently, the number of children in Germany is shrinking, while the number of foreign children, including Muslim Turks, is increasing, and as a result of this conflict, the peace education is strengthened as a conflict resolution program.[14]

3. The role of the Asian Foundation for New Young Adult Education

1. The need for youth peace education in Asia

The diversity of Asia is extremely large, wide and deep. It occupies 30% of the land area of the world land and more than 60% of the population lives in

Asia. In addition, culture, religion, and climate are so many that one does not have the same thing. This diversity is the cause of the conflict. The type, size, and scale of conflict are as diverse as diversity. There is tension everywhere so that war is happening every day. Conflicts between religions are also expanding into major violence, such as war. While the ideological conflict that called the Cold War is alive, conflicts between Asian countries and regions with territories and resources are foreseeing the possibility of World War III. The analysis that the Asian country risk is the highest except for Africa and CIS also shows the potential of conflict in this region.[15]

The United States, China, Russia, India, Pakistan, Japan, South Korea, and North Korea, all of which are the world's strongest military forces, have an army in Asia. It is no exaggeration to say that the number of nuclear warheads these countries have is 99% of the world's nuclear warheads. Among them, India, Pakistan and North Korea are classified as dangerous countries that are not controlled by the international community. There is no mechanism to adjust and coordinate explosive situation owing to territorial disputes among China, Japan, South Korea, India, Pakistan and ASEAN countries. There is no sign of ending religious conflicts in Asia.

In conclusion, the world's largest gunpowder is Asia. Therefore, Asia is the place where peace education is most needed, and peace education for Asian youth is the basis for establishing not only Asia peace but also world peace.

2. Problems of existing peace education

We have described the actual conditions of youth peace education in each country. It is meaningful that the peace education for the youth has begun to be interested now though the peace education in each country is mainly targeted to adults. However, the present situation of youth education for peace can be evaluated as having the following problems.

First, the theme of peace education is simple

As the concept of peace shifts from passive peace to active peace, the theme of peace education is expanded from violence and war to human rights, ecology, culture, and democratic education. However, youth peace education in each country is now on a very simple subject, such as mutual exchange and understanding. This simplicity is not only less scalable for youth peace education, but also loses the interest of youth.

Second, it is overly closed
In other words, even if peace education is concentrated in the country or out of the country, it is limited to the neighboring country or the country of the party. Japan and the United States are dominant in the country, Israel is limited to the Arab and Palestinian countries, and Germany is the neighboring countries such as France. However, the present conflicts and wars are not confined to neighboring countries, but it is a combination of simultaneous and unspecified places. Therefore, peace education should be open.

Third, there is no common field of easy access
The lack of a common forum for the integration of youth peace education also points to the limitations of peace education. The chapter on peace education for youth will be more effective if the contents are made in various languages so that anyone can easily access them, and if there is a place where people can easily interact with other youths in cyber space.

Fourth, youth peace education is being carried out downward
The realization of youth peace education is done by top - down method led by the state or teacher. In other words, it is determined not by the content and method of active participation by adolescents but by the judgment criteria of adults and the education policy of the state. Therefore, most of the content falls away from the youth level. This is a factor for young people to lose interest in peace education.

3. New Youth Peace Education by the Fourth Industrial Revolution

The revolution of the fourth industry is now in life. Tens of millions of people are instantly connected to mobile devices without huge effort and cost, and huge organization is possible by cyber. The fusion of science and technology emerging in a wide range of fields such as artificial intelligence, IoT, and robotics, which are the symbols of the Fourth Industrial Revolution, and the convergence of such organized people / residents are required to be transformed into existing ways of life.[16]

The 4th Industrial Revolution is so different from the previous revolution, that is, the third industrial revolution, that velocity, scope and depth, and system impact are too different.[17] If we introduce the various technologies and features of the Fourth Industrial Revolution into peace education, there are ways to get it easily. In other words, by using the characteristics of the fourth industrial revolution such as super connectivity, super intelligence, convergence, shared economy, on demand (customized service), block chain, etc., the following measures can be sought.

First, accessibility is enhanced

The technology of the Fourth Industrial Revolution is that everything is connected to everything. It is predicted that by 2020, 3 billion people will be connected by the Internet, smart phones and other mobile devices. In particular, young people can connect with more another countries' youths than other generations because mobile is a living thing. In addition, language barriers are also decreasing due to the development of translator and interpreter, and the possibility of access to each other is high.

Second, it stimulates interest in education like games

The technologies of augmented reality and virtual reality (VR) among the technologies of the 4th Industrial Revolution will become commonplace as of now. Augmented reality and virtual reality technologies can bring infinite interest to young people because they are real in the monitor. Educational methods can be applied in a myriad of interesting ways such as games. This method will become a superintendent for many young people to come to their own by converting the content of difficult, overly abstract, peace education to the content of the youth favorite game.

Third, various rich contents

Peace education in general, as well as teenagers, is largely a matter of passive peace. That is why war and violence are central themes. However, in the active sense, because the concept of peace is now top-trend, the content of peace education should deal with infinite topics such as human rights, ecology, and exchange. The technology of intelligence and convergence of the Fourth Industrial Revolution could provide such a variety of themes to young people.

Fourth, customized education will be achieved

The technologies of the Fourth Industrial Revolution can provide a high level of On Demand, ie customized service delivery. A highly customized service means that you can provide the content you want in the time and space you want. Peace education can make a turning point for youth with preconceived notion that if they can provide as much of their content as they want and at the right time,

4. Role of the One Asia Foundation
1. Operator of One Asia Community Platform

As the Fourth Industrial Revolution goes on, power moves from state to nonstate actors, from well-established institutions to loose networks. New technologies, social groups, and interactions between them have enabled virtually anyone to exert influence. It was something I could not even imagine a few years ago. It is the government that is most affected by the increasingly temporary power. Moises Naim said, "In the 21st century, it became easier to gain power, harder to exert, and easier to lose."

With few exceptions, policymakers have been less able to lead change. This is because the role of policy makers is to receive check as the emergence of competitive forces, including transnational organizations, local and regional organizations as well as individuals. This micro-power is now able to control the macro power of the national government.[18]

In other words, the private sector will be able to govern or coordinate the state.

Using the technology of the Fourth Industrial Revolution, non-power activities such as peace education at least in Asia have become possible right now. However, there is a need for discussion and consensus on who should be the main subject. Although there are various requirements of the central subject, the nature of the Fourth Industrial Revolution suggests that a non-governmental organization (NGO), which has wide network, experienced and financially adequate.

On this basis, the One-Asia Foundation is the most appropriate organization.

First, since its foundation in 2009, the One Asia Foundation has been pursuing a peaceful Asia Community through understanding between countries and regions, and the goal remains unchanged.

Second, One-Asia Foundation currently supports 467 universities in 47 countries and regions, including 288 universities and 179 colleges and universities, and is building a strong network.[19]

Third, the goal of the One Asia Foundation is to create 'One Asia Community' in Asia like the EU. Mr. Sato, the founder of One Asia Foundation, has established the idea that a community of 40 countries and 4.4 billion people in Asia has created a one-Asia foundation with a dream of peaceful and abundant life.

Fourth, from a financial point of view, the One Asia Foundation is very strong with about 10, 000, 000, 000 yen (about $ 88, 000, 000) of Basic Funds. When the fourth industrial revolution is more important than money and hardware, ideas and software are more important resources, this level of finance is sufficient.

2. Operation of One Asia Bit Nation

The Fourth Industrial Revolution will revolutionize various socio-economic dimensions by co-opting beyond boundaries through fusion of fields that were formerly disconnected based on information and communication technology (ICT). This confluence makes the boundary of each field unclear. It will maximize the intersection between people, objects, people and things, making the boundary between technology and industry meaningless. In the era of convergence, those that were classified as completely different business systems will compete mutually. Convergence implies that not only is the boundary between industries blurred, but it also means that existing industries can evolve from a totally different perspective.

In addition, ICT technology has made it possible to create a world of their own by creating a perfect black chain. With the development of block chains and bit coins, the main living space will be a self-governing space such as a virtual state or a virtual self-governing body whose own central government does not need intermediation and supervision. Here you will enjoy politics, society, economic life and even cultural life. In fact, some countries have already implemented or are preparing. An example is the case of the Republic of Estonia. Estonia proclaims BitNation and accepts cyber citizens. Over the last few years, Estonia has introduced an electronic residential system. With this system, anyone in the world can apply for a 'transnational digital ID' and certificate to access secure services, electronically encrypt, verify and sign documents.[20]

It is the shape where the boundary of the border or the area gradually collapses. If this phenomenon goes on, then the time has come for the people or residents to become plural citizens and residents without the permission of the central government or local government. The country is breaking the boundaries of territory, the provinces are collapsing the areas of the region.

Since virtual country are characterized by borderlessness, decentralization, and spontaneity, the basis for becoming One Asia Bit Nation is sufficiently formed at present. One Asia virtual nation will be able to issue its own citizenship (e-residency) to build up its own country and expand its economic, social and cultural life as well as the area of economic activity by means of Bit Coin. A real peaceful nation will actually be in front of them. Given the network, human resources, and economy of the One Asia Foundation, building and operating One Asia BitNation will not be a difficult task.

3. Role of One Asia Bit Nation

One Asia BitNation is a virtual country. However, Bitnation differs from existing virtual reality countries in that it can only operate in the cyber world in that block chains are used in real world as well as in virtual world. The fourth industrial revolution is the Cyber Physical System (CPS), a technology that connects cyberspace and reality at the same time. Therefore, One Asia Bit Nation should be able to operate not only on line but also off line. Here are some key suggestions.

First, Center of the peace education and the peace movement

Establishing One Asia is one of the most important reasons to create a peaceful atmosphere in Asia, so peace education and peace movement should be the first goal of Asia. In addition, the basic of all the activities of One Asia Bit Nation are always peaceful. This peace education and peace movement should not be led by any country, organization, or even the sponsor, the One Asia Foundation. Youth should lead theses process. Only the peace education and peace movement, which are carried out by youths for young people, will not only enhance the efficiency of youth peace movement, but will also maintain sustainability.

Second, Role as an intermediary for exchanges

One Asia BitNation is a society that is active on off-line as well as on-line. Current peace education, especially the peace education in Asia, was only an exchange with neighbors, even though there was little or no exchange between youths in the virtual world as well as the real world. It is no exaggeration to say that in large continents like Asia, it was impossible to exchange youths between countries and regions. One Asia BitNation will be able to make active interchange among Asian youths on the first line. Asian youths with citizenship of One Asia BitNation will be able to interact with the desired time and contents through a machine that simultaneously translates almost all national languages and virtual reality, augmented reality technologies in One Asia Bit Nation. One Asia BitNation can promote exchanges with young people on off-line. The convention, which is held annually by the One Asia Foundation, will provide a number of ways to invite youth from each country to create their own programs.

Third, Role of the chapter of data production and its sharing

The life of the platform is the quantity and quality of the content. Therefore, One Asia BitNation should continue to produce and share the best and diverse materials in the world and share these materials and data among Youth of Asia. There are articles that are often quoted like buzzwords related to the Fourth Industrial Revolution. 'Uber, the world's largest taxi company, has no taxis. Facebook, the world's most popular media company, does not make any content at all. Alibaba, the world's most wealthy retailer, has no inventory. Airbnb, the world's largest lodging company, does not have any real estate. Something interesting is happening.[21]

This means that money and hardware-based ownership is less important than ever, and instead, accessability based on ideas and software are becoming increasingly important. Therefore, one Asia Bit Nation does not produce the data directly, but it can create the best data warehouse through sharing with other data and improving accessibility.

Fourth, Role of linking the universities supported with youth peace movement

At present, the number of universities supported by the Asian Community Foundation program is 288, and the number of universities to be supported in the near future is close to 500. If the programs run by these universities are link the local youth peace education program, it is expected that the ripple effect will be very great. Peace education by linking university students with local youth in the region will become a chain of peace and will become a systematic organization of peace education and peace movement.

4. Conclusion

The world that mankind dreams in any age is a peaceful world without war and violence. But humanity has never had a peaceful world. Nevertheless, mankind has never abandoned the dream of continuing to have a peaceful world. Until now, this paper has examined why the peace of humanity should be made constantly and the environment of peace education for young people of future generations. In contrast to the necessity of youth peace education, the reality is that there are too many obstacles. There were so many barriers that prevented the exchange and understanding between Asian youth, such as distance, time, language and culture. It is no exaggeration to say that there is very little exchange between Asian youth and mutual understanding.

However, the technologies and characteristics of the Fourth Industrial Revolution, which is the current amin stream now, are able to eliminate these barriers one by one. Super connectivity, super intelligence, convergence, shared economy and customized on-demand services enable Asian youth to connect and interact with each other in cyberspace and reality. Virtual reality, augmented reality, etc. has increased the fun and experience of peace education.

This study proposes One Asia Bit Nation as a space where Asian youths can make their own peace decision making, experience and live life by themselves. One Asia Bit Nation is a fictitious country that utilizes the features of block chain, statelessness, decentralization and spontaneity, which are one of the technologies of the fourth industrial revolution. However, One Asia Bit Nation is a virtual country, but it can serve as a platform for various exchanges, sharing and understanding among Asian youths by using it as an on line and off line. It is desirable for the One Asia Foundation to operate this platform by taking advantage of the many networks, experiences and operational know-how so far.

It is anticipated that peace movements will be greatly expanded if universities and NGOs, the largest think tanks in the country and region, add to it. This result is intended to find meaning of this proposal in that it can be settled not only in Asia but also as a practical movement to settle world peace.

Notes

1 Jin Chang Nam, Jeju Peace Research Institute, Research Report, 2008. 2, p. 2.
2 Ian M. Harris, Mary L. Morrison, translated by Park Jung Won, Peace Education (Jeju, Oum, 2011), pp. 27–28.
3 The above book, p. 47.
4 Jin Chang Nam, Proceedings, p. 14.
5 Jin Chang Nam, Proceedings, p. 26.
6 I have focused on the following report and book.

Moon Jeong-in, Yang Young-chul et al., Globalization of Jeju Education, Jeju Provincial Office of Education, 1995.

Here we describe the peace education in the country with professors from the United States (K.Mingst, University of Kentucky), Tsai (Singapore National University), and Germany (E. Weede, Professor, Cologne University) Professors in each country see peace education in the same context as globalization education.

Jin Chang Nam, others report.

7 Jin Chang Nam, Proceedings, pp. 61–62.
8 http://peacemaking.history.com/2005
9 Proceedings, pp. 31.
10 Jin Chang Nam, Proceedings, pp. 25–26.
11 Moon Jeong-in, Yang Young-cheol, previous book, p. 175.
12 Proceedings, pp.20–21.
13 Moon Jeong-in, Yang Young-chul, previous book, pp. 215–217
14 Above, p. 24.
15 Jeju Peace Institute, Asian Regional Risk Analysis, 2012, p. 13.
16 Klaus Schub, Song Kyung Jin, The Fourth Industrial Revolution (Seoul: New Current, 2016), p. 112.
17 Abover, 12–3.
18 Klaus Schub, an earlier book, p. 113.
19 http://www.oneasia.or.jp/ en / subsidies / total Number.html
20 Don Tapscott (Alex Tapscott, translated by Park Ji-hoon, BLOCKCHAIN REVOLUTION (Seoul: Kayo Culture, 2017), 353–6.
21 "Tom Goodwin," The Battle for the Customer Interface, "Tech Grunch, MARCH 3, 2015.

Kevin Kelly, quoted from Inneverable.

References

Kim, Min-ji (2016), A Study on the Multicultural Attitudes of University Students toward Multiculturalism and Peaceism, Studies on Peace Studies, Vol. 17, No. 4,
Kim Jin Ho (2017), The Fourth Industrial Revolution by Big Data, North Caravan.
Richard Susquint, Daniel Susquint (2016), Supreme Leader, Future of Profession in the Fourth Industrial Revolution Era, Wise Berry.
Rausch Schub, Song Kyung Jin (2016), Fourth Industrial Revolution, New Current.
Moon Jeong-in, Yang Young-chul et al. (1995), Globalization of Jeju Education, Jeju Provincial Office of Education.

Park Young-sook (2016), Ben Gorce, Artificial Intelligence Name 2030, Double Book.

Ian M. Harris, Mary L. Morrison (2011), translated by Park Jung Won, peace education.

Jeju Peace Institute (2012), Asian country risk analysis.

Jin Chang Nam, (2008), Analysis of the actual situation of peace education programs at home and abroad, Jeju Peace Institute, Research Report.

Korea Information Technology Promotion Agency (2016), Fourth Industrial Revolution and e-Government, D.gov Planning Report.

Don Tapscott (Alex Tapscott), translated by Park Ji-hoon (2017), BLOCKCHAIN REVOLUTION.

http://www.oneasia.or.jp/en/subsidies/totalNumber.html

http://peacemaking.tistory.com/2005

Chapter 12

Research on the Culture of the Formation of General Geographical Places Name in the East Asia Chinese Character Culture

Yu, Fong (Feng Chia University, Taiwan)

1. Introduction

In the historical development of mankind, most of the nouns were "specified". For example, among the 823 proper nouns of places during the Oracle era, most of them were names of specific places. Although there were some commonly used nouns for places, their use was not as universal. (Yu:2013) However, with the increasing complexity of the social division in terms of labor, the names of places, functions, and different categories of have become more and more numerous, and these functions, categories, and attributes of the places cannot be judged from how it is commonly called, and therefore must be something other than the existing nouns to indicate the them ? Commonly Used Nouns for General Places.

"Generic name" is the commonly used nouns of general items, and "General geographical name" is the nouns commonly used for geographical places. The names of a certain place, in addition to existing proper nouns, in order to highlight the attributes of proper nouns, they will be given a commonly used noun and form the name of a place using the format of "actual name + commonly used noun". The use of general geographical name not only facilitates identification, but also strengthens the administrative system. The relationship between general geographical name and proper nouns is not completely tight, and proper nouns do not necessarily need to be combined with generic name. However, when there are too many proper nouns for geographical places, it is necessary to add commonly used words to list their categories or attributes. Thus, the formation of generic name.

The formation of commonly used nouns for general place is an important historic cultural heritage of mankind. Every language has its own unique and different nouns for these general places. For example, in the British street system, there are different names such as "Street", "Avenue", "Road", "Yard", "Place", "Cres", and "Lane". Hong Kong, which used the British system in the early days therefore had adopted such methods and give different nouns for such places namely "道", "路", "街", "徑" and "里" respectively.

Due to the large number of generic name for geographical places, this article only refers to commonly used Chinese characters in East Asian cultural circle to examine the origin and use of Chinese characters, and the use cases of the generic names in the East Asian cultural circle.

2. Examples of General Geographical Name Used to Decribe Place Form of the Nature

The general geographical name refers to commonly used nouns to describe natural geography. This article lists nouns commonly found in East Asian Chinese cultural circle such as *Shan* (mountain/山), *Qiu* (hills 丘), *Yue* (alps/岳), *Feng* (summits/峰), *Shui* (waters/水), *Chuan* (creeks/川), *He* (rivers/河), *Jiang* (rivers/江), and *Xi* (streams/溪).

1. Shan (mountain/山)

"*Shan*" is one of the commonly used name for natural geography in the cultural circle of Chinese characters that depicts a mountain. As early as in the Shang Dynasty, the word "*Shan*" was used as the word mountain, like the shape of three peaks. The shape of the word in the bronze inscription (金文) of the Western Zhou Dynasty inherit the traits of the oracle bones with images of mountains and peaks connected to one another, which in turn affects small seal script(小篆) and the "*Shan*" shape of the Chinese character written today.

As far as the shape of the Chinese character is concerned, the mountain is like a mountain with peaks. The original meaning is mountain, and the *Shuo Wen Jie Zi* (A book that explains the origins of Chinese characters/《說文解字》)emphasizes that *"Shan"* is a high-topography with stones. In the case of Oracle, the characters were mostly borrowed for the name of the person and the object of worship. The Bronze inscription began to use it as a commonly used noun for places, such as *"Han Shan"* (寒山) In literature, the word *"Shan"* was used as a general noun for mountainous areas and peaks.(Yu :2011)

When used as the name of the places, the name *"Shan"* has been widely used in the cultural circle of Chinese characters since the Shang Dynasty. Today, most of the mountain names require the addition of the general geographical name of *"Shan"*, as in China there are *Tai Shan, Huang Shan, Hua Shan*; Taiwan's *Yu Shan, Xue Shan*; Hong Kong's *Tai Ping Shan*; Japan's *Fuji Shan*; Korea's *Hal La Shan* and *Jiri Shan* are all example of *"Shan"* used with proper nouns for names of places to indicate that they are mountain by nature.

2. Yue (alps/嶽/岳)

The structure of the Yue-character is after a *Qiu* (丘) and after a *Shan* (山), where *Qiu* had long existed during the Oracle bones period, *Shuo Wen Jie Zi* interpreted it as a small hilly heights. Oracle bones inscription depicts it as the act of climbing a small hill. In other words, it means that both *"Qiu"* and *"Shan"* needed to be climbed. Therefore, *"Yue"* (岳)'s meaning is related to the mountains. Since ancient times, there have been "Five Sacred Mountains" namely *Dai Shan, Lao Shan, Hua Shan, Heng Shan* and *Tai Shan*. *"Yue"*(嶽) is a mountain that is dangerous and steep. In its later use, the words *"Yue"*(岳) and *"Yue"*(嶽) are in parallel. Japanese characters and simplified Chinese characters are collectively referred to as *"Yue"* (岳); Taiwan's standard characters *"Yue"*(岳) and *"Yue"*(嶽) are still used together.

"Yue"(岳) and *"Yue"*(嶽) are not commonly known as nouns to name places in the ancient China. Most of them use the word *"Yue"* (嶽) to describe mountains that are enormous and appears to leave people in awe at sight.

In the cultural circle of Chinese characters of East Asia, those who use the noun "*Yue*"(岳) as part of the name of a place are most apparent in Japan. Among the names of mountain in Japan, the commonly used nouns along with the proper nouns are "*Shan*" and "*Yue*". In 1978, the Japanese New Wave Agency's "New Wave Library" had one hundred high mountains listed in their article "One hundred Japanese mountains" Among them, 47 mountain names come with the noun "*Yue*" as part of their names, such as the "*Rishiri Yue*", "*Shirouma Yue*" and "*Yari Yue*". In particular, the names of the mountains in Japan are also known as the word "*Yue*"(嶽), such as the names of the mountains, such as the "*Ontake Yue*" and "*Kita Yue*".

3. *Feng* (summits/峰)

The word *Feng* (峰) is after the mountain and the used *Feng* (夆) as its sound radical, it is also written as 峯. *Shuo Wen Jie Zi* interpreted it as a high mountain with a pointy summit. A mountain may not necessarily have only one hill. Each hill has its own name. In order to distinguish between the mountain as a whole and the mountain summits, the name of the mountain is commonly known as "*Shan*", while for the mountains' summits "*Feng*" is more often used.

The use case of the word "*Feng*" was rather late. In the pre-Qin and Han dynasties it was mostly the meaning of both mountain as a whole and the mountain summit. It was not until the Tang dynasty that the "*Feng*" is adapted as a commonly used noun along with the proper nouns to indicate names of summits such as the "*Zhi Ge Feng*" that is mentioned in Du Fu, the famous Tang Dynasty poet's poems.

Therefore, the commonly used nouns to indicate natural geography attributes, in addition to existing proper nouns, form the name of a place using the format of "actual name + commonly used noun (*Feng*)". For example, poems in the Tang Dynasty indicates other summits such as *Xiang Lu Feng*, *Jiu Hua Feng*, and *Min Feng*. These named "*Feng*" are all summits of mountains. *Zi Ge Feng* is a summit of *Zhong Nan Shan* and *Xiang Lu Feng* is a summit of "*Lu Shan*". The usage of *Feng* back then to indicate a summit is the same as the how it is used today.

4. *Chuan* (creeks/ 川)

Chuan is written in the form of rivers. *Shui* was used in the pre-Qin and Han periods as "*Shui*" looks like a river. The "big rivers" is called "*Chuan*".

The *Shuo Wen Jie Zi* recorded that the name of the small river was "〈", followed by "〈〈", and the great rivers was "川". The three words "〈, 〈〈, 川" were used to indicate the size of the river. In ancient times, "*Chuan*" was widely used in geographical nouns, referring to the great rivers. In the pre-Qin literature, there were many "*Shan Chuan*" and "*Chuan Ze*". For example, the "Book of Changes" mentioned: "If a man is modest, he could cross even the greatest *Chuan*."

In the same way as the word "*Feng*", the word "*Chuan*" is widely used in literary words and is gradually used as the concept of commonly used nouns of places with the attribute of a great river. Therefore, the name of the rivers in the Han Dynasty, namely, "*Ying Chuan*", "*Zi Chuan*", "*Ji Chuan*", "*Guang Chuan*" uses the format of "proper nouns + commonly used nouns (*Chuan*)". The names of Japanese rivers are known by their names. They all use the word "*Chuan*", such as "*Shika Chuan*", "*Chiyoda Chuan*", "*Tama Chuan*" and "*Ara Chuan*".

5. *He* (rivers/ 河)

The word *He* is formed after the water character carrying the sound of *Ke* (可). In the Oracle, the word "*He*" refers to the "*Huang He*" and also refers to the "God of *Huang He*" The word "*He*" was used as the name of the "*Huang He*" from the Shang Dynasty to the Han Dynasty.

At the present stage, in China and Taiwan, river names are often mainly referred to as "*He*". However, in the context of historical development, *Shui* was used as names of rivers in the pre-Qin and Han periods, and "*He*" was used as the proper noun *Huang He*. It could be added to the commonly used nouns for waters, *Shui* and become "*He Shui*". In the Northern Wei Dynasty, the name of the rivers recorded in the *Shui Jing Zhu*, also named after "*Shui*".

Until the Tang Dynasty, "*He*" was no longer the proper noun of the *Huang He*, and it gradually changed into a commonly used noun for rivers. For example,

"*Huai Shui*" was renamed the "*Huai He*" and "*Ju Yang Shui*" was renamed as "*Ju Yang He*" and it was later used in that sense until the modern times. At present, the river systems of the *Huang Hai* (yellow sea) and *Bo Hai* can also be known as "*He*", such as "*Tuo He*", "*Ying He*", "*Xiao Qing He*" and "*Hai He*". Taiwan's mountains and rivers are highly water-tight, and rivers often use "*Xi*" for their names, and only a few uses the word "*He*", such as the "*Dan Shui He*"

6. *Jiang* (rivers/江)

The word "*Jiang*" is formed after the water and uses *Gong*(工) as its sound radical, in the East Zhou Dynasty bronze inscription, it means the *Chang Jiang*. Just like the word "*He*", the ancient word for "*Jiang*" refers specifically to the proper noun of the Chang Jiang. Therefore, It could be added to the commonly used nouns for waters, *Shui* and become "*Jiang Shui*", just as it is written on *Han Shu*.

The period of time when the usage of "*Jiang*" as a commonly used noun is similar to that of the word "*He*". It gradually increased during the Tang Dynasty and was mainly concentrated on the basin of *Chang Jiang*. The *Chang Jiang* itself has many tributaries. The early tributaries also used the word "*Shui*" as their name; and the "*Jiang Shui*" itself has long been known as *Chang Jiang* due to its long rivers. The "*Chang Jiang*" was originally a structure of adjectives + nouns (proper nouns). By the Tang Dynasty, tributaries of the *Chang Jiang* were gradually renamed as "Jiang", such as "*Min Jiang*", "*Jia Ling Jiang*", "*Jin Sha Jiang*", etc., in response to "*Chang Jiang*". Up to the Song Dynasty, almost all of them used the name "Chang Jiang" and it is less often called "*Jiang Shui*".

In the modern East Asian Chinese cultural circle, rivers using the name of "*Jiang*" are: 1. Referring to the area of the *Chang Jiang* basin and its southern region, such as "*Zhu Jiang*", "*Long Jiang*" and "*Jiu Long Jiang*" and each tributary of the *Chang Jiang* basin.; 2. The rivers in South Korea are also called "Jiang", such as the "*Han Jiang*", "*Jin Jiang*", "*Rong Shan Jiang*", and "*Luo Dong Jiang*".

7. *Xi* (streams/溪)

The word "*Xi*" is formed after the water and uses *Xi* (奚) as its sound radical. Its original word is *Xi* (谿). *Shuo Wen Jie Zi* depicts it as the valley because there are often small streams in the valley, they are later referred to as streams.

Xi is largely used for valley streams in the Tang dynasty, such as *"Qing Xi"* which often appears in Tang poetry. At the end of the Sui Dynasty and the early Tang Dynasty, the literati Wang Ji's *"Traveling to Bei Shan Fu"* had a large number of instances where *"Xi"* was used as a commonly used noun of the place with streams. Examples include *"Niu Xi"*, *"Bai Niu Xi"* and *"Qing Xi"*. At present, in the cultural circle of Chinese characters, most rivers in Taiwan and in the southeast coast of Fujian Province are known by the name *"Xi"*, especially in Taiwan, which has high mountains and high water levels, except for a few like *"Dan Shui He"*, *"Dong Shan He"* and so on where *"He"* is a commonly used noun, and the rest are all known as *"Xi"*. The longest river is the *"Zhuo Shui Xi"*, and there are *"Da Jia Xi"*, *"Gao Ping Xi"* and *"Tou Qian Xi"*. There are no examples of river names such as *"Chuan"* and *"Jiang"* in Taiwan.

3. Examples of General Geographical Name Used to Decribe Place Form of the Humanities Category

The humanities category refers to the commonly used nouns of geographical places formed as a result of the needs of humanistic activities. Such nouns do not describe the phenomenon of natural geography, but describe local systems, local divisions, etc. in human geography. With the increasing complexity of humanistic activities and the organization of social organizations, the number of culturally-known geographical names has increased and the level has increased. This has affected the culture of Chinese characters in East Asia.

1. *Guo* (country/國)

The meaning of *Guo* in the ancient time is domain. The meaning of the word was later expanded. The foreign countries known as the *"Fang"* in the Shang Dynasty were called *"Guo"* when it comes to the Qin and Han dynasties. The *"Guo"* of the pre-Qin and Han periods included the *Zhu Hou Guo* (feudal princes, esp. the monarchs (dukes or princes) of the several vassal states/諸侯國) of the pre-Qin period, the vassal states of the Han dynasties, and "*Xi Hu Guo*" of the foreign states.

At present, the usage of "*Guo*" in the cultural circle of Chinese characters directly corresponds to the English language. It refers to the country, such as "*Zhong Guo*" (China), "*Han Guo*" (Korea) and "*Mei Guo*" (the United States of America). It is a relationship of "proper nouns + commonly used nouns (*Guo*)." The kingdoms and *Hou Guo* in the ancient feudal system were no longer seen in the modern society. Therefore, the meaning of the "*Guo*" became a commonly used noun for the names that specifically referred to the country with governmental authority.

2. Xian (county/縣)

"*Xian*" is an important unit of the local system in East Asia. The ancient "*Xian*" was the *Tian Zi* 's (emperor) federal territory, and it was originally located in the surrounding area of *Zhou Tian Zi* in the early days. It had the meaning of "hanging" in it. Therefore, the name "*Xian*" was used as the name of the division. (Zheng: 1995) The area of counties in various early vassal states was indefinite. The documents in the *Jin Guo* and *Chu Guo* were all resettled. Until *Qin* unified the county system, the organizational norms of the county were clearly and clearly documented and became an important unit of the local system. (Yu:2011)

After the implementation of the county system, the "*Xian*" has an influence of more than 2, 000 years. The descendants are either three-tier systems such as "*Zhou, Jun Xian*"(states, divisions, counties/州、郡、縣) or four-tier systems "*Sheng, Dao, Fu, Xian*" (provinces, roads, prefectures, and counties/省、道、府、縣) The counties maintained their window of "connecting the local government to the central government". Up till today, China, Taiwan and Japan have been maintaining the "county" system.

3. Shi (City/市)

In the ancient local system, the business district was restricted to the scope of the *"Shi"*, and the perimeter of *"Shi"* was built with walls and separated from the residential area. The *Chang An* and *Luo Yang* capitals in the Han and Tang dynasties are basically two cities, namely, the *"Dong Shi"* (East City/東市) and the *"Xi Shi"* (West City/西市) This is the first time that the *"Shi"* was used for as the commonly used noun of geographical names for humanities, but no proper nouns was given at the time. Simply use the position words of "East" and "West" to describe it. The content of the *"Shi"* at that time was equivalent to the current "commercial zone" and was different from the meaning of *"Shi"* today.

Although the ancient capitals, counties, and counties in ancient China all had a certain scale, none of them was named after the noun *"Shi"*. The *"Shi"* system of the modern Chinese character culture circle originates from Japan. In 1888, Japan issued the "Municipality and Machino System", which set 36 cities such as Tokyo, Kyoto, Osaka, and Gifu as a *"Shi"* and corresponded to the concept of "City" of the western countries. At the time, Taiwan, which was still under Japanese rule back then, also set up a *"Shi"* system in Tainan in 1903. After the founding of the Republic of China, China was promulgated in 1921, which stipulated that *"Shi"* should be established in capitals, provincial capitals, commercial ports, counties, and other places with a population of 10, 000. (Huang:1980)

The use of *"Shi"* to correspond to the meaning of "City" should be related to the concept of *"Shi"* in Chinese. Even the ancient *"Shi Ji"* (the historical records/史記) has already recorded the word *"Shi"*, and *"Shi"* is referred as the area surrounded by city walls. It is also used as a place name, such as *"Huai Yang Shi"* and *"Chang An Shi"* Although *"Shi"* has not been given the role of a formal local system, plus Japan town is also called *"Shi"*, such as "Kumamoto Town" and "Osaka Town" are referred to as *"Shi"*. It is not Kumamoto City or Osaka City, but the ancient town left behind. If the new "city" is named after *"Shi"*, it will be confused with the existing "city" concept. Therefore, the word *"Shi"* is used as a commonly used noun in the local system.

4. *Dao* (road/道)

The word *Dao* was found in West Zhou Dynasty bronze inscription, such as "巤道", "*Yuan Dao*" and "*Zhou Dao.*" "Dao" has two meanings in ancient times. One is the name of the road, and the other is the name of the local system. The local government's "*Dao*" system began in the Han Dynasty. There was no visible system before the Han dynasty. However, "*Dao*" itself carries the meaning of a road. Therefore, the "*Dao*" of the bronze inscription refers to the road system.

The earliest "*Dao*" was listed as a local system and was found in the West Han Dynasty. In the dynasty after the West Han Dynasty, the position of "*Dao*" was different. For example, *Shi Dao* of the Tang Dynasty were positioned above the prefecture and county level. The local system of modern mainland China and Taiwan has no "*Dao*"; South Korea still maintains the "*Dao*" system and its status is similar to that of the province, such as the use cases of "Gyeonggi-Dao", "Gangwon- *Dao*" and "Gyeongsangbuk- *Dao*"; There are seven "*Dao*" in Japan since the Nara period, including Higashiyama, Tokaido, Hokuriku, Sanyo, Sanyo, Hokkaido, Hokkaido, and Hokkaido. After the reform of the local system in 1889, only "Hokkaido" maintained the "*Dao*". system.

5. Zhou (states/州)

The *Shuo Wen Jie Zi* shows that the word *Zhou* stands for alluvial sands that can be found in the water are high places surrounded by water. In the *Yu Gong* chapter of "*The Book of Odes*", the earth is divided into nine *Zhou*, and later in the book of "*Zhou Li*" and "*Er Ya*", there were recordings concerning the nine Zhou, but their names are not the same and have not been formally implemented. *Han Wudi* imitated the system of the nine *Zhou* and added the "*Zhou*" system to the prefecture state. It divided the world into thirteen states. Each state has a provincial government which during the initial period was merely dummies, and later became part of the local system.

The word "*Zhou*" is used in the local system and has a very long term impact. From the Han to the Qing dynasty and even Japan and South Korea, there was a system of "*Zhou*". Although each state and jurisdiction of the "*Zhou*" is not the same, the term is still used. The *"Zhou"* system has the same long-term local system as *"Xian"*. However, in the early 19th century, countries such as China, Japan, and South Korea successively abolished the *"Zhou"* system. In the use for determining names of places, there are still *"Zhou"* known by their names, such as *"Kyu Zhou"* and *"Hon Zhou"* in Japan; The single-syllable names of the mainland are co-operative with the *"Zhou"* to indicate a state, such as *"Zheng Zhou"* and *"Liu Zhou"*.

6. *Xiang* (village/鄉)

The *"Xiang"* character of the oracle bone is like two people facing each other and in the *"Shuo Wen Jie Zi"*, it is described as the units that are designated by the local government under the *Zhu Hou Guo*.

The word *"Xiang"* is used as a geographical name and is found in the literature. When the *"Shi Ji"* documented the *Shang Yang* Reformation, the collection of small townships became a county. This was the beginning of the county system under the county jurisdiction.

The *"Xiang"* system has been a small-scale local system since the Han Dynasty. It is usually located in units below the prefecture level. At present, the *"Xiang"* system still exists in mainland China and Taiwan, and mostly in agricultural areas.

7. *Zhen* (town/鎮)

The *Zhen* character is formed after gold and uses *Zhen*(真) as its sound radical, and *Shuo Wen Jie Zi* explained it as a bet also means the bet when gambling. The *"Zhen"* in the *Classics* is often used in military terms such as guarding and repression. The *"Zhen"* is only a borrowed word and has nothing to do with the formation of the word structure.

In the Middle Ages, the term *"Cheng Zhen"* was found, and it was similar to the meaning of "city". However, the organized *"Zhen"* mostly belonged to the military zone. Until the early 19th century, the Qing Dynasty promulgated the *"law of local self-government in towns and villages"*, and then The Republic of China and the People's Republic of China set up *"Zhen"* units under the *"Xian"*, and it is a tertiary administrative district.

8. *Ding* (town/町)

The word is formed after field and uses *Ding* as its sound radical. There is no record of this word both in the oracle bones inscriptions and bronze inscriptions. The *"Shuo Wen Jie Zi"* explains it as the places where farmers can cultivate their fields. In ancient China, there was no example of the use of the word *"Ding"* as a commonly used noun for a place name. In the East Asian cultural circle however, Japan is known for using *"Ding"* commonly. In Japanese, it is called "まち ma chi." The *"Ding"* system is similar to Taiwan's township unit; the city's sub-district also uses *"Ding"*. Taipei's *"Xi Men Ding"*, is a place left during the Japanese occupation named is in the format of the "actual name + commonly used noun (*Ding*)".

4. Conclusion

Due to some formatting constrain and word count requirements, this article had not listed the commonly used nouns after all the names of places in the East Asian Chinese character cultural circle. It is based on commonly seen and commonly used nouns such as *"Shan, Yue, Feng, Chuan, He, Jiang, Xi"* and humanities the noun of *"Guo, Xian Shi, Dao, Zhou, Xiang, Zhen and Ding"* is known as the mainly used common nouns after places.

Each name for places has its own history and allusions, such as *"Shan"*, *"Xian"*, and *"Guo"*. These were all commonly used nouns. They have been used for a long time and they are still used to name places. In particular, the "Xian" system of the pre-Qin period affected the "division-county system" of the *Qin Guo*, which in turn affected China, Japan, and Taiwan in the modern society. *"Xian"* is still the main identification of local zoning.

In the ancient period, some of the generic names were merely geographical terms, such as *Feng, Chuan, Xin, Guo and Shi*. The use of later generations added the direction "east, west, south, and north" as bearing words. Then, with the development of time, the bearing words were replaced with proper nouns of geographical names, so that the nouns that originally belonged to geography were transformed into geographical nouns and influenced many countries in the East Asian cultural circle.

REFERENCES
Huang, Da Shou (1980), *Chinese Modern History Program*. Taipei.
Zheng, Dian Hua (1995), 'County(郡縣) source research'. *Beijing Library Journal*, V1/2, p. 22.
Yu, Fong (2011) 'Research on General Geographical Name of the Shuo Wen Jie Zi'. *The 22nd International Symposium on Chinese Philology*, Wu-Nan, Taipei.
Yu, Fong (2013) 'Research on General Geographical Name of the Shang Dynasty Oracle'. *Retrospect and Forward-looking International Academic Seminar on Digitization of Chinese Characters*, E.C.N.U., Shanghai.

Chapter 13
Promoting Global Citizenship Education, Multicultural Education, and Civic Education to a Peaceful Asian Community

Dasim Budimansyah (Indonesia University of Education, Bandung, Indonesia)

1. Introduction

Globalization and modernity encompass almost every aspect of our lives. In the field of education, there is a disputable question of what sort of education prepares someone to be a global citizen. We cannot be citizens of the world in the way that we are citizens of a nation, adding that being a citizen now takes an active role (Davies & Pike, 2008). The UK Oxfam Curriculum for Global Citizenship defined a 'global citizen' as someone who: (a) is aware of the wider world and has a sense of their own role as a world citizen; (b) respects and values diversity; (c) has an understanding of how the world works economically, politically, socially, culturally, technologically and environmentally; (d) is outraged by social injustice, is willing to act to make the world a more equitable and sustainable place; and (e) participates in and contributes to the community at a range of levels from the local to the global (Ibrahim, 2005).

Globalization pushes every nation and individual to be more competitive. Economically, politically and socio-culturally, globalization may pose a threat to traditions, religious beliefs and even question the notion of citizenship and nationalism. With these challenges, teacher education institutions play a crucial role in the education of the youth. As stated, citizens now need to take an active role and learn how to become citizens of the world (Anderson, 2006).

Launched in September 2012, Global Citizenship Education became one of the strategic areas of work for UNESCO's Education Program (2014-2017). For UNESCO "Global Citizenship Education equips learners of all ages with those values, knowledge and skills that are based on and instill respect for human rights, social justice, diversity, gender equality and environmental sustainability and that empower learners to be responsible global citizens. GCE gives learners the competencies and opportunity to realize their rights and obligations to promote a better world and future for all (Balta, 2014). The concept of multiculturalism, on the other hand is crucial in understanding the challenges brought by globalization and modernity. One must understand the culture, the diversity of culture, ethnicity and religious freedom. It is expected that everyone can be fair to himself, others and his environment. No more hatred can control every act (Reardon, 1988). The objective of Citizenship Education is qualified and responsible participation in political and community life at the local, state, and national levels (Branson, 1998).

Providing Global Citizenship Education (GCE), Multicultural Education (ME) and Civic Education (CE) is very useful in a much globalized world. With the advent of ASEAN Integration, South East Asian nations particularly ASEAN Teacher Education Institutions must prepare policies, curricular programs, faculty development, and learning environments that can help ensure the development of civic minded, global citizens, and culturally proficient teachers. This research is pivotal in determining the policies, curricular programs, faculty development activities, and students' learning environment of selected ASEAN Teacher Education Institutions in GCE, ME, and CE.

The objective of the research is to delineate the policies, curricular programs, faculty development activities, and measures on learning environment of selected ASEAN Teacher Education Institutions implemented in their respective universities. More specifically, the research team members of the Universitas Pendidikan Indonesia (UPI) otherwise known as Indonesia University of Education were encouraged to build some descriptions based on the descriptive analysis with respect to issues of university policies, curriculum and instruction, faculty development programs, and learning environment in support of the implementation of GCE, ME, and CE that will benefit prospective teachers in the forthcoming ASEAN Integration.

2. Conceptual Review

It was agreed that the emphasis given to citizenship education i.e. GCE, ME, and CE in the curriculum has effectively contributed to the development of values and attitudes of students as prospective teachers. It is strongly believed that the inclusion of GCE, ME, and CE in the curriculum of teacher education will immensely contribute to the development of values and attitudes related to the essence of GCE, ME, and CE of students, which finally will contribute to their professionalism as teachers in schools. It is argued that educating prospective teachers for future generation has been accepted as an integral part of the national human investment.

From the other point of view, citizenship education, as Potter (2002), and Osler & Starkey (2006) identified, appears to be an educational program that all the countries in the world are so much concerned to prepare students to be democratic and responsible citizens. For Indonesia it was noted that since 1960's there have been dramatic changes in civic education program at least six times along with the changes of the school curriculums throughout the country. On the other side, in Australia and world-wide citizenship education is widely acknowledged as a necessary part of the school curriculum for various reasons, including the perception that it can be a useful cure for the 'social ills' often associated with young people: that is, tendencies for anti-social behavior and political apathy among young people (describe as 'youth deficit')."

At the local community level, Sigauke (2013) assumed that social and environmental problems can best be resolved through an understanding of what it means to be a citizen. However, beyond the local community, global events such as the World Trade Centre attack of September 2001, the January 2010 earthquake in Haiti or the tsunami that devastated parts of Japan in March 2011, in Sigauke's analysis, have made it necessary for both old and young people to be aware of what is happening in other parts of the world and take action where and when they can. Sigauki then examined the nature of and the extent to which citizenship ideas and citizenship education are covered in the social science subjects of the teacher education curriculum program offered to preservice teachers at one Australian university.

Generally, contents of educational documents such as teacher education programs and schools' syllabuses are mainly products of government policies on education that may, as Scott (2000) observed, operate to influence public opinion on the agendas of powerful groups in society. They are in fact formulated by people in positions of power and as such may be ideological. They use various language devices to conceal their own interests. Thus even where there is little need to ask, readers are advised to ask themselves questions about intentions of documents; their ideological underpinnings and the relevance of policy agendas to learners, practitioners and society in general (Scott, 2000).

As they pass through the bureaucratic chain, down to the school level, educational policies are sometimes misinterpreted or completely changed as they are implemented as school, college or university syllabuses. These views are important for the present study that seeks to understand the nature of civics and citizenship education in the social science program at the teacher education level; to have some insight about who develops policy in teacher education programs; and the level of control teacher institutions have on programs they develop and teach" (Sigauke, 2013). Viewed from the idea of social transformative pedagogy such condition, Sigauke (2013) underlined, would stimulate and raise consciousness in learners, allowing them to be active and responsible participants; and for them to recognize oppressive, violent and exploitative conditions. Correspondingly, Grundy & Hatton's (1995) research has shown that the nature of ideological discourses at the teacher education level is important in determining what education (including civics and citizenship education) can do to change the status quo. It was also the case in a study in Australia by Grundy & Hatton (1995) which identified two ideological discourses in teacher education i.e. social transformation and social.

On a different note, Thomas (2009) viewed that education needs to adopt the

Freirean socially transformative "dialogical, liberatory or critical/constructivist pedagogy"; a knowledge creating, learning and collaborative process between teachers and learners that illuminates and acts on the realities of everyday problems. It seems that this is similar to what Connell (1993) referred to as "social justice in the curriculum", a counter-hegemonic curriculum that takes into account interests of the socially disadvantaged. It is an approach that leads to social justice during which students and teachers jointly contribute in decision-making to resolve community problems". On the other hand, critical or constructivist pedagogy considered it not just the "deposition of knowledge" (banking process) from elsewhere into learners (Hinchey, 2004) but a liberating process that empowers students to build a just and equal society: that is, equality between races, sexes and cultures; involving parents, teachers and students in school governance and policy making (Shor, 1990).

Consequently, a democratic teacher using a social transformative approach teaches for equality and critical knowledge; s/he adopts student-centred, participatory and problem-solving approaches. Thus, classroom teacher-student interactions in socially transformative environments are essentially based on democratic discourse approaches where students bring in their everyday experiences for discussions and research on conditions of everyday life in communities" (Sigauke, 2013). A teacher who uses critical pedagogy is not authoritarian, permissive, silent nor passive but is mainly a facilitator of democratic processes who encourages students to challenge teachers and to speak freely as partners in a democratic project; as what Kemmis referred to as "socially-critical schooling" (Sigauke, 2013). Further the school is regarded as a learning community within the community and is characterized by collaborative action, negotiation and self-reflection (Kemmis et al., 1983).

3. Methodology

UPI as one of the ASEAN Teacher Education Network (ASTEN) members was the focus of the study. The respondents came from the different functions and/or roles in UPI as one of the 11 biggest and oldest institutions of teacher education in Indonesia. An initial assessment of the UPI's policies, curricular programs, faculty development activities, and measures on learning environment of selected stakeholders in terms of GCE, ME, and CE were undertaken. To meet the research objectives the ASTEN instruments were utilized to outline the policies, curricular programs, faculty development activities, and measures on learning environment of the UPI as one of the ASTEN-member Teacher Education Institutions including faculty members and administrators. The instruments were especially used in conducting focused group discussions in UPI and interviews with the UPI administrators, and other stakeholders.

4. Findings and Discussions

It is vitally important to underline the activities of GCE, ME, and CE developed in UPI which were basically intended for the preparation of all prospective teachers from UPI to embrace global perspectives. Among the activities promoted so far are Student Group Practicum in Australia and Thailand and students acting as teacher aides in schools in Australia. It is of importance to note that not all GCE, ME, and CE activities are yet organized in a single subject. In fact, all operational activities dealing with the ideals of GCE, ME, and CE have been actualized within the university living cultures. Discourses on the idea of organizing GC, ME, and CE into a single disciplinary subject need further inquiry.

When the ideals of GCE, ME, and CE are formally developed as formal subjects, they might lose the essence of each of the subject as a vehicle for living values education. Those ideals will significantly turn into formal subjects requiring more academic criteria rather that of living values. And yet, UPI as a teacher education institution will still have to actualize its educational system and culture in harmony with living values development through its educational endeavors. All prospective teachers educated in UPI should have both national and local perspectives and global perspective as well.

From pedagogical perspectives, a number of factors need to be considered in selecting methods and techniques in teaching GCE, ME, and CE. Among those factors were: future orientations/visions; child characteristics; competencies to be developed; learning facilities needed; teachers' competencies; hands-on experience to be created; future trends of working place; related government policies; world trends in science and technology; and regional changes. Institutional commitments in UPI must be strengthened in order that GCE, ME, and CE can be embedded into all related subjects in addition to their systematic inclusion with each of the General Education.

Various modes of learning materials have been used in delivering GCE, ME, and CE. Some of them were supplied by the Government or institutionally developed. To mention some, these include: various printed materials (textbooks, modules), web/video/recorded based learning materials; open education resources (web-based, internet access), local library; community/society (local, regional, and global) as an open and global classroom.

Specifically in the provision of training and instructional materials, book allowances and subsidies either in the form of travel grants to cover airfare, accomodation or registration fees when participating in conferences or trainings related are seen as of the importance for GCE and CE. On the other hand, the provision of adequate trainings and seminars to upgrade students' knowledge and skills in teaching were catered for GCE and CE but it was not to be the case for ME. Thus far UPI has made various collaborations with both domestic and international educational agencies. A number of Memorandum of Understanding (MoUs) have been established with a wide range of universities around the globe. Among the subjects of cooperation revolve around academic, administration, teaching, research, publishing, and student learning. While most of collaborations were still at preliminary stages, further efforts need to be made to ensure that all university collobarorations would give impact or benets to the development of UPI.

To guarantee the quality of learning materials, a special committee needs to be established. Unfortunately, until recently the committee has not been formally set up. Instead a group of experts in a certain area of learning was assigned to do some reviews of learning material developed by a or a group of lecturer - a colleagueal reviewer.

It was found that there was no problem with religious perspective(s) related to learning materials. In fact, each individual lecturer in Indonesia must have his/her religious creed according to his/her belief and do worship according to his/her religion as well. In daily living anyone should uphold the value of tolerance within the *Pancasila*'s (The Five Principles of Ethics) way of living. Religious perspective is outonomous for any individual. It is noteworthy that learning materials are not yet gender sensitive/diverse. Basically all learning materials are geared for all students regardless of their gender. All learning materials must be coherent with the values inherent in the philosophy of the subject the lecturer is academically and pedagogically responsible for.

Table 13-1 Effects of GCE, ME, and CE programs to develop the charactor of UPI students as prospective teachers

Nu	Citizenship Characters that Appears	Pedagogy Instruments
1	Civic responsibility	General subjects, i.e.: • Pancasila and Civic Education • Religion Education • Indonesian Language • Student organizations • Enggagement activities
2	Civic knowledge, Civic disposition, and Civic Skills	• Lectures • Workshops • Projects • Civic misson (e.g. youth, music, sport, dance, competion, debate)
3	Patriotic citizenship	• Lectures • Workshops • Projects • Civic misson (e.g. youth, music, sport, dance, competion, debate)
4	Environmental sustainability	General subjects, i.e.: • Socio-cultural Education • Basic Science • Basic Humanities • Student organization • Enggagement activities

Source: Suryadi, Budimansyah & Winataputra (2017)

To cater for the needs of learners from indigenous communities, UPI generally has accomodated a small number of students coming from *Baduy Dalam* (Banten), *Anak Dalam* (Jambi), *orang Tengger* (East Java) who can get along with the general society and willing to get formal education. There is no exclusive treatment yet, but these indigenous people are immersed in the general student groups, intentionally to make them get more and more inclusive.

Analysis of the existing documents as well as FGD and interview reports reveals that all the three programs i.e. GCE, ME, and CE have proved themselves respectively to be the effective means in building citizenship characters in the following ways (see Table 13-1).

Detailed descriptions of the effects of GCE, ME, and CE on developing the citizenship character of UPI students as prospective teachers are described as follows. Civic responsibility has been developed pedagogically through General Subjects (*Pancasila* and Civic Education, Religion Education, and Indonesian Language) and student government/engagement activities. Civic knowledge, civic disposition, and civic skills are introduced and learned through lectures, workshops, projects, civic missions (e.g. youth, music, dance, competition, debate). It indicates that civic responsibility of students and prospective teachers as well have significantly emerged and developed during their stay on campus as well as off campus programs.

Likewise, patriotic citizenship also has been pedagogically developed in the same way. It indicates that just like civic responsibility, patriotic citizenship of students and prospective teachers as well have emerged and developed harmoniously during their stay on campus and as reported particularly, during the campus activities such as during their student community service learning programs.

It is also has been the case with environmental sustainability. The issue was developed generally through General Subjects, i.e. Basic Social Sciences, Basic Humanities, and Basic Sciences and student government/engagement activities. Civic commitment, civic confidence, and civic competence are all believed to be the main components of patriotic citizenship and civic responsibility actualized through civic mission, i.e. community services as a part of service learning. It indicates that just like civic responsibility, patriotic citizenship of students and prospective teachers have emerged and developed in their perceptions, behavior, attitudes and habits of caring and looking after university environment such as buildings, rooms, parks, pathways, ponds, the performing arts building, sport facilities; all of which simbolize a clean and green campus of UPI.

Student government system in UPI covers varied activities/focuses organized within activity clusters: Student Activity Unit; Faculty Student Government; Student Resilience Program; etc. All of them are basically designed and facilitated to generate ideas and prospects in relation to GCE such as international collaboration of students. All those citizenship characters are believed to have the most significant pedagogical and sociocultural impacts of GCE, ME and CE programs and their related activities.

There are problems in teaching of GCE, ME, and CE particulalry in dealing with content coverage, learning activities, and student participation/enggagement. Attempts have been made to address these problems by way of planning and organizing learning experiences based on the ideas of democratic citizenship ideals. No crucial problems dealing with content coverage have been uncovered as those issues are closely bound to the content coverage of the curriculum and those subjects which are open to current issues and resources available in various learning resources including those available in Open Educational Resources (OER). The only problem is in how to generate various model of learning which are able to stimulate student partiipation in CGE, ME, and CE.

Further development of the ideas of GCE, ME, and CE in UPI have indicated that new paradigm and related policy for GCE and MCE are needed. Emphasis on CE as the academic field offering a full-fledged academic program needs to be enriched by refocussing and redeveloping both GCE and ME to upgrade their statuses from the embedded substance to become a more structured educational program with specific goals.

The study of civic education should be academically and pedagogically enhanced in the following ways. It needs to realign and redevelop the existing CGE, ME, and CE in UPI in order that all those educational endeavours would be more useful and meaningful for student teachers. Further, more innovative strategies of CGE, ME, and CE are urgently needed for all teacher educators in UPI. Thus, they will become even more and more competent and they personally could become models of good and smart citizens. It is also noted that introduction and training on more innovative strategies of CGE, ME and CE are imperative for all teachers in schools used as teacher training facilities in order that student teachers from UPI would be increasingly more qualified and serve as the models of good and smart citizens at school level.

Attempts are needed to enrich GCE, ME, and CE in UPI by giving advocacies and religious holidays which officially have existed within the academic calendar e.g. Human Right's Month, Women's month, Ramadan, Christmas, and etc. Moreover, in Indonesia more holiday/festivities days related to almost any kind of human activities, community celebration, national festival could be used as socio-cultural references in planning and conducting CGE, ME, and CE in and off campus setting. Further promotion of GCE, ME, and CE within the context of the implementation of ASEAN 2015 vision is in order as well. To meet the end, full energy and all possible supports are necessary to realign and redevelop CGE, ME, and CE so that those programs will facilitate collaboration and friendship among ASEAN people through developing global understanding for global citizenship. Accordingly, relevant prospective teacher education program to support the development of ASEAN identity has a strategic role.

Dealing with the promotion of Multicultural competencies, it has already been stipulated in the National System of Education (Referring to the National Education Act No. 20 Year 2003, specifically in the three legal imperatives, i.e. Foundation, Function and Objectives, and National Principles of Education that the essences of CGE, ME, and CE must become the national credo of the Indonesian educational process. Thus, initiatives as well as further development of CGE, ME, and CE are absolutely needed. It is to be noted that issues around women's rights, LGBT rights, indigenous people rights have been discussed widely in the institution. Among the three issues, the LGBT one is considered as a heated issue due to its religious and political considerations. The other two issues, i.e. Women's rights and IP rights have been guaranteed by Laws.

Given that GCE, ME, and CE are a whole-institutional program, supportive facilities and services such as Assistive Rails Language, Interpreter Elevator/Lift Access, Ramp Access, Restroom for People with Disabilities (PWD), Trash bins segregated accordingly, and Worship Center have already been made available in UPI Campus. However, breastfeeding station, recycling facility, restroom for LBGT, Sign language interpreters, and women help-desk are not yet available.

Naturally and humanly the roles of woman and men are arguably different with their uniqueness and commonality. These need to figure in nondiscriminatory treatments in the university. Community expectations to deal with women and men in the family and society are to be taken into consideration in university management.

Furthermore, it was noted that the availability of all religion worships has historically and sociologically related to the number of each of religious believers needing special religious facility. For Moslem believers, the university built a Big Mosque integrated within the Tutorial Building, but it has not been the case yet for other religious believers due to limited number of their believers. Certain rooms; however, has been made available for doing religious their religious activities as needed. Legally no restriction exists to build those needed religious sites.

All activities have been recognized as an important component to amplify the development of values that are inherently included in GCE, ME, and CE to foster future teachers. Future teachers are those who have the capacity to educate young people not only to be good citizens for their country but to be global citizens who are able to fill the world peacefully. In the Asian context, promoting GCE, ME, and CE in the teacher education curriculum will be a smooth road for the realization of a peaceful Asian village.

The teacher education curriculum that GCE, ME, and CE accommodate to realize a peaceful Asia should contain an ideological perspective, supported by a set of key concepts, perspectives and key contexts, and pedagogical issues that contain key issues in teaching and learning (Davies, 2018). Referring to Davies' view, Indonesia University of Education within the framework of ASTEN establishes a teacher education curriculum with strategic components as presented in Table 13–2.

Table 13-2 The strategic components of the GCE, ME, and CE curriculum at Indonesia University of Education towards a peaceful Asia

Ideological Perspectives	Key Concepts	Principal Perspectives and Contexts	Pedagogical Matters
1. Nationalism 2. Globalism 3. Internationalism 4. Transnationalism 5. Cosmopolitanism 6. Post-colinialism 7. Indigenousness and indigeneity	1. Justice 2. Equity 3. Diversity 4. Identity and belonging 5. Sustainable development	1. Economics 2. Politics 3. Culture 4. Morality 5. Environment 6. Spirituality and religion 7. Race/ethnicity 8. Gender and sexuality 9. Migration 10. Social class	1. Religion education 2. Pancasila and civic education 3. Indonesia language 4. English 5. Socio-cultural education 6. Music, visual and performing art 7. Physical education and sports 8. Service learning 9. Social media 10. Study abroad 11. extracurricular activities

Source: Davis, et al. (2018); Suryadi, Budimansyah & Winataputra (2017).

5. Conclusion

The terms of Global Citizenship Education (GCE), Multicultural Education (ME), and Civic Education (CE) have been defined in a variety of ways for different orientations i.e. as ideals; a program and a process of education; a mindset; an education policy; issues; attitudinal change; a developmental stage to deal with the ways citizenship educational ideals, principles, programs, and process are designed, implemented, and evaluated within the context of higher teacher education institution. GCE, ME and CE have been carried out through the teaching of General Education subjects as well as all co-curricular and extracurricular activities in producing graduates who are capable of being competitive in the global community. The GCE, ME, and CE activities developed in UPI are primarily intended for the preparation of all prospective UPI graduate teachers to embrace a global perspective and to become future teachers, i.e.

prospective teachers who have the capacity to educate young people into human beings who can spread peace in the world.

References

A. Osler & H. Starkey, Education for democratic citizenship: a review of research, policy and practice 1995–2005 1. *Research papers in education*, 21 (4), 433–466, 2006.

A. Suryadi, D. Budimansyah & U.S. Winataputra, Pedagogical Profile Of Global Citizenship Education, Multicultural Education, And Civic Education In Indonesia University of Edcation, *UPI-Asten Policy Research*, 2017.

A.T. Sigauke, Citizenship Education in the Social Science Subjects: An Analysis of the Teacher Education Curriculum for secondary schools. *Australian Journal of Teacher Education*, 38 (11), 2013.

B. Anderson, *Imagined communities: Reflections on the origin and spread of nationalism*. Verso Books, 2006.

B.A. Reardon, *Comprehensive peace education: Educating for global responsibility*. Teachers College Press, 1234 Amsterdam Avenue, New York, NY 10027, 1998.

D. Scott, *Reading Educational Research and Policy*. London, Routledge Falmer, 2000.

H. Hinchey, *Becoming a Critical Educator: Defining a Classroom Identity, Designing a Critical Pedagogy*. New York, Peter Lang Publications Inc, 2004.

I. Davies et.al. (eds), *The Palgrave Handbook of Global Citizenship and Education*, https://doi.org/10.1057/978--137-55733-5_2.

I. Shor, Liberation education: An interview with Ira Shor. *Language Arts*, 67 (4), 342–352, 1990.

J. Baltà, Evaluation of Enesco's standard-setting work of the culture sector. In *Part IV-2005. Convention on the Protection and Promotion of the Diversity of Cultural Expressions. París, Francia: Organización de las Naciones Unidas para la Educación, la Ciencia y la Cultura*, 2014.

J. Potter, *Active Citizenship in Schools: A Good-Practice Guide to Developing a Whole-School Policy*. London: Kogan Page, 2002.

L. Davies & G. Pike, Global citizenship education. *Handbook of practice and research in study abroad: Higher education and the quest for global citizenship*, 61–78, 2008.

M.S. Branson, The role of civic education: A forthcoming Education Policy Task Force position paper from the Communitarian Network. Center for Civic Education, 1998.

P.D. Thomas, Revisiting Pedagogy of the Oppressed: Paulo Freire and Contemporary African Studies. *Review of African Political Economy* 36: 120, 253–269, 2009.

R.W. Connell, *Schools and Social Justice*. Leichardt: Pluto Press Australia, 1993.

S. Grundy & E. Hatton, *Teacher Educators Ideological Discourses. Journal of Education for Teaching International Research Pedagogy*, 21 (1), 7–24, 1995.

S. Kemmis, P. Cole & D. Suggett, *Orientation to Curriculum and Transition: Towards the Socially-Critical School*. Clifton Hill, Victoria Institute of Secondary Education (VISE), 1983.

T. Ibrahim, Global citizenship education: Mainstreaming the curriculum?. *Cambridge Journal of Education*, 35 (2), 177–194, 2005. this region is where diverse geopolitical conflicts and cooperation converge.

Section 5

Perspectives towards an Asian Community – Part 3
Culture, Arts and Media

Chapter 14

Hybrid Food Culture through Migration:
Case of Ethnic Koreans in Central Asia

Jean Young Lee (Inha University), Sun Ah Kim (Cordia)

1. Introduction

Globalization and migration across national borders are making a world smaller than ever. Foodways of migrators who have their own food culture are mixed together with foodways of the host countries. A new hybrid foodway represents a new identity of the migrators. Korean food in Central Asia by the Korean migrants who were enforced to move to the Central Asia in 1937 is a good example. *Peranakan* or *Nonnya* food culture in Malaysia by the early Chinese settlers are well known. Some Chinese immigrants to Indonesia who had firstly moved to Surinam in Latin America and moved again to Holland created a 'newly styled hybrid Dutch food'. Hybrid food culture is a symbol of integration and a representation of identity in a certain migration group in the globalized world.

'One Asia' is not only a matter of political or economic integration, but also a cultural fusion of Asian people. Food culture is essential in making One Asia here. The goal of One Asia is a peaceful co-existence and mutual development through recognition of diversity. Recognition of diversity is only possible through mutual understanding and reciprocal acceptance of other cultures. Food culture, here, is a powerful tool for mutual understanding. Through migration, food cultures become mixed together and a new hybrid food culture as a sub-culture of a host society is emerged. This new hybrid food culture can be a *very* good notion of peaceful coexistence of a certain society.

Here, in this paper, food culture of Koreans in Central Asia will be discussed. Through series of migration from the Korean peninsula, *Koryeo saram* (Ethnic Koreans in Central Asia) set a unique food culture in Central Asia, which is hybrid with Russian and Central Asian foodways. Migration into a new world is a big cause of making the unique food culture of Koreans in Central Asia. Therefore, history of migration and how it is connected with food culture of the Koreans in Central Asia will be discussed. In doing so, changes of foodways and making a new food culture of them will be illustrated. In discussing hybridity or re-ethnicization of food culture of them, the implication for One Asia will be illustrated as a conclusion.

2. Migration of Koreans and Making *Koryeo saram* foodways in Central Asia

History of a unique formation of foodways of ethnic Koreans in Central Asia can be divided into four parts in connection with their migration history; 1) Origin: *Hamkyeong* Province (1863-1923), 2) Adaptation to the Russian food culture (1923-1937), 3) Enforced migration and Formation of *Koryeo saram* foodways, and 4) Re-migration and globalization (1991-).

1. Origin: *Hamkyeong* Province (1863–1923)
1. Migration of Koreans into the Russian Far East

Koreans in Central Asia are descendants Koreans who migrated from the Korean peninsula since 1860s. Due to the Treaty of Beijing of 1860 between Russia and Qing China, Russia starts to share a border with Korea. Korean immigration to the newly formed Russian Far East started with 13 families from nearby *Hamkyeong* Province in Northeastern part of the Korean peninsula. However, along the newly marked border between Korea and Russia, some Koreans had already settled. Some of them were irregular, seasonal or illegal migrators due to the poverty caused by severe famine and draught of the northern parts of Korea in the 1860s. The population of Koreans in the Pos'yet area near the southern reaches of Ussuri River increased rapidly, because there were fertile lands for farming and few Russian settlers. Until the Treaty of Seoul in 1884, there was no official regulation to stop the migration Koreans into new Russian soil by the Russian authorities. It is because Russia needed workforce to cultivate the land and more time to induce Russian settlers from faraway European part of Russia. Anyway, the population of Koreans reached almost 10, 000 when the first policy by the Russian authority to the Koreans was initiated in 1888. Russian authority permitted citizenship to the Koreans who entered Russia before June 25, 1884. As a result, a new group was emerged; Koreans in Russia, later called as *Koryeo saram*.

By 1923, more than 100, 000 Koreans were settled down in Russia. Among them, only 20 to 30% were able to obtain Russian citizenship. Most of Koreans were from nearby province of Korea, *Hamkyeong* Province. But Koreans from other parts of the peninsular migrated after the Sino-Japan War in 1894 and Japan-Russia War in 1904. Advance of Japanese imperialism into the Korean peninsula after the victories of these wars enforced Korean independence activists to flee Korea and made the Russian Far East as the base for the Korean independence. Until the formation of the USSR in 1922, guerilla-style fights by the Korean Righteous Army or pro-Bolshevik communists were activated in the Russian Far East. Korean nationalism was strongly emerged in the region at that time.

2. Foodways of Koreans in the Far East

However, the first settlers to Russia were mainly from nearby Hamkyeong Province. Moreover, they were citizens of Russia and formed Korean villages in various regions of the Far East. Koreans from other parts of Korea were the second immigration group after a generation of the first settlers from Hamkyeong Province. Therefore, life style of Hamkyeong province was prevailed in the Koreans of the Far East.

Most Koreans were farmers. Some Koreans who obtained citizenship were living in cities. Russian way of life had become accepted to some Koreans, but most Koreans had maintained Korean style of life. Even in cities like

Vladivostock, a Korean quarter called Sinhanchon, New Korea Town, was formed.

Life in small agricultural villages were not very different from the life in Korea. Houses, clothes, and foodways were almost same as Hamkyeong Province. Rice cultivation was started by the Koreans in the Far East. Vegetable cultivation was also started by the Koreans who sold these to Russians in cities. Rice, sorghum, oat, corn and barnyard millet were cultivated. Cabbage, radish, eggplant, oyster, potato, carrot, red pepper, onions, spring onions and garlic for preserved foods such as Kimchi were also cultivated. Cows, chickens and pigs were raised. Sea cucumber, crab and various seaweed were caught from the sea by the Korean seamen whose population were already reached to 3, 000 in 1904. Wheat was not cultivated. Also, sheep was not raised. It means that Koreans maintained their own foodway in the Far East.

Local Hamkyeong province food style was also apparent. Gruel made of barnyard millet and potato were a staple food. Breakfast and lunch were made of cooked millet and dinner was millet porridge with potato. This was a typical foodways of Hamkyeong province differentiated from other regions of Korea. Halibut preserved with salt, pollack preserved with milk and seaweed soup with crab flesh were unique foods of the province. Pork was the favorite meat for the Koreans in the Russian Far East. Therefore, it can be said that food origin of Koreans in Russia was from Hamkyeong province food and it is still apparent in food of Koryeo Saram.

2. Adaptation to the Russian food culture (1923–1937)

At the end of 1922, the USSR was formed and sovietization was started in the all sections of societies in the Far East. The Korean Counseling Board was created in 1923, and a new development plan was carried out from 1924. By 1925, most Koreans obtained Soviet citizenship and the population of Koreans reached 190, 000.

According to a Korean newspaper, *Sonbong* (Avant-garde), traditional Korean way of life was banned in the name of anti-socialism. Commemorative rites of ancestors were kicked off in the name of 'anti-religious movement.' Rice cakes,

Korean wines, and Korean plays were also banned. National holiday such as *Chuseok*, Korean Full Moon Day, was also alternated as 'Communist Youth Day.'

The most serious challenge was from re-location of Korean villages. Korean villages were collectivized to several big villages. New Russian style houses were built and Koreans were enforced to live there. Korean sedentary lifestyle was substituted as stand-up styles. A stand-up meal in a table became a standard. This was a revolutionary change of lifestyle in Koreans. Also, bread and corns with milk were encouraged to eat as a Soviet foodway. Coffee and teas were rapidly penetrated into Koreans. Collectivization rate was almost 94% in 1929 in the Koreans, and it means that Russian foodway became important in ethnic Korean foodways in Russia.

3. Enforced migration and Formation of *Koryeo saram* foodways

However, everything was changed in 1937. Transfer of Koreans from the Soviet Far East to Central Asia was abruptly carried out in 1937. New environment was suddenly emerged and Koreans were enforced to adapt for living.

1. Enforced Migration of Koreans into Central Asia

In autumn 1937, Koreans were suddenly transferred to Central Asia within 3 days of a very short notice. 95, 256 Koreans of 20, 170 family household were enforced to move to Kazakhstan. 76, 525 Koreans of 16, 272 were sent to Uzbekistan by force. Manner of transfer and resettlement were apparently brutal and hostile. Although Koreans were very cooperative to the Soviets and contributed to the establishment of the Soviet Union, it seemed that the Soviet authorities did not trust the Koreans. It was mainly because of aggressive policy of Japan at that time in Northeast Asia. Japan invaded Manchuria and set up the puppet Manchukuo government in 1932, and confronted the border with newly formed Soviet Union. Moreover, Sino-Japan war broke out in 1937, and Stalin felt insecure on the border and loyalties of ethnic Koreans who came from then colonized Korea under the rule of the Japanese empire. But, these cannot explain the barbaric treatment and cruelty to the Koreans of transfer in

1937.

Before the mass transfer, at least 2, 500 Korean cadres were executed or sent to the gulag. Koreans were loaded and packed into train wagons and had to be endure almost a month journey to the Central Asia. There is no way of expressing tragedy of the transfer. But the settlement was also very harsh because they were brought down in no-man's lands or deserted areas.

But life should go on. Koreans should adapt the new situation in Central Asia which was totally different from the Russian Far East. Fauna and flora were not same in the Central Asia. Kazakhstani life was based on nomadic life. It was totally different from the Koreans. Hot and Islamic agricultural Uzbekistan life was also very different from the Korean style of living. Koreans loved pork but Muslims did not. There were quite many fishermen in the Far East, but there were no seas here. Collectivization in kolkhozes also provided a new style of living. Korean started to live with other nationalities such as Kazakhstanis, Uzbeks, Germans or Russians. A new style of foodway was emerged. It is hybrid foodway mixed with Russian and Central Asian foodways, but very unique. Formation of *Koryeo saram* foodways was started.

2. Formation of *Koryeo saram* foodways

Until the early 1950s, a new form of foodways in Koreans of Central Asia was emerged. Foodways of Hamkyeong Province is the basis here, and Russian and Central Asian influences are added.

First of all, food names and cooking methods are from Hamkyeong Province. Instead of saying *bab* (meal), local dialect of Hamkyeong Province, *babi*, is used. *Tsai* (tsang), *sirakjangmuri* (siraekiguk), *buktsai* (doenjang), *miyeokiguk* (miyeokguk), *guksi* (guksu) and *babimuri* (mulbab) are used. Side dishes are also different. *Chimchi* (Kimchi), *mulgokihae* (preserved fish), *jilgumche* (fried bean sprouts), *oechae* (seasoned cucumber), *gamjicha* (seasoned potato), *jelgumichae* (seasoned chives), *mintujae* (mixed vegetables) and other dialect names are easily found. Material names such as *ssari* (rice), *gamji* (potato), *ttubi* (tofu), *ttyai* (bean paste), *ttiroi* (soy bean sauce) and *nokdi* (mug beans) are not easy to understand for Koreans who speaks only standard contemporary Korean.

New menus are invented here in Central Asia by the Koreans. *Kuksi* (Korean noodle), *pegodya* (dumpling) and Koreans salads are very different from counterpart foods in the Korean peninsula.

Koreans in Central Asia are enjoying Russian food. Several dishes such as *kasha* (porridge), *borsht* (soup), *bullion* (radish beef soup), *zakuski* (hors d'oeuvres), *kalbasa* (sausages) and *pelmeni* (dumplings) are widely consumed in everyday table. *Ukrop* (dill) and *smetana* (dairy product) are also widely used as sauces added to Korean food. Tomato is added almost all Korean *guk* (soup). These are Russian influences on the everyday Korean food in Central Asia.

Central Asian influences are more evident than Russian influence. *Beshbarmak* (boiled noodles mixed with finely chopped meats and onion sauce, usually served with *shorpo*, mutton broth), *baursaki* (Kazakhstan fried bread), *bareniye* (jam) are influence of nomadic Kazak people. Uzbek influence is very strong, probably because they are agricultural people like Koreans. *Non* or *lepyoshka* (bread), *plov* (pilaf, rice cooked in a broth) and *shaslik* (skewered cubes of meats) become also main dish to Koreans.

Shaslik and *samsa* (savoury meat pastry), *kuksi* and *pegodya*, and *borsht* and *kalbasa* are coexisted in the Korean dining. From chopsticks to fork, from sitting tables to standing tables, from Korean bowls to western dish, dietary life is greatly changed. In breakfast, Russian style is common, but *kuksi* with bread and dumplings are also common in lunch time. At dinner, *shaslik* party with other mixed dishes are also very common.

But, it is noteworthy that unique *Koryo saram* style are easily found; mainly Hamkyeong province food with Russian and Central Asian influences. Formation of *Koryo saram* foodways was formed which is very different from the foodways of Koreans in the peninsular.

3. Re-migration and globalization (1991–)

1. Domestication and globalization of *Koryeo saram* food

Soviet Union was dissolved in 1991. Soviet republics became independent republics. Koreans in Central Asian countries, formerly called *Koryeo saram*, were enforced to be new citizens of independent republic respectively. Uzbek Koreans became different from Russian Koreans. Due to the conflicts and nationalism in Central Asian countries, Koreans moved again and started to settle down in different places, mainly Russia and former republics such as Ukraine and Baltic countries. This migration was started from the early 1970s but accelerated after the 1990s. In 2002, 148, 558 Koreans were living in Russia. Some returned their homeland in the Far East, but many of them are living in southern part such as Volgograd and Rostov. Ironically, however, this re-migration shows expansion of Korean foodways and localization of *Koryeo saram* foodways were enabled.

In Moscow, it is not difficult to find restaurants every corner of the city run by *Koryeo saram*. Menus here are mixture of typical *Koryeo saram* dishes mainly constituted with some Russian and Central Asian dishes. In markets of almost all big cities in Russia and former republics, it is easy to find *Koryeo saram* seller to sell Korean salads in *Koryeo saram styles*. Carrot, string beans, kid beans, squash, sea weeds, or fish are the main ingredients of a particular local product. *Koryeo saram* mixed with these and made salads with Korean seasonings. Therefore, if Koreans from South or North Korea see these Korean salads in the market, they would say those are not traditional Korean style. In reality, these salads were invented by *Koryeo saram* and distributed every corner of the former Soviet Union by the series of migration of *Koryeo saram*. Therefore, these foods were domesticated gradually and got the citizenship there. These are now called as Russian food with Korean style or *Koryeo saram* food in Russia. There is no need to differentiated these foods as Korean or Russian.

Other interesting phenomenon is that these so-called Korean salads are found in the supermarkets of the former Soviet Union or even in Eastern Europe. In some supermarkets, separate section for Korean salads are easily found. Also, consumers can purchase these foods in internet easily. Commercialization of *Koryeo saram* food was successful and now it can be said as globalization of *Koryeo saram* food.

2. South Korean influence and changes of foodways

Recently, however, the most powerful influence to the foodways of *Koryeo saram* was from South Korea. Relations with South Korea were cut off until the collapse of the Soviet Union. When the normalization with South Korea occurred in 1992, a huge influence was landed with South Korean businessmen. Korean fast food shops were open in cities of Central Asia, and *bulkogi, kimbab, tteokboki* and other foods such as instant noodles or even chocolate pies were popular among ethnic Koreans here. Soon, imports of Korean goods such as seasoning sauces were increased from the 2010s. It means that South Korean foodways are penetrated into the foodways of *Koryeo saram*. Foodways of *Koryeo saram* are now adapting to this new situation and trying to make a new formation.

However, South Korean influence is limited. Even *Koryeo saram* who were settled in South Korea are consuming more foods of *Koryeo saram* rather than South Korean food. In Ansan or in Gwanghwidong of Seoul, there are lots of *Koryeo saram* restaurants in the name of Russian or Central Asian restaurants. Korean salads are also sold here in Korea to the 50, 000 *Koryeo saram* settlers. New generation of *Koryeo saram* usually do not eat sea food such as octopus and shrimp which are very popular to South Koreans. Homesick food, usually symbol of identity, of *Koryeo saram* is now regarded as meat dish such as *shaslick* with *plov* but *Koryeo saram* style. They came from Central Asia.

4. Conclusion

During the last 150 years, series of migration were occurred to the *Koryeo saram*. Their identity was also changed from Korean citizens to Russian citizen, and from Soviet citizen to each republic citizen of the former Soviet Union. Now, some were returned to South Korea and migrated again. In accordance with the migrations, foodways of *Koryeo saram* were also changed. Originated from Hamkyeong Province food of Korea, foodways of *Koryeo saram* soon became influenced by Russia and from the Central Asia after the enforced migration in 1937.

However, *Koryeo saram* adapted to new environments and invented new style of foods and finally formed a *Koryeo saram* foodways which are different from the foodways of historical motherland in 1970s. Hybrid foods were soon domesticated and spread to all corners of the former Soviet Union with the re-migration of *Koryeo saram*. Commercialization and globalization is now very evident in *Koryeo saram* foods. Hybrid food culture of *Koryeo saram* is unique but shows a symbol of peaceful integration to the host society. But a representation of identity in a certain migration group is not disappeared but more evident in the globalized world. Therefore, food culture of *Koryeo saram* case can be a good example to make 'One Asia' with peaceful coexistence.

Chapter 15

Forming One Asia Community:

Asian Value and Growing Up Research Atmosphere [1]

Eko Hadi Sujiono (Department of Physics, Universitas Negeri Makassar (UNM), Indonesia. One Asia Lecture Coordinator at UNM Indonesia),
Helmy Pratiwi (One Asia Lecture Committee at UNM Indonesia.), and
Yasser A. Djawad (One Asia Lecture Committee at UNM Indonesia)

1. Introduction

Asian nations comprise of the population that has different cultures, ethnicities, religions, and languages. However, some Asian countries have almost similar culture and language because they come from the same ancestors. The diversity can be seen as an advantage in many respects, for instance, economics, technology, and education. In addition, Asian countries have a huge population making up 60% of the world's current population and occupying 30% of the world's land area. Such a huge population and land area can be seen as a potential market for products, but it can also generate some serious problems like poverty and pollution [1]. To benefit from these potentials, Asian countries need to come together as a community and collaborate among themselves. It is now become urgency among Asian countries to form such a community in order to support the vital pillars: economic, technology, and education. So that, Asian countries are not left behind from the Western countries. As it can be seen, Asian country such as Japan, China, Korea, and Indonesia be in top 20 list countries who have high *Gross Domestic Product (GDP)* in 2016 [2].

Indonesia is an archipelagic country that has enormous potential in the field of natural resources and human resources. Indonesia has more than 17, 000 thousand islands with huge and varied natural resources. In addition, the human resources potential of more than 250 million is an asset if managed well and correctly will produce progress in various fields. In addition, Indonesia also has a variety of cultural and noble values are very diverse. These noble values are one part of the values of Asia that is worth very noble. The values that will be developed in One Asia lecture at the Department of Physics, State University of Makassar to cultivate the interest of researching which is still very lacking. The current research atmosphere in Indonesia is lacking. This results in innovative products that are the benchmarks of a nation's success are still very less. It is hoped that with One Asia lecture, it can generate research interest among students as well as generate innovative products that can improve the welfare of Indonesian society and align themselves with the advanced Asian peoples.

There are many potential areas in which Asian countries can collaborate as a community. These include agriculture, manufacture, and education. Therefore, thoughts, ideas, and suggestions are needed to explore the problems and to find solutions for the idea of forming an Asian community. The idea of forming an Asian community could be started from universities, where all the experts are in. The information could be widely spread by the students to others while they are still studying and even when they have graduated; they are able to spread the idea to their surrounding working environment. In 2016, the Asian Community Lectures provided a series of lectures at *Universitas Negeri Makassar (UNM)* based on the theme **of Asian Value, Culture and Science Technology in the Asian Community**.

2. The Preparation of Lecture Series at UNM

This lecture series designed to create a campus-wide conversation, the University Lecture Series gives second-year students an opportunity to interact with leading members of the faculty, scholars, scientists, who are nationally and internationally renowned. All students, faculty, alumni, are invited. This lecture series is the 4th year funded by the One Asia Foundation Japan and name it as One Asia Lecture Series UNM.

The Asian Community Lectures provided a series of lectures based on different topics and issues such as culture, Asian values, migration, languages, and education, which were delivered by various lecturers who are experts in their respective fields. The lectures explored the problems and the advantages of the diversity in the Asian nations. At the end of the lectures, it was expected that those students were able to have an understanding and provide some thoughts about the idea of establishing an Asian Community. By the end of this lecture, students from UNM can be able to talk and speak up about the Asian countries and community, moreover UNM as the University which its core is on teacher training so that the students directly go to the school to have teaching-learning training experience. By those direct training, it is expected that the UNM students can spread the information to the junior and senior high school students about the forming of Asian Community.

The preparation for this event was started by inviting the dean of faculty mathematics and Natural Sciences and all heads of department at the Faculty in a meeting to spread the information and also to get some ideas about how the Asian Community Lecture series should be running. After the third year, this lecture becomes a permanent course at Department of Physics. The result of the meeting was that the lecture would conduct as permanent course and integrated into the curricula of Physics study program at the fifth semester which is 2 (two) credits semester. Other participants would be obtained from other students using proportion systems representing all departments at the faculty of mathematics and natural sciences. To help us manage the lecture series, three volunteers from our alumni were recruited. The volunteers had a number of tasks, for instance, to make an invitation letter, to prepare the equipment for the lecture series and to service the lecturers during the event. In order to spread the event information widely, a website (http://oneasia.unm.ac.id) was also developed to help students get further information about this event [3]. At the same time, some articles were published in our official university website and also the other way to socialize this event is on social media such as Facebook and

Instagram. In total, 200 students were designated as permanent participants of the Asian Community Lecture Series at UNM. During the preparation, some journalists from different local newspapers were invited to a press conference to publicize this event.

In total, there were 11 lecturers presenting in 12 lecture events. The lectures were conducted each month from September 2016 to February 2017. All students at fifth semester in the department of physics, faculty of mathematics and natural sciences were invited to attend the third lecture series. The lecture was attended by around 100 students. Furthermore, the information about the lecture was continuously informed using Facebook and email to permanent participants. The lectures were attended by only permanent participants. They were very curious and interested in following the lectures. The participants had a lot of questions to the lecturers. The lecturers eventually did not have enough time to answer all questions. The lectures method was so interactive; there were two ways of communication. So, the source of knowledge was not merely from the experts but also from the students. They were all given a topic and involved in a deep discussion. Moreover, the experts shared their experiences while they were students and how they drowned themselves in research. This lectures method was so enjoyable and chill for students; it is proven by their participation in submitting their testimonial essay about this lecture series.

The aims of this paper are described a course result of One Asia Lecture has conducted at UNM. The course explored values, cultures, and language of the Asian countries to give better understanding and perspective to the students. At the same time, the values, cultures, and language of Asian countries could be used as a base to enhance and mastering of science and technology. As we know, Indonesia is still lack in science and technology compared to developed countries in Asia. After this course, the students are more motivated to explore their self to learn and pursue their degree in the Asian countries. The students understand about Asian values from various perspectives like socials, cultures, politics, and economics. The students also understand more details of how the development of science in Asia especially in Indonesia, understand about how developed Asian countries are leading in the economy through research. A case for Indonesia has discussed to obtain the drawbacks and opportunity of Indonesia to improve its research and be a leading line in research terms.

The last lecture was presented by Adviser of One Asia Foundation Prof. Dianni Risda and was attended by all permanent students. The lecture was presented in Indonesian, and subsequences in Japanese and translated to Indonesian. The Lecture series has conducted at Department of Physics, UNM as shown in Figure 1, 2, 3 and 4, respectively. A lot of questions were raised by students. However the time was too short, and only a few questions could be answered by the lecturer. The lecture was closed by Dean of Faculty

Figure 15-1 A lecture by Mr. Yoji Sato [OAL 2014/2015]

Figure 15-2 A lecture by Mr. E. H. Sujiono [OAL 2016/2017]

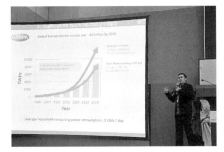

Figure 15-3 A lecture by Mr. Ariando - NUS [OAL 2017/2018]

Figure 15-4 A lecture by Mr. Risa Suryana - UNS [OAL 2017/2018]

mathematics and natural sciences.

The lecturers material were collected and can be accessed through our Learning Management System (LMS)http://lms.unm.ac.id [4].The committee also asked the permanent participants to fill out a questionnaire to give their feedback regarding the lecture series. The results were that the students gave positive feedback to the lecture series and that they have gained the idea of the Asian community formation.

Based on the curricula that we always propose in every proposal we submit to One Asia Foundation, there are 8 key points which are going to achieve after the end of every lecture:

1. The students understand about Asian values from various perspectives like socials, cultures, politics, and economics. The lectures also discuss how to face the challenges in the context of forming of the Asian community and the role of Indonesia to be involved in the development of Asian community.
2. The students understand about cross-cultural communication in the Asian community. The course explores an aspect of communication in verbal and non-verbal ways in the Asian community. The understanding of cross-cultural communication could be used to have a better experience during travel or study in the Asian countries.
3. The students understand the importance of language education. The need to improve a language is very important to understand nation from different countries. Asian nations comprise of many languages that are quite different. Students should take this into attention to gain better future.
4. The students understand the role of language that can improve the student mobility in the world, especially in the Asian countries. Students have to develop their self in order to increase their personal quality and language is one way to for it.
5. The students understand how is the mobility of students in Asian countries. The lectures also explore the ways for students to increase their

mobility. Such ways like scholarship, internship, students' exchange and youth camp are also discussed. The characteristics of the education system in Asian countries are also described.

6. The students understand more detail of how is the development of science in Asia, especially in Indonesia. The lectures are focused on how to maximize the potential of science to gain the benefit for the future of a country and to unite countries in Asia.

7. The students understand how developed Asian countries are lead in the economy through research. The lectures reveal the step of how research can be one of the factors of economic growth in a country. Case for Indonesia is discussed to obtain the drawbacks and opportunity of Indonesia to improve its research and become leading in research.

8. The students understand about various tools in ICT that can be used to share different resources like documents, libraries, and software. The lectures have also explored the drawback and the advantage of the demographic, geographic, economic and social potential to enhance the development of ICT.

3. Asian Value and Growing Up Research Atmosphere

Indonesia is one of the countries that has a big population. This population as human resources is an advantage for economic growth. For many years, this resource has not been explored well for many reasons. The aim of the course is to explore values, cultures, and language of the Asian countries to give better understanding perspective to the students. In the same time, the values, cultures, and language of Asian countries could be used as a base to enhance and mastering of science and technology. As we know, Indonesia is still lagging in science and technology compared to developed countries in Asia. After this course, it is hoped that students are more motivated to explore their self to learn and pursue their degree in the Asian countries.

Indonesia is a country that has many cultures and languages spread across the island in Indonesia. Different cultures and languages do not become separators between the people of Indonesia and even a unity that tightens the ropes of brotherhood among the people of Indonesia. These values need to be transformed to the younger generation to be used in the catch up in the field of science and technology from other Asian peoples by developing science through research.

These noble values need to be preserved because the young generation is a generation that is still unstable and easily affected by negative things. The role of parents and educational institutions is very important in maintaining these noble values as the successor of a nation that continues to preserve these values. Values can be transformed through educational institutions in which educational institutions are not only a place to study but also as a place to transfer moral and ethical values that are a reflection of the nation's personality. These values teach us to be humanistic and unselfish. Another value that is characteristic of the Indonesian nation is deliberation and mutual cooperation. Deliberation is to take important decisions by conducting discussions with several people to produce decisions acceptable to all parties. While "gotong-royong" is cooperation in completing a job to be completed quickly and well. In mutual assistance, there are many values of togetherness that can be used to solve various kinds of difficult and difficult problems for the Indonesian nation. These values are now beginning to be forgotten by the younger generation. For that, it takes a variety of businesses. Efforts that need to be developed include: developing mutual respect and help each other. In addition, there should also be an attitude of maintaining unity and unity as a nation. This effort can be made by developing character education which means the development of values among the younger generation is not only at the level of theory but also must be implemented in everyday life. With the planting of education that characterizes the younger generation is expected to make this Indonesia as a nation of great and dignified.

The development of character for young generation is very important in developing science. Because the Indonesian nation is made up of many tribes, races, and religions, it takes a common view of cultural values and the character of a nation. By instilling a characteristic education based on local culture, it is expected that the young generation who become the successor of this nation can realize prosperity and prosperity for the nation of Indonesia. The One Asia lecture conducted in the physics department provides an understanding of character education by elevating the noble values of local culture so that students can develop their existing capacities to develop knowledge by cooperating with various parties and institutions. This course also provides the development of science in the field of physics from several experts from various universities in Indonesia to provide a broad insight into the development of the existing physics today. At the same time, these experts also provide an understanding of the noble values that exist through the experiences they have gone through in order to encourage and motivate students to develop knowledge.

To support the long-term economic development proclaimed by the Indonesian government, one of the supports that can accelerate this is the solid research foundation. This can encourage the achievement of skilled workers, innovation power, and a strong investment climate. It's just one of the obstacles faced is the university in Indonesia is still more priority teaching activities than research. As a result, the university does not see any problems that occur outside the university environment. This has resulted in weak links between universities and the public and industry sectors. This problem is coupled with the lack of bureaucracy at universities to support research. In addition, Indonesia does not have a funding scheme for the development of science and technology. The Indonesian government only allocates 0.8% of Gross Domestic Product (GDP) for research activities. These problems lead to the weak capacity of human resources in Indonesia to conduct research. One of the main factors hampering research in Indonesia is the lack of a good funding scheme to support research. This is coupled with a rigid research reporting system that causes researchers in Indonesia to be less productive because it is preoccupied with how to report research results and not on how to produce quality research results. Finally, the research is burdened with administrative burdens that are generally unnecessary. As a result, the concentration of researchers to produce quality research becomes divided with administrative requirements that accumulate. This requires steps such as improving research funding and simplifying the process of access to funds and research reports (Brodjonegoro and Greene, 2012).

The Government of Indonesia has sought to disburse 1.7 Billion from the State University Operational Aid (BOPTN) and Non-Tax State Revenue (PNBP). This fund is dedicated to cultivating innovative research in science and technology to improve international publications and patents. This resulted in a significant increase in the number of international publications indexed on Scopus by 9, 501 in August to 12, 098 in October 2017. In addition, there was a significant increase in journal journals indexed in the Directory of Open Access Journal (DOAJ) from 76 to 931 journals (Kemristekdikti, 2017).

The Indonesian government must change its strategy to improve research that can improve the economy. This increase can ultimately change people's lives. This change should involve various parties including industry by encouraging educational institutions to generate more research and upgrading of existing devices in the laboratory to produce reliable researchers. In addition, the less developed research climate in many universities became the main obstacle plus the lack of writing ability of the research results in English which became one big obstacle. In addition, inter-institutional cooperation and industry need to be improved and strengthened in order to synergize together to produce more quality research. Currently, there is still little cooperation between universities and industry, whether from the small, medium or large scale. This also happens because in general, the existing industry in Indonesia is an import-based industry. Increased cooperation with overseas institutions also needs to be improved both in terms of quantity and funding.

One final result of the research is scientific publication in the journal so that the public knows the results of the research that has been done. On the other hand, the publication also has a function as a means of control whether the research has been done properly and correctly because it has passed the review process of experts who come from the same field. Scientific publications in international journals also show an index of contributions to science. This contribution index is not seen from the number of researchers or the number of funds spent. The significant obstacles faced by researchers in Indonesia are not having enough understanding and experience in writing scientific articles.

This resulted in the low number of scientific articles produced by researchers in Indonesia published in reputable international journals. While on the same side, a country whose researchers are able to produce good scientific articles becomes a benchmark for generating innovative products that can be used by the wider community.

The Ministry of Research and Technology and Higher Education is also expected to encourage universities to create more internal journals within the university. This journal is expected to receive research articles produced by lecturers within a university. Furthermore, these internal journals are accompanied to increase their level into peer-reviewed journals nationwide. And furthermore, the grant may proceed to a higher level until it becomes a reputable international journal. This step is done to accommodate the results of research in the form of scientific articles from researchers in Indonesia. Researchers who are required to publish their research results in reputable international journals can gradually improve their abilities. The guidance to the lecturers to improve their ability is strived to keep them from publishing their research results in an internal journal made by the faculty.

Another issue that needs attention is the absence of research management conducted on research groups conducted by lecturers in universities in Indonesia. Even on many occasions, the lecturers carry out their own research which resulted in less efficient results of research conducted. The research management in question is the existence of a research manager consisting of administrative staff, research staff, financial managers and others. It is necessary to manage the research professionally in order to produce quality research. Research output in the form of scientific articles in national or international journals, articles on conferences, papers, and research reports should be used as the main benchmark of research results. However, currently, there are still many researchers who have not made as the main benchmark of research results given the time given to carry out research is very short.

The government has tried to do various ways to improve the research output. Law No. 12/2012 Article 89 of Higher Education states that about 30% of BOPTN can be used for research funding, but this mechanism can not improve the results of existing research at the university. Another scheme is the certification of lecturers, which gives incentives to lecturers to be more focused on implementing the tri dharma of higher education has not had a big impact on the quality of research in Indonesia. In addition, the Credit System used in the university as a standard lecturer's career path using assessment of lecturer performance based on the college tri dharma that is teaching, research and dedication do not give a strong impetus to produce quality research. This is because the low number of credits given for research is not worth the effort spent on research.

Barriers that occur in improving the results of research can be overcome by growing the values of Asia that have been faded in some circles including among academics. The low number of researchers in Indonesia is due to the low salary for researchers and low investment for research resulting in a lack of funding for researchers capable of producing quality products. This resulted in the absence of incentive standards for researchers who successfully publish their research results in reputable international journals from the university as well as from the ministry. And in general, the university does not provide an allocation of funds for its lecturers who successfully published results in reputable international journals. Existing research funds are from the government, and few come from private parties.

Another effort that has been done by the Indonesian government to stimulate Indonesian researchers is to cooperate with foreign institutions and universities overseas. Kemristekdikti has provided financial support to research groups at the University to initiate cooperation with overseas universities through the Consortium Grant scheme. With this consortium grant scheme, existing research groups at universities in Indonesia are being transacted to conduct research collaborations with several research groups abroad. It aims to improve the ability to research and produce publications of research results in cooperation with researchers who already have experience abroad. Furthermore, with the consortium is expected to form the Center of Innovation (CoI). CoI intends to unite all the potential that exists to produce product innovations that industry, the whole society, and the government can use. This can be done by building cooperation with domestic and foreign partners. Inter-institutional coordination and synergy are expected to contribute to delivering the right product of innovation. For that required mapping needs from market demand. This mapping is based on the theme and strategic issues contained in the national development plan implemented by the government. The Government has also established a functioning agency to manage research funds in Indonesia under the name of the Indonesian Science Fund (DIPI). This institution is an independent institution that provides research funding to existing researchers in Indonesia by cooperating with existing research institutes abroad such as Newton Fund.

On the other hand, Asian Value is a theme that UNM as a host of Asian Community Lecture Series raised to be taught in a class. It is viewed that this terminology is urgent to be discussed and implemented in students' daily life. Mahathir Mohamad and Lee Kuan Yew whom the Prime Minister of Malaysia and Singapore were particularly vocal advocates of Asian Values. The main Asian values argument is: a set of values is shared by people of many different nationalities and ethnicities living in East Asia. Asian values are today usually associated solely with East and Southeast Asia. These values include a stress on the community rather than the individual. The privileging of order and harmony over personal freedom. There are some points of view about Asian Value: 1) refusal to compartmentalize religion away from other spheres of life, 2) a belief that government and business need not necessarily be natural adversaries, 3) a particular emphasis on saving and thriftiness, 4) an insistence on hard work, 5) a respect for political leadership, 6) an emphasis on family loyalty. In order to find out the in-depth definition of Asian value, there were two comparisons of Asian value to Asian Economics and Asian Politics. In the viewpoint of Asian values and Asian Economics, it is a belief that in seeking to understand the economic success of certain Asian societies, credit must be given to the role of these 'Asian values.' It is not appropriate to analyze Asian economic success in culture-free economic terms. It is not appropriate to characterize Asian economic success as a result of the adoption of specifically Western values. In the other side, Asian values on Politic side can be seen as like this: Modern political systems in Asian societies should be grounded in the specific Asian cultures in which they are to be situated, and it is not acceptable to reform or criticize Asian societies solely on the basis of liberal-democratic forms developed in Western societies.

4. Conclusion

The lecture series was successfully conducted and was attended by all students was registered at semester fifth in Department of Physics Faculty of Mathematics and Natural Sciences, Universitas Negeri Makassar (UNM). The theme of the lectures was based on the Asian Value, Culture and Science Technology in the Asian Community and this had been discussed from various points of view according to the disciplines of each of the lecturers. The participants had gained a lot of information about the idea of the establishment of Asian Community from value, cultural, science and technological perspectives, based on how to grow up research atmosphere at University.

Acknowledgment

The One Asia Lecture Committee at UNM Indonesia acknowledge and many thanks to the One Asia Foundation for the funding. Specials appreciation to Mr. Yoji Sato as Chairman the One Asia Foundation for his lecture and cooperation.

Note

1 Presented at One Asia Convention, Nagoya, Japan, 4–5 August 2017.

References

[1] Asian Development Bank (ADB), Key Indicators for Asia and Pacific 2014 Highlights, 2014; http://www.adb.org/sites/default/files/publication/43030/ki2014-highlights_1.pdf

[2] Development Team, 50 years of Universitas Negeri Makassar, 2012, Badan Penerbit UNM.

[3] One Asia UNM Committee, One Asia Lecture Series UNM 2014, 2015, and 2016.
http://oneasia.unm.ac.id

[4] ICT Center UNM, Learning Management System UNM, 2016.

http://lms.unm.ac.id
[5] *Hibah Kompetensi*, research grant report, Directorate of Research and Community Services, Directorate General of Research and Development, Ministry of Research and Higher Education, Republic of Indonesia, 2015 and 2016.
[6] World Bank Open Data, 2016.
https://datacatalog.worldbank.org/dataset/gdp-ranking
[7] Indonesian International Publication keeps on shooting, Nasir appeals to keep it real. https://ristekdikti.go.id/publikasi-ilmiah-internasional-indonesia-terus-melesat-nasir-himbau-untuk-jaga-momentum/
[8] Brodjonegoro, Satryo Soemantri, and Greene, Michael P., 2012, *Creating an Indonesian Science Fund*, Indonesian Academy of Sciences, World Bank and AusAID, Jakarta.

Chapter 16

Cultural Acculturation for One Asia United in Diversity

Vo Van Sen[1] (University of Social Sciences and Humanities
Vietnam National University Ho Chi Minh City),
Tran Cao Boi Ngoc[2] (University of Social Sciences and Humanities
Vietnam National University Ho Chi Minh City)

1. The New World Order

The past centuries saw major powers dominating the world stage, acknowledging that a new global order has gradually shaped the world since the end of the Cold War. Therefore, politically, refining the world situation after the Cold War sprouts up rapidly in the world at large, making it a hot issue for every country in every region. Will one major power dominate the future? Or two major ones will? Or has the post-Cold War period already entailed a fast-evolving multi-polar era when at least five major powers – the United States, Europe, China, Japan, and Russia – will call the shots and run the show to emerge as economic powers? These countries will form alliances politically, economically, or both. Others countries are struggling for the position of additional poles of growth. What will the impact be politically or economically? In reality, whichever major powers the political ambivalence toward today's development models that now characterizes, the new world order means shifting markets in trade, investment and opportunity. Moreover, together with globalization, economies which are not fully industrialized are enabled to harvest the benefits of industrialization to become integrated into the world markets. In fact, the new order, deep down, is characterized by engagement and mutually beneficial interests.

In 2012, the Obama administration announced that it was going to be intensifying its focus to the Asia-Pacific in a policy popularly known as the "rebalance to Asia." The policy signaled that the US would be refocusing its interests and resources toward the Asia-Pacific region by investing and developing new capabilities, strengthening existing alliances and investing in key partnerships.[3]

Asia's economies were huge beneficiaries of the open trading system that was set in place in the post-war period. Asia's revival of growth can be seen especially in terms of economy and trade with Asia being a big winner. According to Voice of Asia[4], leading economic indicators show the growth has turned more positive.

The G3 economies (the United States, Europe, and Japan) are all maintaining or increasing their rates of recovery. India continues to surprise by maintaining growth above 7 percent in the face of global headwinds. China is stabilising thanks to aggressive policy action to offset that nation's headwinds. Large emerging economies such as Indonesia are poised to accelerate. [....] Export-oriented ASEAN economies stand to gain as well: Malaysia has a competitive currency and a strong base of export-oriented manufacturing, and trade is a big share of the Malaysian economy – one of the world's highest such ratios. Thailand, too, will be a winner, as will Vietnam, although the Philippines and Indonesia are less competitive in export-oriented manufacturing.

2. Cultural Exchange and Acculturation

Agner Fog, in the book *Cultural Selection* (1999)[5] has clearly stated,

"*Transmission of cultural traits can follow different patterns: vertical transmission is from parent to child; horizontal transmission is between unrelated persons; group socialization is the concerted influence of many (older) group member on a child or new group member; and the one-to-many transmission pattern is the influence of a teacher or a leader on a group.*"

Cultural exchange assists humans to develop relationships, understand a broader range of perspectives, and develop the knowledge and skills needed for participation in globalized multicultural society. In addition to cultural exchange, assimilation plays a major part in the course of history. As its name implies, acculturation can be understood, in the simplest terms, as

"When alien culture traits diffuse into a society on a massive scale, acculturation frequently is the result. The culture of the receiving society is significantly changed. However, acculturation does not necessarily result in new, alien culture traits completely replacing old native ones. There often is a syncretism, or an amalgamation of traditional and introduced traits. The new traits may be blended with or worked into the indigenous cultural patterns to make them more acceptable." [Dennis O'Neil 1997–2006]

3. One Asia - Unity In Diversity

Currently, after the collapse of the bipolar world, and the rising of the multipolar world, economists recognize an accelerating power shift from the advanced countries to Asia, and expect Asia to play the leading role in guiding world economy into strong growth with deep pools of capital and new business expertise invested. Frank, Andre Gunder, in his book ReOrient stated that

"If any regions were predominant in the world economy before 1800, they were in Asia. [...] 'Leadership' of the world system – more than 'hegemony' – has been temporarily 'centered' in one sector and region (or a few), only to shift again to one or more others. That happened in the nineteen century, and it appears to be happening again at the beginning of the twenty-first, as the "center" of the world economy seems to be shifting back to the 'East'."

Cultural diversity is one of the main factors leading to multiculturalism. The key to the success of multiculturalism is inclusiveness. Every citizen has the right to be active and gives equal participation to the multifaceted society while still maintaining their cultural traditions, to maximize the benefits of a multicultural society united in diversity, to address the challenges in order to build on achievements as a peaceful and prosperous community.

The *history of Asia* can be seen as the collective history of several distinct civilizations of the world's earliest known, with each region developing its own early civilization. The civilizations in Asia shared many similarities including cultural and religious practices, among many other aspects. Undeniably, the rise of China and India once again marked their global success in the fields of economy, culture and technology, in particular. Together with the rise of China and India, other countries deeply imbued with original cultural identities such as Korea, Japan and Vietnam are playing important roles in the development of worldwide economy, culture and politics accentuating the image and significance of Asia. Throughout the course of history, cultural exchanges and cultural acculturation have asserted its integral part in the history of mankind in general, in the development of Asia in particular. The formation of Asia was a thick book of colorful historic pages painted with major events of cultural exchanges leading to *Sinicization (Sinisation) –De-Sinicization, Hinduization–De-Hinduization, Westernization–De-Westernization*, etc. These cultural exchanges within what is now Asia formed Asia of Ancient Age, Middle Age, and going on into modern and contemporary Ages with deeply-engraved features of Buddhism, Islam, Hinduism, etc.

The most meaningful of these events can be vividly seen in the three following great phenomena[6] of cultural exchanges:

• The first phenomenon was *"Sinicization and De-Sinicization"*. Vietnam was invaded and dominated by Chinese feudal dynasties during ten centuries (from 111BC to 938AD). This was the periods when Sinicization took place in a powerful way. This phenomenon consisted of cultural assimilation and normal cultural exchanges. In order to fight against cultural assimilation and at the same time to absorb the positive factors of Chinese culture, Vietnam carried out De-Sinicization. The history of Vietnamese culture can be summarized in only two categories *Sinicization* and *De-Sinicization*. Cultures and civilizations of Vietnam, Korea and Japan in the Old and Middle Ages etc., basically, were formed and developed in the cultural exchanges and acculturation with Chinese culture. Moreover, in Vietnam, especially in the Central and South of Vietnam, the process of cultural exchanges occurred under strong influences of Indian culture.

• The second phenomenon was *"Hinduization (Indianization) and*

De-Hinduization (De-Indianization)". Indian interests in Southeast Asia increased when India and China began to trade with each other in the second century B.C. The trip through the Malacca Strait between Malaya and Sumatra was the quickest and easiest way to travel between Asia's two main centers of civilization. This way, expansion of Hinduism in Southeast Asia soon took place. Indeed, from about the 1st century, India started to strongly influence Southeast Asian countries. For more than a thousand years, Indian Hindu/Buddhist influence was therefore the major factor that brought a certain level of cultural unity to the various countries of the region. From the 5th to the 13th century, South-East Asia had very powerful Indian colonial empires and became extremely active in Buddhist architectural and artistic creation.

Throughout the history of Southeast Asia, there are a number of early Indianized kingdoms namely Funan, Champa, Khmer, Srivijara which covered nearly all of the South Asian areas at that time from the 1st Century to the 13th Century. Hinduization is exemplified in just some of hundreds of illustrations[7]

1) "Indianized faiths and beliefs can be seen in Funan, situated along the Mekong delta, where the earliest record found there were rock-inscriptions in Vocanh, Buddhist documents in Sanskrit and a south Indian script belonging to the first half of the third century. Furthermore, the Hindu cult of Siva worship and its coexistence with Buddhism was supposedly well established by the fifth century. Indianized faith can also be seen in the Sanskrit inscriptions of Quang Nam and Phu-Yen and the three rock inscriptions found in the Tra-kieu, a presumed area of Champa capital, that tell of the founder of the worship of the Shiva Bhadreshavara shrine. (Coedes, 1966, pp.64). In the case of Cambodia, the still existing grand temples reflect the worship of Siva, Vishnu and Buddha during the time of the Khmer kingdom. Meanwhile the establishment of Mahayana school, Siva cults and Brahman temple were recorded in the Sanskrit inscriptions found in Malay Archipelago (Harrison, 1967, pp.25)."

2) "Secondly, taking a look to the language and literature influence, it is obvious that nearly all of inscriptions found in Southeast Asian countries are written in Sanskrit. All of the local variety and adaption, the alphabets used today for Burmese, Thai, Laos and Cambodia all derive originally from Indian prototypes (Majumdar,

1963, pp.18, 28). A large number of inscriptions discovered in different parts of the Southeast Asia are written in Sanskrit and in Indian alphabets of about the fourth and fifth century. Indians literature and Indian mythologies have delighted generation of Southeast Asians. Puppet shows, shadow plays, and live dramatic performances based on the tales of the Ramayana have been popular everywhere. The Indian epics, the puranas and the Jakarta tales have been taken over. The art and sculpture of Southeast Asia have utilized themes from Indian literature, and their forms clearly show the influence of Indian style (Burling, 1965, pp.69)."

3) "The art and architecture of Southeast Asia were also adopted from the Indians. The temples from Cambodia are the sound evidence reflecting the patterns of India. Since pre-Angkor period, they directly borrowed the Indianized culture but after the Angkor period, the architecture was localized by modifying Indian features. So also, the remaining Indianized temples such as in Thailand, central Java, Malay Peninsula and Pagan in Burma indicated that the undeniable influence of Indianized architecture in Southeast Asian region. Taking at some examples throughout mainland and peninsula Southeast Asia , Borobudur , Bodisatva Avalokitesvara, Mendut, Lara Jongorand in Java, Phra that temple in Malay peninsula, Po Rome temple, Po Klong Gorai temple in Champa, Anada temple in Burma and other scattering around the Southeast Asia, it can also determine the extent of Indianization in Southeast Asia (Majumdar, 1963).Though after 13 century, there architecture designs were varied according to the local modification, it is not questionable that the fundamental art and architecture derived from India."

4) In addition, evidences are also found in Indianized kingship, codes of law and public administration; in Indianized codes of law and administration; in the adaptation of Indian societal construction by the practice of caste system in Southeast Asian countries.

Basically "De-Hinduization" was a peaceful process as it did not take place in political and military expansion, but mainly through commerce and religion. Therefore, De-Hinduization in Asia was a localization process with normal cultural exchanges. India had vague trace of struggling against assimilation; thus, it could be disseminated more easily without being fought against. Throughout history, Hinduization and De-Hinduization flourishing civilizations enriched cultures from nations in South Asia, especially Southeast Asia.

• The third phenomenon in the history of Asia was *"Westernization and De-Westernization"*. The 15th and 17th centuries saw Westernization as the role and place of European influence on the superstructure of Southeast Asian beliefs. Westernization was previously perceived as having much impact on Southeast Asia. However, studies of anticolonial movements, economic systems, nationalism, rituals, and identity deemphasized the impact of Westernization in order to balance the roles of both the West's and Southeast Asia's cultural integrity. With distinctly Asian identities, Western superpower imposition is strongly influenced by Asian consciousness. With this shift in perspective, the notions "the Orient Wind blows away the West Wind" or even "the West Wind blows away the Orient Wind" are outdated as the Orient and the West are now on the same par with interactions of equal impacts. Scholars now view more balance in acculturation and cultural exchanges which mean learning from each other, mutual understanding, regional integration between the West and the Orient. Modernization and industrialization from Japan, technological innovation from India, the four tigers in Asia are precious experiences learnt from the interactions between the Orient and the West, redefining the relationship between what is perceived as Western influence and what is not[8].

Therefore, due to Westernization, a certain indigenous cultural element of the traditional Orient is replaced by the penetrating Western element. With Westernization and De-Westernization, the Orient saw the transformation from an agricultural culture to the utilization of modern science and technology, advanced educational system, industry, national defense among many others as a product of human progress.

The course of history proves that cultural exchanges will create big opportunities for the development of Asia, which continues to take place at the moment! In reality, many countries are taking on more importance in the development of Asia where stunningly rapid economic growth and deep cultural acculturation is taking place between Asia and the West[9]!

4. Sinicization and De-Sinicization in Vietnam

In ancient times, the present-time territory of Vietnam included three countries: Giao Châu – Northern Vietnam, Champa and Funan.

From 111BC to 938AD, Northern Vietnam was occupied by the Chinese. The Chinese sent in their own governors, officers to govern Northern Vietnam and impose Chinese social, cultural and religious values on the Vietnamese people. This long domination resulted in

1. Assimilation (compulsory exchanges)
2. Normal Exchanges

Buddhism came to Vietnam by the maritime route from India and from China by land. The noted Vietnamese scholar, Tran Van Giap in his work "Le Bouddhisme en Annam, Des Origines au XIII Siecle" published in "Bulletin de L'Ecole Francaise d' Extreme Orient XXXII, 1932 (1933) p. 205", insists that Buddhism could be found in Tonkin (North Vietnam) in the 2nd Century A.D. Mou Po (in Chinese; Mau Bac in Vietnamese) is highly appreciated for introducing Buddhism to Vietnam. As Tonkin was on the direct sea route between China and India, it became a center for the propagation of Buddhism and the translation of Buddhist sacred scriptures.

Nowadays, in Vietnam, Buddhism fills the need of many people, bringing to life the Four Noble Truths, the Five Commandments or Prohibitions, the Twelve Principles of Buddhism, the Five Buddhist Virtues represented by the five colors of the Vietnamese Buddhist flag, etc. In addition, the system of Chinese beliefs was engraved in Northern Vietnam everyday life. The most prominent was *Confucianism* – a philosophy and system of ethics based on the teachings of Chinese philosopher Confucius (551–478 BC). Confucianism was introduced into Vietnam early during the Chinese rule, promoting the worship of Heaven, the honoring of the Emperor, the commemoration of great men, the veneration for ancestral rite practices where filial piety is the basic virtue. In addition, he encouraged *three obediences* (三从, tam tòng): obedience to father until married, obedience to husband while married, obedience to eldest son when husband is dead = "在家從父. 出嫁從夫. 夫死從子." "*Tại gia tòng phụ. Xuất giá tòng phu. Phu tử tòng tử*".); also, **the four virtues** (四德, tứ đức): morality (婦功, Fùdé, phụ công), modest manner/appearance (婦容, Fùróng, phụ dung), proper speech (婦言, Fùyán, phụ ngôn), and diligent work (婦行, Fùgōng, phụ hạnh). In addition, the **three social bonds** (三綱, tam cương) referred to the servant-emperor, father-son, husband-wife relationships; and **the five constant virtues** (五常, ngũ thường) to benevolence, righteousness, proprieties, wisdom and fidelity (nhân, nghĩa, lễ, trí, tín).

Apart from Confucianism, introduced into Vietnam through Chinese cultural influence and occupation, **Taoism** is regarded as "a law of life" requiring that man adjust to nature in order to have happiness. Lao-Tze, founder of Taoism, lived about 600 B.C. in China, taught that man needs to have a natural life which could be achieved only when in relation and in harmony with nature. For instance, Taoist concepts are to be observed in non-western medical practices; in marital arrangements which necessitate consulting horoscopes; in ceremonies of worship as they pertain to the Spring, the Fall, the ploughing of the ground, the planting of seeds, etc.

Though under assimilation, Vietnamese people were very flexible and skillful in the way to adopt Chinese elements into their culture and life. *As the process of De-Sinicization, for exchanges with active selection of the best-fit values and properties*, Vietnam proved itself to be very creative, dynamic with high spirit of patriotism, sense of self-defense, etc. Measures for improvements of farming and production technology were taken. Vietnamese people learned the positive elements from the Chinese such as adopt know-how to forge tools of iron and bronze; to make ceramics with enamel coating; to do the furrowing with iron ploughshares on wingploughs drawn by oxen or water buffaloes replacing cultivation in burned out clearings; to cure diseases by way of Chinese medicinal herbs and plants; among many others. Vietnamese handicraft such as weaving, basket-making, glass-making techniques, etc. underwent great development. As the word "exchange" implies, the Chinese also learned from Vietnamese people in that they began to plant sugarcane crops, adopt two-crop cultivation practices, etc.

Vietnam's feudal social structure took shape during the period of Chinese rule. The historical page of Vietnam witnessed whole-hearted efforts to preserve the national identity against foreign invaders, etc. They rose to flexibly fight against assimilation from the Chinese invaders. Under this spirit of the Vietnamese, the Chinese government's assimilation policy was confronted with a stubborn resistance which meant the Vietnamese people were not assimilated to melt into another culture. For instance, the Vietnamese's popular literature still developed its vitality going hand-in-hand with a learned literature written in classical Chinese; together with Confucian rites and precepts, Vietnamese's local traditions continued hold the Vietnamese ancestors in veneration; the making and use of bronze drums during great ceremonies still remained; Dong Son art was still clearly seen with its decorations and statuettes; the Vietnamese language was largely borrowed from the Chinese, but the words had been "Vietnamized" to enrich the Vietnamese vocabulary. In fact, the ideographic script of the Chinese was taught at schools and used in literature and art for about twenty centuries, but Vietnamese intellectuals devised the Nom script, derived from Chinese, in order to record the actual sound of Vietnamese. The others just learned the script for writing and reading abilities, not the pronunciation for oral communication.

The Vietnamese intellectuals also created the Vietnamese sound for each Chinese word, called "Han-Viet pronunciation". For example, 使用 (= to use), in Chinese, is pronounced [shǐyòng], but in Vietnamese "sử dụng"; 大学 (university), in Chinese, is pronounced [dàxué], but in Vietnamese "đại học". Other examples of De-Sinicization could also be seen in the resistance against negative values such as the despisal for women. A lot of the traditional Chinese characters with bad denotation were coined with the word "female" in them, which was best exemplified in:

1. 婪 LAM (Han-Viet pronunciation) in 貪婪 THAM LAM = greedy
2. 嫉 TẬT = envy, hate
3. 妒 ĐỐ in 妒嫉 = be jealous of
4. 嫌 HIỀM = ill will, suspicion
5. 妄 VỌNG = absurd, preposterous, presumptuous, rash

6. 妖 YÊU = evil spirit, demon
7. 奴 NÔ = slave
among many others!

To fight for these fossilized prejudices, the Vietnamese cultural dialogue developed such concepts as "Wife first, Heaven second!" It was one of the typical examples of cultural dialogue between Chinese and Vietnamese.

Many Vietnamese created the best combination of three religions – Taoism, Confucianism and Buddhism (Tam Giáo Đồng Nguyên, The Three Teachings of the same Root). It was one of the unique phenomina of the religious history in the world. Taoism is for adjustment to the natural world, Confucianism is for the social world, while Buddhism is utilized for harmony with the universe of which man is a part and for preparing for future existences. Under Ly-Tran Dynasties, we recognized the highest development of the combination of the three religions. In 1169, Emperor Ly Anh Tong (1138–1175) established a school for the study of the three religions – Confucianism, Taoism and Buddhism. The same ruler gave recognition as the official state religion to Buddhism, and granted it high privileges. By the close of the eleventh century, Buddhism had planted its roots so deeply into Vietnamese culture that it was no longer considered an imported religion. It had been introduced and utilized as a court religion; now it had filtered down to the villages and hamlets. Here mixed with Confucianism and Taoism, it became an indigenous part of the popular beliefs of the common people.

Undoubtedly popular Confucianism in Vietnam is quite different than the original teachings of the sage, but its effect on the culture and people of Vietnam is undeniable.

5. Hinduization and De-Hinduization

Besides the two processes of *Sinicization and De-Sinicization*, and *Westernization and De-Westernization*, the process of *Hinduization and De-Hinduization* exerted a great influence on the history of Asia. The phenomenon of *Hinduization and De-Hinduization* in Southeast Asia occurred in the first centuries BC[10] through cultural exchanges in a peaceful manner. Indian people's interests in Southeast Asia began to go up when India and China began to trade with each other in the 2nd century B.C. In addition to the three main routes for trade between India and China, Indian merchants searched for the quickest and easiest water route and they found it in Southeast Asia's seas. This was the sea lane through the Malacca Strait between Malaya and Sumatra, Indonesia.

This sea lane quickly paved the way for Hindu wave penetration into Southeast Asia. Indeed, from the first century AD, India has exerted strong effects on the culture of Southeast Asian nations. According to written records, the clergy and Indian traders gradually spread knowledge and culture of the immense Indian Ganges civilization (including hand writings, carving techniques, dances, heroic epics, and even worship rituals to honor the gods of Hinduism and Buddhism) into Southeast Asian societies where resided kingdoms of Champa, Chenla which are the Central and South of Vietnam today. In the ancient nations of Southeast Asia, Hinduism and Buddhism became the official religions and brought about economic stability, culture and society. After these two great religions introduced into this region, the worship of the deity with supreme power changed to a kind of religion mixture with the traditional beliefs of Mau worship and of prosperous worship of wet rice agriculture. Hinduization and De-Hinduization were embodied in various aspects such as economy, literature, art, religion, etc. of the ancient feudal nations in Southeast Asia, in which, in particular, aspects of religion left the most imprints.

Through maritime trade routes passing through the Strait of Malacca, Indian religious gained conditions for intrusion and developments in the ancient nations, also known as the ancient kingdoms of Funan, Champa, Chenla, Srivijaya[11], etc. Firstly, one of the two major religions of India Ganges civilization – Buddhism followed Indian monks into Southeast Asia and was recorded on artifacts dating back to the ancient Oc Eo culture kingdom of Funan. According to Chinese historical records, Funan is a powerful empire spreading across and downstream Mekong Delta, and survived from the third century to the sixth century (corresponding to the southern region of Vietnam). Remnants of the existence of the Funan Empire and the early introduction of

Buddhism in the first century can be found in the inscriptions on both sides of Vo Canh Inscription – the oldest inscription plate in Southeast Asia which was recognized national treasures of Vietnam, and is currently on display at the National History Museum. The inscriptions on the edge of Vo Canh Inscription were studied, showing that the writing style is very similar to the inscriptions in Amaravati in South India.

At the same time, in the coastal area of central Vietnam appeared a powerful kingdom – the kingdom of Champa. Prior to the fifth Century, the deep impact of Indian culture has been clearly shown through the parallel existence and practice of Shiva (Shiva cult) and Buddha (大乘, Mahāyāna) worship of the Cham kings. Therefore, in the 18th and 19th centuries, the French archaeologists excavated and found many artifacts related to the process of Hinduization of Champa kingdoms. For example, those written in the Cham and Sanskrit languages engraved on inscriptions and on the surface of the stone temples in the provinces of Quang Nam, Phu Yen, or the three stone slabs at Tra Kieu – the place previously served as the capital of the kingdom of Champa, which told about the founder of Shiva Bhadreshavara temple [Coedes, George 1966].

6. Cham art, architecture and sculpture in Vietnam

At the end of the 4th century, the influence of Hinduism was soon formed and created profound impacts on the Cham culture, religion and art.

Religions from India, once penetrating into the socio-cultural life of ancient Champa, were forced to adopt changes and adjustments to the original (De-Hinduization). Although the Cham entered a period of royal state and regime, traditions still lived in matriarchy with women playing a huge role in family. With the arrival of Hinduism, goddesses of Hinduism were transformed into goddesses of the native population. Although the names may come from the Indian originals, in the minds of Cham residents, those goddesses were indeed the images or the reincarnation of the goddesses in Cham beliefs.

Some examples of the Hinduization and De-Hinduization phenomena still survive the test of time and can be seen through Vietnam cases: the simultaneous appearance of Buddha, Shiva, Vishnu and the local gods of Southeast Asian population, e.g. Goddess of the Upper Sky (Mẫu Thượng Thiên), Goddess of the Highlands (Mẫu Thượng Ngàn), etc. on holy altars; the application of "Buddhist elements" into the goddesses' images in indigenous beliefs, e.g. Man Nuong Mother Buddha (Phật mẫu Man Nương); the "feminized" image of Avalokitesvara (Phật Bà Quan Thế Âm, Bodhisattva image), or the reincarnation of Bodhisattva into the female forms for human beings salvation, etc.

7. Westernization and De-Westernization

France colonized Cochinchina (Mekong Delta), as southern Vietnam was then called, and by 1864 established a protectorate over Cambodia. Following a victorious war against China in 1884–1885, France also took Annam. Located south of China and east of India on the southeastern-most peninsula of the Asian continent, Indochina comprises the modern-day countries of Vietnam, Laos, and Cambodia. After European contact, the future country of Vietnam was divided into three main provinces: Tonkin in the north, Annam in the center, and Cochinchina in the south. After their establishment in the Southeast Asian countries in the mid-nineteenth century, the French sought to build new infrastructure to increase the productive capacity of the colony. Among the countries under the Chinese cultural sphere of influence, Vietnam where Chinese scripts were used for centuries replaced them with a phonetic alphabet thanks to Mr. Alexandre de Rhodes. Not long after 1917, Vietnamese intellectuals and politicians were quick to recognize *quốc ngữ* as an efficient means to educate the masses." From 1853 to 1954, Vietnam was a French colony. Vietnam's colonial past has left an indelible mark on the country's language. Consequently, a lot of the French language terms went into Vietnam's daily life. The Vietnamese word for *cheese*, for example, *phó-mát*, comes from the French word *fromage* and *cake* is called *ga-tô*, from the French word *gateau*. The word for *butter – bơ –* comes from the French word *buerre*.

Vietnam is the point of convergence of elites from all the three processes ***Sinicization–De-Sinicization, Hinduization–De-Hinduization, and Westernization–***

De-Westernization towards a Vietnam united in diversity. For instance, the central region of Vietnam – the location of Champa Kingdom – was the cradle of the interference between the cultural and religious waves of Asia. Being benefited from the growth of economic activities on sea among China, India and Southeast Asian countries, the cultural exchange process was being promoted intensively. The excavated historical remnants shows that the amalgam between the non-indigenous and indigenous cultural values of Champa Kingdom's people resulted in the formation of unique spiritual products, which contributed to diversify cultural and religious treasures of Vietnam.

The Vietnamese people's active minds, flexibility, wisdom and creativity have resulted in refreshing Vietnam with a new life imbued with original cultural identities. It is certain that there will be a considerable increase in world population. The best estimates are for eight billion people by 2030. To avoid continued poverty and isolation, Asian nations must increasingly undertake multi-faceted exchanges so that they can work together to weave interrelated needs into a seamless experience full of possibilities and potentials. In other words, they must be organized into ONE MULTICULTURAL ASIA – united in diversity. The diversity of the Asian population will bring to each Asian nation important economic and cultural benefits, and a greater understanding of the globalised world. In fact, diverse cultural expressions enrich all nations, making them more vibrant and creative.

In conclusion, Asia is a multiplicity of pluralistic societies: multi-cultural, multi-lingual, multi-ethnic and multi-religious. The new world order, regionalization, globalization have exerted dramatic effects on the 21st century in all aspects including higher education. Higher education institutions (HEIs), hence, should act as research and innovation hubs for local, national and international collaborations, for a world of peace without clashes of any kind, without endangerment of nature. To actively accelerate international integration of higher education and improve institutional quality, the state should create supporting mechanism and publish appropriate policies to form a network of Asia's HEIs where every university can seize the opportunity and proactively build up a world-class university model in accordance with the assurance in educational quality, international integration and social responsibility commitment.

The new world order, "multipolar" or "one superpower plus many major powers", with a lot of conflicts leading to struggles and alliances intertwined with and into each other, creates opportunities as well as posing challenges to every people, especially Southeast Asian peoples. HEIs, with all their significant functions, play the major and decisive role in the enhancement of possibilities and in the surmounting of challenges for sustainable development of our peaceful world. In that new world order, in the development of Southeast Asian history in general and of Vietnam in particular, the process of acculturation which was *Sinicization and De-Sinicization, Hinduization and De-Hinduization, Westernization and De-Westernization* took place very early and left a lot of bold imprints.

With an aim to cultivate unity within diversity, build a culture of social inclusion, embrace equality within all communities in Asia towards accentuating the image and significance of One Asia, every citizen has the right to give equal participation to the multifaceted society while still maintaining their cultural traditions, to maximize the benefits of a multicultural society united in diversity, to address the challenges in order to build on achievements as a peaceful and prosperous One Asia.

Notes

1 Prof. Dr., University of Social Sciences and Humanities, Vietnam National University Ho Chi Minh City
2 Dr., University of Social Sciences and Humanities, Vietnam National University Ho Chi Minh City
3 Atlantic Council 2018, *India and the Emerging World Order*, retrieved from the World Wide Web http://www.atlanticcouncil.org/elections?view=article&id=2 3353:india-and-the-emerging-world-order
4 Voice of Asia, *Four things you need to know about Asia in 2017*, retrieved from the World Wide Web https://www2.deloitte.com/insights/us/en/economy/voice-of-asia/january-2017/insights.html#endnote-sup-1
5 Agner Fog, *Cultural Selection*, 1999, published at Kluwer Academic Publishers, retrieved from the World Wide Webs http://www.springer.com/gp/

book/9780792355793 and https://link.springer.com/content/pdf/bfm%3A978-94-015-9251-2%2F1.pdf

6 *The Spread of Chinese Civilization: Japan, Korea, Vietnam,* retrieved from the World Wide Web http://wps.ablongman.com/long_stearns_wc_4/0, 8725, 1125407-, 00.html

7 *"Indianization in Southeast Asia History Essay"* retrieved from the World Wide Web http://www.ukessays.com/essays/history/indianization-in-southeast-asia-history-essay.php

8 *"This new Asian identity has social, cultural, economic and political implications. After decades of reserve on the international stage, Japan is now poised to assume a permanent seat on the U.N. Security Council, which would raise its diplomatic profile and influence. Efforts by Indonesian President Suharto to sustain and rejuvenate a post-Cold War version of the Nonaligned Movement bespeak a regional confidence and desire for autonomy. So does the conflict between Asia and the Western nations at the U.N. convention on human rights this year in Vienna. It made some participants, like Singapore Foreign Minister Wong Kan Sen, realize the extent of their Asianness for the first time. A few Asian nations, including Japan and Korea, supported the stand for universal rights taken by the United States and European countries, but India and the Philippines, two Asian democracies, were among those who argued that human rights must be considered in the context of the right to economic and social development. Charges of human-rights violations presented by other countries, they argued, were attempts to intervene in their domestic affairs. Most Asian political leaders maintain that the most desirable mode of democratization emerges spontaneously from economic growth, which sparks political consciousness among a middle class."* (*The Asianization of Asia*, by Yoichi Funabashi, http://www.foreignaffairs.com)

9 Coedes, George, *The "Korean Wave" only laid the foundation for the "Asian Wave",* The Making of Southeast Asia. Publishers: Routledge & Kegan Paul, p. 64, 1996

10 "Indianization In Southeast Asia History Essay", retrieved from the World Wide Web http://www.ukessays.com/essays/history/indianization-in-southeast-asia-history-essay.php

11 "The Kingdom of Srivijaya: on the Indonesian island of Sumatra, directly to the west of the city of Palembang, are ruins and artifacts that appear to date back to the Kingdom of Srivijaya. Indications are strong that the Palembang region of south Sumatra formed the heartland of the kingdom. Srivijaya (Sri Vijaya) was a maritime kingdom of Sumatra that existed from circa 500 CE until the late 1300's, although it possibly had roots going back as far as 200 CE." Retrieved from the World Wide Web: http://www.ancientworlds.net/aw/Article/543335

References

VIETNAMESE

1. Arlo Griffiths, Amandine Lepoutre, William A. Southworth and Thanh Phan (compiling), The Inscriptions of Campa at the museum of Cham Sculpture in Da Nang. HCMC Vietnam National University Publisher, 2012
2. Barry Eichengreen, Charles Wyplosz, and Yung Chul Park (edited), *China, Asia, and the New World Economy,* Oxford University Express, 2008
3. Bui Thanh Thuy, "Preservation, Development cultural Values in the Context of Globalization". Culture and Arts Magazine (No. 351, September 2013). Ministry of Culture, Sports and Tourism
4. Dinh Ba Hoa, *Champa Ancient Pottery, Binh Dinh,* Khoa hoc Xa hoi Publisher, 2008
5. Ngo Van Doanh, *My Son Sanstuary,* Tre Publisher, p. 83, 2003
6. Nguyen Duy Ty and Le Minh Phong, "Archaeological Examination on Cham Culture in Ninh Thuan in 1993", New archaeological discoveries in 1993, pp. 284–285, 1993
7. Nguyen Tien Luc, *Japan and Vietnam. Civilizationalization Movement at the end of 19th Century and at the beginning of the 20th Century.* Vietnam Education Publisher, 2012
8. Phan Huy Le (chief compiler), *History of Vietnam* (volume 1), Vietnam Education Publisher, 2012
9. Tran Ky Phuong, Nguyen Van Phuc, "New Cham Remains discovered in Chiem Son Tay Valley (Quang Nam – Da Nang)", 1991
10. Tran Ngoc Them, *Searching back to Vietnam Cultural Identities.* HCMC Tong Hop Publisher, 2006
11. Tran Thi Thuy Phuong, Pham Huu Cong, *365 steps around the Museum of Vietnamese History in HCMC.* Department of Culture, Sports and Tourism, 2008
12. Truong Quoc Binh, "Preservation and Development of Cham Cultural Heritage in Vietnam – the Bridge for Vietnam-India Diplomatic Relationships". Proceedings of the international conference *Indian Imprints in the Process of Cultural Acculturation in Vietnam and Southeast Asia.* HCMC Vietnam National University Publisher, 2013
13. Xuan Diem Le and Vu Kim Loc, *Artefacts of Champa,* HCMC National Culture Publishing House, 1996

ENGLISH

1. Andrew Hardy, Mauro Cucarzi and Patrizia Zolese, *Champa and the Archaeology*

of Mỹ Sơn (Vietnam), Singapore: NUS press, 2009
2. Anne-Valérie Schweyer, *Ancient Vietnam – History and Archaeology*. River Books Guides, Bangkok, 2011
3. Anne-Valérie Schweyer, "The Birth of Champa", 13th International Conference of the European Association of Southeast Asian Archaeologists, vol. 2 : Connecting Empires and States, Berlin, pp. 102–117, 2012
4. Avind Kumar Singh, "Cham Culture of Vietnam: Tracing the Indian Roots". Proceedings of the international conference *Indian Imprints in the Process of Cultural Acculturation in Vietnam and Southeast Asia*. HCMC Vietnam National University Publisher, 2013
5. Bruce M.Lockhart, "Colonial and post-colonial constructions of "Champa", in The Cham of Vietnam – History, Society and Art, ed.Tran Ky Phuong and Bruce M.Lockhart. Singapore: NUS Press, pp. 1–53, 2011
6. Burling, Robbins, *Hill Farms and Padi Fields: Life in Mainland Southeast Asia*, Prentice Hall, Englewood Cliffs, N.J., 1965
7. Coedes, George, *The "Korean Wave" only laid the foundation for the "Asian Wave"*, The Making of Southeast Asia. Publishers: Routledge & Kegan Paul, p. 64, 1996
8. Coedes, George, *The Indianized States of Southeast Asia*. East-West Centre Press, 1968
9. Danny Wong Tze Ken, *Vietnam-Champa Relations and the Malay-Islam Regional Network in the 17–19 Centuries*. Department of History, University of Malaya. This project was funded by a SEASREP-Toyota Foundation Regional Collaboration Grant, 2007
10. Ellen L. Frost, *Asia's New Regionalism*, Lynne Rienner Publishers, 2008
11. Emmanuel Guillon, *Hindu-Buddhist Art of Vietnam: Treasures from Champa*, Weatherhill Publisher, 2001
12. Emmanuel Guillon, *Cham Art, Treasures from the Da Nang Museum, Vietnam*, Thames & Hudson Publishers, 2004
13. Geetesh Sharma, India-Vietnam Relations – First to Twenty first Century. Publishers: Dialogue Society, 2004
14. Geetesh Sharma, *Traces of Indian Culture in Vietnam*, Publishers: Banyan Tree Books Pvt.Ltd., 2009
15. Graham Allison, Robert D. Blackwill, Ali Wyne, Henry A. Kissinger, "*Lee Kuan Yew: The Grand Master's Insights on China, the United States, and the World*". MIT Press, pp. 2–3, 2013.
16. Harrison, Brian (third edition), *South-East Asia: a Short History*, London: Macmillan and Co Ltd., 1966

17 Zbigniew Brzezinski, "*The Grand Chessboard: American Primacy and Its Geostrategic Imperatives*". Basic Books Publisher, pp. 151–193, 1997
18 Majumdar R.C., *Ancient Indian Colonization in South-East Asia*, Baroda: B. J. Sandesara, 1963
19 Majumdar R.C., *Hindu Colonies in the Far East*, Baroda, : B. J. Sandesara, 1963
20 Majumdar R.C., Champā: *History & Culture of an Indian Colonial Kingdom in the Far East*, 2nd-16th century A.D. Delhi: Gian Pub. House, 1985
21 Michael Schuman, *The Miracle – Châu Á thần kỳ. Thiên sử thi về hành trình tìm kiếm sự thịnh vượng của Châu Á* (translated from *The Miracle: the Epic story of Asia's Quest for Wealth*, 2009), Thoi Dai Publisher, 2010
22 Neelima Dahiya, "Dynamics of Culture Interaction between India and Champa during 2nd Century CE to 15th Centure CE: Some Reflections". Proceedings of the international conference *Indian Imprints in the Process of Cultural Acculturation in Vietnam and Southeast Asia*. HCMC Vietnam National University Publisher, 2013
23 Ooi Keat Gin (editor), *A historical Encyclopedia*, from Angkor Wat to East Timor, 2004
24 Po Dharma, *The History of Champa* (paper)
25 Proceedings of the seminar on Champa, ed. P. B. Lafont. University of Copenhagen on May 23, 1987; Southworth, William. *The origins of Campa in Central Vietnam: A preliminary review*, PhD.diss, SOAS, 2001; The Cham of Vietnam – History, Society and Art, ed.Tran Ky Phuong and Bruce M.Lockhart. Singapore: NUS Press, 2011
26 R.C. Majumdar, "The Vo-Canh inscription" in Studies in Asian history and culture, presented to Dr. B. R. Chatterji on his eightieth birthday by Prakash Buddha (ed.), pp. 152–157, 1970
27 R.C. Majumdar, Champā, *History and Culture of an Indian Colonial Kingdom in the Far East*, 2nd-16th Century A.D.. Book III. Delhi: Gyan Publishing House, 1927, reprint: 1985
28 Richard Münch and Neil J. Smelser (editor). *Theory of Culture*. University of California Press, Berkeley · Los Angeles · Oxford, © 1993 The Regents of the University of California, 1993
29 Samuel P.Huntington, *The Clash of Civilizations and the Remaking of World Order*. Simon & Schuster, 2007
30 The National Intelligence Council, *Global Trends 2025: A Transformed World*. US Government Printing Office, 2008
31 Tran Ky Phuong and Bruce M. Lockhart, *The Cham of Vietnam*. History, Society and Art. Singapore: NUS press, 2011

32 Tran Ky Phuong, "The wedding of Sītā: a Theme from the Rāmāyaṇa represented on the Tra Kieu pedestal" in Narrative Sculpture and Literary Traditions in South and Southeast Asia by Marijke J. Klokke (ed.), pp. 51–58, 2000

33 Tran Ky Phuong, *Vestiges of Champa Civilization*. Ha Noi: The Gioi Publishers, 2004

34 Tran Ky Phuong, *Cultural Resource and Heritage Issues of Historic Champa States in Vietnam: Champa Origins, Reconfirmed Nomenclatures, and Preservation of Sites*. Working Paper Series No. 75, Asia Research Institute, National University of Singapore, Singapore, 2006

35 Ummu Salma Bava, *New Powers for Global Change? India's Role in the Emerging World Order*. Friedrich-Ebert-Stiftung, 2007

FRENCH

1 Abel Bergaigne, "L'ancien royaume de Campā, dans l'Indo-Chine d'après les inscriptions, " Journal Asiatique, series 8, 11 (1888), 5–105, 1888

2 Anne-Valérie Schweyer, "La royauté au Campā d'après les inscriptions" in Les apparences du Monde : Royautés hindoues et bouddhiques de l'Asie du Sud et du Sud-Est by B. Brac de la Perriere and M.-L. Reiniche (eds.), pp. 119–183

3 Anne-Valérie Schweyer, "Po Nagar de Nha Trang, " Aséanie 14, 109–140, 2004

4 Arlo Griffiths, Amandine Lepoutre, William A. Southworth and Thành Phần, "Épigraphie du Campā 2009–2010: prospection sur le terrain, production d'estampages, supplément à l'inventaire, " BEFEO, 95–96, 435–497, 2008–2009, published 2012

5 Coedes, George, *Inventaire des inscriptions du Champa et du Cambodge*. Publisher: Impr.d'Extrême-Orient, 1908

6 Coedes, George, *Histoire ancienne des États Hindouisés d'Extrême-Orient*. Hawaii: East-West Center Press, 1944

7 Coedes, George, *Les peuples de la péninsule indochinoise: histoire, civilisations*. Dunod editions, 1962

8 Georges Maspéro, 1928, *Le Royaume de Champa*, rev.ed. Paris and Brussels: Van Oest, 1928. English version: The Champa kingdom – The history of an extinct Vietnamese culture, translated by Walter E.J. Tips. Bangkok: White Lotus Press, 2002.

9 Philippe Stern, *L'art du Champa (ancien Annam) et son évolution*. Toulouse and Paris: Les Frères Douladoure and Adrien-Maisonneuve, 1942

10 Pierre Baptiste and Thierry Zéphir (eds.), *Trésors d'art du Vietnam. La sculpture du Champa Ve-XVe siècles. Paris: Réunion des musées nationaux and Musée des arts*

asiatiques Guimet, 2005

11 Plubplung Kongehana, Chainarong Sripong, *L'état des connaissances des Etudes Cham en Thaïlande*, pour la 6ème Conférence Annuelle du monde Musulman (Les 22 et 23 mai de 2013)

12 Po Dharma, *Le Pāṇḍuraṅga (Campā) 1802–1835: Ses rapports avec le Vietnam*. Pulications de l'Ecole française d'Extrême-Orient (EFEO), 1987

13 Po, Dharma, "Survol de l'histoire du Campa, " Le Musee de Sculpture Cam de Da Nang. Paris: Association Française des Amis de l'Orient (AFAO), Ecole Française d'Extreme–Orient (EFEO). Editions de l'AFAO. pp. 39–55, 1997

WEB SITES

1 A Glorious Hindu Legacy: Indic influence in Southeast Asia, retrieved from the World Wide Web http://www.hinduwisdom.info/Glimpses_XIV.htm

2 Agner Fog, Cultural Selection, 1999, published at Kluwer Academic Publishers, retrieved from the World Wide Webs http://www.springer.com/gp/book/9780792355793 and https://link.springer.com/content/pdf/bfm%3A978-94-015-9251-2%2F1.pdf

3 Atlantic Council, 2018, India and the Emerging World Order, retrieved from the World Wide Web http://www.atlanticcouncil.org/elections?view=article&id=23353:india-and-the-emerging-world-order

4 Dennis O'Neil, Acculturation, retrieved from the World Wide Web http://anthro.palomar.edu/change/change_3.htm , Copyright © 1997–2006

5 East Asia and the Pacific in the 21st Century: Geopolitical and Economic Dimensions, retrieved from the World Wide Web http://interactioncouncil.org/node/69

6 Evan A. Feigenbaum, 2015, The U.S. must adapt to Asia's new order, retrieved from the World Wide Web http://www.eastasiaforum.org/2015/03/22/the-us-must-adapt-to-asias-new-order/

7 http://anthro.palomar.edu/change/change_3.htm

8 http://whc.unesco.org/en/list/949

9 http://www.ancientworlds.net/aw/Article/543335

10 http://www.archives.gov.vn

11 http://www.mongabay.com/history/south_korea/south_korea-daoism_and_buddhism.html

12 http://www.sacha-champa.org

13 http://www.ukessays.com/essays/history/indianization-in-southeast-asia-history-essay.php

14 Indianization in Southeast Asia History Essay, retrieved from the World Wide Web http://www.ukessays.com/essays/history/indianization-in-southeast-asia-history-essay.php
15 James Blake Wiener, 2013, Deciphering Ancient Cham Art, retrieved from the World Wide Web http://www.ancient.eu.com/news/3128/
16 Jashaklikei, "Mối quan hệ Đại Việt - Champa trước thế kỷ XI (Dai Viet – Champa Relationship before the 11th Century)", Quan hệ bang giao Đại Việt – Champa: một cách tiếp cận mới (Dai Viet - Champa Diplomatic Relations: a new way of approach), Posted March 24, 2014 onto the World Wide Web http://jashaklikei.wordpress.com/2014/03/24/quan-he-bang-giao-dai-viet-champa-mot-cach-tiep-can-moi-2/
17 Muthiah Alagappa, 2010, Regionalism in the 21st Century Asia, retrieved from the World Wide Web http://www.eai.or.kr/type/panelView.asp?bytag=p&code=eng_report&idx=9502&page=75
18 Peter Drysdale, 2012, Asia's economic and political interdependence, East Asia Forum, retrieved from the World Wide Web http://www.eastasiaforum.org/2012/05/28/asias-economic-and-political-interdependence/
19 South Korea – Daoism and Buddhism, retrieved from the World Wide Web http://www.country-data.com/cgi-bin/query/r-12289.html
20 The Asianization of Asia, by Yoichi Funabashi, retrieved from the World Wide Web http://www.foreignaffairs.com
21 The Spread of Chinese Civilization: Japan, Korea, Vietnam, retrieved from the World Wide Web http://wps.ablongman.com/long_stearns_wc_4/0, 8725, 1125407-, 00.html
22 Voice of Asia, Four things you need to know about Asia in 2017, retrieved from the World Wide Web https://www2.deloitte.com/insights/us/en/economy/voice-of-asia/january-2017/insights.html#endnote-sup-1
23 Yoichi Funabashi, Japan and the New World Order, retrieved from the World Wide Web https://www.foreignaffairs.com/articles/asia/1991-12-01/japan-and-new-world-order
24 Yoichi Funabashi, The Asianization of Asia, retrieved from the World Wide Web http://www.foreignaffairs.com
25 Zbigniew Brzezinski, 2011, As China rises, A new U.S. Strategy, the January/February issue of Foreign Affairs, retrieved from the World Wide Web http://www.wsj.com/articles/SB10001424052970203413304577088881349304486

Chapter 17

A Study of Japan's New Ocean View and Marine Education from *Coexistence with the Ocean* by Tomoya Akimichi

Demin YANG (Shanghai Ocean University),
Yanhong ZHOU (Shanghai Ocean University)

Introduction

One of the seven books in *Series of the Translated Book Series on Marine Culture* by College of Foreign Languages, Shanghai Ocean University, *Living with the Ocean: the Ethnology of the Ocean Men* is written by Tomoya Akimichi (1946 -), a famous Japanese anthropologist and marine ethnologist, who is the professor emeritus at Research Institute for Human and Nature, National Museum of Ethnology, and the Graduate University for Advanced Studies, Japan. Professor Kawashima, from Tohoku University Japan comments on *Tokyo Shinbun* (September 8, 2013) that this is the first research work on rejuvenation of aquaculture in the disaster-stricken ocean waters after the 3·11 East Japan Earthquake and that this latest achievements in natural science are concise and easy to understand. Professor Kawashima points out that the opinion proposed in this book - integration of every aspects into marine research - is of great importance, especially in the process of marine rejuvenation after tsunami and nuclear leakage caused by the great earthquake. To put into specific words, the point is that issues related to the natural science and social science should all be comprehensively put into consideration. "Science is not a matter of all-purpose. This is what we have learned from the tsunami"(Kawashima 2013). "In the course of marine rejuvenation, how to protect marine recourses is our first concern"(ibid.), "the linkage among forest, ocean and villages"(ibid.) should not be hindered.

In the Chinese version, the following three major opinions in the book are to be introduced: coexistence (two theories are included), new ocean view and marine education.

1. Coexistence

1 Coexistence of the ocean and ocean men

What does coexistence with the ocean mean? The author re-examines the relationship between the human society and the ocean from various aspects. Men are land animals but seek supplies from the ocean. Many sorts of marine lives are used for food and tools or raw materials for industrial products in the human world. Although the relationships between the two parties vary in accordance to place and time, one thing remains definite, that is, the human society gets what they want from the sea. In this book, the author refers those people or groups who directly related to the ocean as 'ocean men', with its written form '海人' and its pronunciation 'kaijin' in Japanese. This term not merely refers to those in Japan, but people or groups in the vast areas spreading from the Bering Strait to the southern Pacific Ocean, from the North Sea to the Mediterranean, even including those living around the Indian Ocean. Their expedition go beyond the coastline and shallow waters of the sea and reach the faraway places across the ocean, well beyond the national and continental bounders. And thus their activities are characterized by the feature of 'transboundary'.

Ocean men have created various forms of wisdom and fishing techniques. These wisdoms have been passed on to later generations to familiarize them with marine life and its ecology. As early as the Paleolithic era, ocean men in Japan have learned the techniques for fishing tuna or salmon. The history of fighting between humans and marine life is, at the same time, the history of human's adaptation to the ocean and conquering the ocean. They add a thick touch of color to the human history.

Should the ocean men be regarded as the destroyer or protector of the marine resources? The author argues that there is no a simple answer. The relation between them is dynamic, which is seen as the second nature of the ocean men: 'changing'. In other words, the influence from nature and human society have a direct control over the activities of ocean men. They have to adapt to their changes and alter the way they act. Let's try and analyze this topic in a more visible way.

Based on the fact that it is the ocean men who is the subject that coexists with the ocean, the author attaches great importance to this perspective of the ocean men. As researchers mutually hold that in the professional field relating to various types of the relationships between the human society and the ocean, the ocean men integrate these relationships into their daily lives. It is through this perspective that the book attempts to portray the true image of ocean men.

Marine race in this book does not mean its narrow sense, but refer to all the creatures across national borders living off the ocean. Consequently, all of the nationalities in the world are in the range of marine race. From the perspective of bio-ecology, all the living things in the ocean are included in the great marine race as well. In this sense, marine ethnology in this book takes the view that the human society is not the dominator of the ocean, instead, they are one of the creature living off it. So they should coexist with other marine races, treating other marine races in a more humble way.

2 Two theories

1. Romantic relationship between forests and the ocean -- sustainable development of marine resources

Forests provides rich organic salts for the lower-level creatures and thus properly and efficiently maintains the food chain and ecological cycle. The preservation of forests equals to the preservation of the sustainable marine resources.

1) Interconnection and rejuvenation of forests and the ocean

Mr. Shigeatsu Hatakeyama, an oyster farmer in Miyagi Prefecture, is the first one who proposes this theory: "Forests are the lover of the ocean" (Hatakeyama

2006). Over the past 25 years, he has been actively advocating tree planting. This theory has been succeeded by Professor Tanaka and Professor Yamashita from Kyoto University and has thus developed into a new branch of science: Study of the interconnections between the Caspian Sea and forests.

2) Sea floor springs and sea water circulation

Rivers are not the sole route to carry nutrients to the ocean. Rainfalls dissolve some constituents of the underground rocks before reaching the ocean. Finally, these nutrients run out with the springs.

Case studies show that there are two ways to bring biogenic nutrients to coastal waters. One way is that nutritious waters flow from the forest to the sea through the river; the other way is that the freshwater spray directly from the sea floor. The latter contributes more in the course of nutrition supply.

2. Teleconnection and wind-bucket theory

Global atmospheric pressure variation stimulates repeated changes between two faraway places, like the work of a seesaw. In the interim, atmosphere and the ocean are correlatively involved in the process, leading to climate changes. This is Teleconnection. One typical case can be the ENSO: the change of the surface temperature of the Pacific Ocean results in the altering amount of rainfall in India and South Africa.

In addition to the influence on natural phenomena, Teleconnection also exerts a direct effects on fishery and agriculture etc. However, the human race have no controlling power over these dynamic changes.

The wind-bucket theory is from a well-known Japanese saying: if the wind blows, the bucket shop gains. Strong wind rolls up the sand, which increases the number of the blind people; then the musical instruments Shamisen are in great demand by the blinded, which are made of cat skins. Killing of cats in great numbers leads to suffering of buckets in families due to the epidemic of rats. In the end, the bucket shops gain profits.

Seemingly uncorrelated phenomena are closely related ecologically. This concept shares the similar sense with the above-mentioned theory. The only difference between them is that the wind-bucket theory, the ecological correlation, can be applied in the study of natural phenomena, economy, politics, culture and human bodies etc; while teleconnection obviously does not have such wide applications.

2. Japan's new ocean view

1 Nuclear power generation and marine science

Soon after the East Japan Earthquake, Fukushima nuclear plant leaked 530 tons polluted water of high density. A large amount of radioactive substances ran into the sea. Although the Japanese government once issued security declaration, claiming that the ocean pollution is within the range of control. But later, a check of the sea catch from the local waters revealed that the radioactive substances exceeded the tentative reference value. So far, all the fishing and selling of seafood has been strictly banned within Fukushima Prefecture. There is no doubt that the density of the radioactive substances in the sea water continuously decreases after the leakage. However, some fish species take in higher density radioactive substances while other fish species take in lower density radioactive substances. Unfortunately, we mankind do not have relevant knowledge and ability to distinguish them. Nor do people know why there are differences among the fish species on taking in the different density of radioactive substances.

One more thing that the Japanese government facing nowadays is ways of handling nuclear power generation. So far, Japan has relied too much on nuclear power generation. A official tracking survey was conducted by the government in 2012, in which the percentage of nuclear power by the year 2030 was set as 0%, 15%, 2–25% respectively and 6894 candidates were inquired before and after their discussion with experts. The final results revealed only slight difference: 32.6% chose 0% in the first survey; after their discussions with relevant experts, it went up to 46.7%. But those who prefer 2–25% remained the same in the two surveys. On the opinion hearing held in Fukushima around the same period, 28 among the 30 participants insisted abolition of nuclear power.

As time elapses, statistics relating to polluted marine lives caused by the nuclear leakage alters, and it is the same with those numerical results in the social survey. However, should the government bear the role in judging the authenticity of these figures, announcing the criteria on the safety of fish and shellfish, or abolishing nuclear power? It should be understood that it is important to verify the figures derived from natural sciences and social sciences. Only in this way, can researchers approach forward. A modest attitude must be adopted in tackling ocean issues The latter is the touchstone that will determine the future of Japan and the world.

2. Integrated coastal management

In 2007, Japan formulated the Ocean Basic Law. According to this law, the Ocean Basic Package came out in 2008, but is not well implemented, from what is seen today. Inadequate administrative management at the lower and upper levels of the relevant prefectural offices is the main reason. New edition of the Ocean Basic Package was issued in 2013, aiming to eliminate the administrative drawbacks. Major problem involved is that no sufficient comprehensive consideration of the marine policies were mentioned in the former version. According to the new law, mutual cooperation and cross-impact of relevant businesses are to be carefully considered.

The new edition of the Ocean Basic Plan was developed under the leadership of the former president of Tokyo University, Professor Komiya, the speaker of the Integrated Marine Policy Division Conference. Marine Policy Division consists of five specialized project teams, focusing on the following fields respectively: (1) Innovation and rejuvenation of marine industry, (2) Unification and publicity of marine information, (3) Talent development, (4) Integrated management and planning of coastal sea areas, (5) Marine safety and security. Fields (1), (3) and (4) just focus on the post-disaster reconstruction of Sanriku area, an tsunami-stricken area in eastern Japan.

In order to rejuvenate the aquaculture in Sanriku coastal waters, formulation of a new coastal waters management model is expected from the Japanese government. However, this topic has not been explored in full range. Now, first of all, consultants should be promoted who are familiar with local conditions. These consultants play a key role in the communication between countries and regions. They can reflect to the country whether or not the Ocean Basic Plan is effective in its implementation in various regions. They can find ways to reflect the wishes of the local residents faithfully. They not only play a role in regulating the interests of various parties, but also provide guidance on political judgments of the administration. Their suggestions are flexible and persuasive. The implementation of a comprehensive management policy in the coastal waters, namely "integrated coastal management", is the main thrust of the book and the fundamental issue that concerns the relationship between the human society and the ocean. Therefore, integrated coastal management can be said to be the touchstone for the creation a bright future for the ocean.

People engage in various activities in the coastal waters. As for the fishery alone, there are several types of fisheries. There are sea areas set as shared fishery zone; there are fishing grounds consisting of fishing nets areas or areas for aquaculture; there are special marine reserves. On the seaside, there are fishing ports, fish markets, fishery co-operation, ice-making facilities, refrigerated and frozen warehouses, and gas stations. In addition to fisheries, there are marine sports areas and experimental waters for research. Harbors in these coastal areas are well developed. Besides shipyards, some ports are often built for sightseeing boats and cargo ships' landing offshore. In some areas along the coast, various fish processing plants, aquaculture-related facilities, cold storage and freezing facilities, seafood specialty shops and hotels are established. In addition, in the downstream areas of rivers, tidal barriers, embankments, and water gates should be built in some places. These facilities can not only regulate the flow of water from the river, but also block waves, surges and tsunami. The coastal environment, in a broad sense, includes all the natural environments and hardware facilities mentioned above. The most important aspect of integrated coastal management lies in ways to protect these coastal environments and promote the activation of regional industries. The first issue is to determine who, among all the stakeholders in the coastal area, will lead the planning process, who will implement the plan, and who will control the entire plan frame. In the post-earthquake reconstruction process after the earthquake and tsunami, the state, local governments, local residents, corporate parties, and fishermen all participate in the whole reconstruction process. Therefore, when planning for the establishment of a recovery plan, it takes time to adjust opinions and reach consensus, which sometimes results in delaying the implementation of the plans.

The Japanese government established the Revival Office on December 9, 2011, which is expected to be repealed on March 31, 2021. Under the Revival Office, various departments were set up to deal with different issues. Specifically, there are the following departments: Department of co-operation promotion, Department of command and planning, Department of regional affairs and Fukushima affairs, Department of special zones and grants affairs, Department of infrastructure construction, Department of residents support, and Department of industrial promotion. At the same time, a local agency, the Revival Bureau, was established in three prefectures in northeastern Japan. Namely, Iwate Revival Bureau, Miyagi Revival Bureau and Fukushima Revival Bureau. In addition, Recovery Offices were also established in Hachinohe, Aomori Prefecture, and Mito, Ibaraki Prefecture.

On the other hand, Japan's Ministry of Land, Infrastructure and Transport, the Ministry of the Environment, the Ministry of Economy, Trade and Industry, the Ministry of Agriculture, Forestry and Fisheries, as well as other ministries and offices have jointly participated in the revival project. Japan's relief funds allocated for the post-disaster recovery are not all used in post-disaster reconstruction. Some relief funds are used in other non-affected areas. In the post-disaster reconstruction process, it is not clear who and how to allocate the national disaster relief funds. Therefore, there are certain reasons for the government to be criticized by all circles. It is hoped that there is no disagreement among the governments at all levels in the country, prefectures, cities, towns and villages and jointly promote the post-disaster reconstruction. However, this is not an easy task. The author holds that in order to implement the idea of decentralization, smooth implementation of post-disaster reconstruction must be politically and strongly promote.

Comprehensive management, the realization of the revival of various industries after the disaster, is called the integrated management (ICM) of coastal waters. In one word, it is a method of integrated governance. Therefore, the author insists that in order to realize the industrial revival of the coastal waters in Japan and to realize the goal of comprehensive management, the most important thing is to formulate an overall plan. As shown below, first, as the basic condition for planning, the chain relationship between the sea and forests must be guaranteed. To ensure that the nutrients in the forest soil on the land are diverted through the river and flow unimpededly into the coastal waters. Second, a careful plan and a good job should be conducted in preventing disasters in the river basin and protecting the surrounding environment. Special attention should be paid to protecting forests in the upstream area because they not only prevent floods but also maintain the service function of ecosystem. At the same time, dams cannot be installed in the upstream basin. Dams, etc., will prevent nutrient salts from flowing into the sea. Third, projects in the coastal areas like land reclamation, post-tsunami reclamation projects, restoration of wetlands after seawater reclamation, and building of embankments, etc., have a very remarkable influence on the state of nature. Therefore, special attention should be paid to implementing such projects without hindering the natural ecological cycle. It takes more than 10 years to revive industries after the disaster. It will take longer time to fully restore the natural ecological cycle.

Frankly speaking, if a variety of service functions in the ecosystem are not maintained, the natural cycle will be interrupted, and more seriously, the coastal areas may be abandoned and the aquatic industry will decline. There are abundant spring water resources in many places in Japan. The state should formulate relevant laws and regulations and restrict the development of coastal areas. This can effectively prevent environmental degradation and at the same time, achieve the purpose of "spring legacy will be left behind". Since comprehensive management is advocated, not only the normal operation of the ecosystem should be protected, but also the local industries should be revitalized and the loss of population be prevented. These are the major prerequisites for achieving comprehensive management. And only on the basis of fulfilling these preconditions can a truly comprehensive judgment be possible.

3. Japan's future marine education

What is the most important issue in marine education? The Ministry of Education, Culture, Sports, Science and Technology of Japan will review the textbook a few years later. The biggest task facing Japan now is how to clearly demonstrate the importance of marine education in textbooks. Only after doing a good job in this matter can a fine report be submitted to the Central Education Review Council in a few years. Since the content of marine education is very broad, general and vague explanations will only leave people with a general and ambiguous impression. If so, it will not help. The author believes that there are abundant marine knowledge and interesting marine areas. When considering marine education, it is necessary to comprehensively consider the interrelatedness of various marine areas and various fields.

When considering land issues, people often ignore that the ocean issues are , in fact, closely associated with them. From an oceanic perspective, land issues must be considered as well. Forests and the ocean form an ecological cycle. In addition, crew members use "YamaTate" methods from the sea to determine the location of their vessels. Japan is located on a relatively small island and has to be aware of the surrounding sea. The Okinawa islands, in the Middle Ages and the modern period, once deviated from the sea and implemented agrarian policies. However, as long as the ocean is concerned, it is a broader world before the nation.

The book also collates the topics related to marine education, among which are some modern topics. There are five main groups: (1) How to prevent disasters caused by tsunami and big waves; (2) After the atomic energy leakage accident, the importance of developing and utilizing natural regenerative energy is exposed, such as natural renewable energy sources, including wind power, tidal power, sunlight, biological energy, and the like; (3) Appropriate use of seabed minerals, oil, natural gas and other energy issues and biological resources; (4) Safety and equity issues in the sea area and territorial waters; (5) Maintenance of marine biodiversity and protection of the natural environment. The above five groups of issues are related to each other, but not independent of each other. This is also an important feature of them. From primary and secondary education to high school education, the degree of difficulty and guidance of ocean knowledge for all grades should be arranged in a flexible way. Among the five topics that should be included in school education, in the author's opinion, there is a common theme, namely, water and life. The earth is called the "water planet." No living body on earth can sustain life without water. Water, including fresh water, seawater, and fountains, is the source of all life. All living bodies are connected by the same water. Handling this point in a proper way is an important guide to help Japan educate the next generation. The implementation of marine education is conducive to cultivating the next generation, not only in the aspect of the biological and ecological knowledge, but also in that of the sentimental and ethical aspects as well as the formation of students' rich personality.

Nature does not tell us any information. The most important thing is that we humans actively learn and cultivate the ability and qualifications to perceive the information of the nature. And this is the goal that the marine education is to achieve. The tsunami that occurred on March 11 was a natural phenomenon. It did not tell people any information in advance, but give us so many lessons. So what can people learn from these lessons? This is the question the author has been thinking about. Many chapters in this book devote to the tsunami issue from various perspectives, to mention a few: local governments actively participate in the post-disaster recovery; the tsunami has turned the natural world upside down and has caused serious damage to the ecosystem. people worry about the future of aquatic products from this area due to the atomic energy leakage accident; the development of the aquaculture industry and the issue of public ownership; how to use the trading network in a flexible way for the circulation of seafood products, etc. The Education Committee of Ōtsuchi, Iwate took essays from all local elementary and middle school students in the local town and compiled them into a book. The essays by the students truly recorded the actual scene of the earthquake and tsunami. Readers feel so touched and sad. It is expected by the author that students in other parts of Japan read this book as well, some of whom may be troubled by abuse and corporal punishment. However, in northeastern Japan, people are deeply suffering from natural disasters and have left indelible wounds in the hearts of local children. From the position of teaching and educating people, the local teachers are working hard with the children to sum up lessons from the disaster. It can be said that marine education has been in full swing in the schools of northeastern Japan.

What shall be done next? New guidelines should be rethought and formulated to solve a variety of problems concerning the ocean, including various issues related to land. We must not rigidly adhere to the land. Instead, we should attach importance to the interlinkage between the forests and the inland sea, cross the national borders, and better understand the structure of marine ecosystems including that of the unknown species. Knowledge in these areas falls into the realm of education. Most people think that it is difficult to put forward a strong factual basis. But this is not the case. This is a good opportunity to increase children's curiosity about the unknown world and the passion for the exploration of complex ecosystems. In short, we must realize that we should not be too confident in the great forces of science. On the contrary, the focus is to continue searching for the unknown world and stimulate people's academic interest. This is especially important for marine education. In the last chapter of the book, the author also emphasizes that it is the fundamental purpose of implementing marine education to develop a critical attitude towards general conclusions and data.

4. Conclusion

All human beings live off the sea, thus the term "marine race." Ocean is not only a sea of human beings, but also the sea of marine life that we use as our food. For a sustainable development of these marine resources, the most important thing is to co-exist with these marine lives.

The field of marine ethnology advocated by Professor Akimichi integrates the previous research achievements in both fields of anthropology and marine biology. This is a comprehensive study of anthropology and marine biology from a broader perspective. There is no similar research in China and a relatively new research area in the world. The new ocean view on nuclear power generation and integrated coastal management, especially Japan's marine education concept, has provided other countries with useful information. The concept "ocean race" can evoke our great sense of humanity. We should jointly defend the mutual homeland - the Earth.

From the day when the 3·11 Great East Japan Earthquake took place to now, Japan has been responding to the issue of post-disaster reconstruction. As is well-known, Japan is located between the plates. Since the ancient times, Japan has accumulated a lot of experience in responding to the earthquake and tsunami. Therefore, the loss of people's lives and property in the recent earthquake is also the smallest. In contrast, earthquakes have occurred frequently in some areas in China in recent years, and casualties and property losses are more severe. China should learn from Japan in prevention of disasters as well as post-disaster relief.

Professor Akimichi emphasizes that the perspective of marine ethnology should be the starting point in the promotion of the post-disaster reconstruction and revival, while taking into full account of the ecological links between the oceans, forests, and rivers, aiming to protect the sustainable resources. To convey this advanced concept to the Chinese people is also one of the fundamental purposes of translating this book. Professor Akimichi's research results are mostly based on data obtained from field surveys conducted in various sea areas around the world. They are detailed and available for investigation. Therefore, they have a high reference value for Chinese experts.

Selected references

H. Kawashima, Possibility of human knowledge about the Caspian Sea, *Tokyo Shinbun*, 2013

S. Hatakeyama, *Forests are the lover of the ocean*, Bungeishunshu, 2006

T. Akimichi, 1995. *Study of marine race*, Tokyo: Tokyo University Press Association, 1995

T. Akimichi, *Anthropology of commons*, Jinmonshoyin, 2004
T. Akimichi, *Who's the whale?* Tsukimo Books, 2009
T. Akimichi, *Knowledge on sphere of influence and mutual Cooperation - An ecological and historical understanding of circle, environment, and academia*, Showato, 2011

Section 6

Appendix

Number of Universities that received the Course Grant by Country/ Region

As of 22 June 2018

Countries/Regions	Course Started	Preparations in Progress	Total
Japan	61	48	109
South Korea	71	26	97
China	110	30	140
Hong Kong	4	3	7
Macau	0	1	1
Taiwan	13	7	20
North Korea	0	1	1
Singapore	1	2	3
Thailand	4	4	8
Mongolia	3	6	9
Vietnam	5	2	7
Myanmar	0	4	4
Nepal	0	2	2
Philippines	0	3	3
Cambodia	7	6	13
Indonesia	8	4	12
East Timor	1	0	1
Malaysia	2	1	3
Sri Lanka	1	0	1
India	1	5	6
Pakistan	0	1	1
Bangladesh	1	1	2
Laos	2	0	2
Bhutan	0	1	1
Kyrgyz	6	0	6
Kazakhstan	4	2	6
Turkmenistan	0	1	1
Uzbfiistan	0	2	2
Tajikistan	0	4	4
Australia	5	1	6
USA	4	4	8
Canada	2	0	2
Mexico	0	1	1
UK	1	2	3
France	0	2	2
Ireland	1	0	1
Italy	1	0	1
Spain	2	1	3
Austria	1	0	1
Russia	2	0	2
Ukraine	1	0	1
Poland	1	1	2
Belarus	0	1	1
Slovenia	0	1	1
Lithuania	1	0	1
Turky	2	2	4
Egypt	0	1	1
Congo	1	0	1
Total (48 Countries/Regions)	330	184	514

Note: Of all the above, 128 universities in 19 countries/regions have set up a course on Asian Community as a standing subject.

Introduction of Former Conventions

One Asia Convention
Tokyo 2011

1 July 2011

One Asia Convention
Incheon 2012

6~7 July 2012

One Asia Convention
Bandung 2013

22~23 March 2013

One Asia Convention
Jeju 2014

1~2 August 2014

One Asia Convention
Shanghai 2015

31 July~1 August 2015

One Asia Convention
Phnom Penh 2016

5~6 August 2016

One Asia Convention
Nagoya 2017

4~5 August 2017

About the Authors

Glenn D. Hook (Chap. 1)
University of Sheffield, United Kingdom

Eiji Makino (Chap. 2)
Hosei University, Japan

Asunción López-Varela (Chap. 3)
Universidad Complutense Madrid, Spain

Shoutong Xu (Chap. 4)
Sanya University, China

Bahadir Pehlivanturk (Chap. 5)
TOBB University of Economics and Technology, Turkey

Tung-Chieh Tsai (Chap. 6)
National Chung-Hsing University, Taiwan

Whanbhum Song (Chap. 7)
Seoul Women's University, Republic of Korea

Seok-won Song (Chap. 8)
Kyung Hee University, Republic of Korea

Kwangsoo Park (Chap. 9)
Wonkwang University, Republic of Korea

Narangoa Li (Chap. 10)
The Australian National University, Australia

Young-chul Yang (Chap. 11)
Jeju National University, Republic of Korea

Fong Yu (Chap. 12)
Feng Chia University, Taiwan

Dasim Budimansyah (Chap. 13)
Indonesia University of Education, Indonesia

Jean Young Lee (Chap. 14)
Inha University, Republic of Korea

Sun Ah Kim (Chap. 14)
Cordia, Republic of Korea

Eko Hadi Sujiono (Chap. 15)
Universitas Negeri Makassar, Indonesia

Helmy Pratiwi (Chap. 15)
Universitas Negeri Makassar, Indonesia

Yasser A. Djawad (Chap. 15)
Universitas Negeri Makassar, Indonesia

Van Sen Vo (Chap. 16)
Vietnam National University Ho Chi Minh City, Vietnam

Cao Boi Ngoc Tran (Chap. 16)
Vietnam National University Ho Chi Minh City, Vietnam

Demin Yang (Chap. 17)
Shanghai Ocean University, China

Yanhong Zhou (Chap. 17)
Shanghai Ocean University, China

Towards Asian Community—Peace through Education—
（アジア共同体へ向かって―教育を通じた平和―）

■発　　行――2018年8月3日初版第1刷
■編　　者――一般財団法人ワンアジア財団
■発行者――中山元春　〒101－0048東京都千代田区神田司町2－5
　　　　　　　　　　　電話03－3293－0556　FAX03－3293－0557
■発行所――株式会社芦書房
　　　　　　　　　　　http://www.ashi.co.jp
■印　　刷――新日本印刷
■製　　本――新日本印刷

©2018 One Asia Foundation

本書の一部あるいは全部の無断複写，複製
（コピー）は法律で認められた場合をのぞき
著作者・出版社の権利の侵害になります。

ISBN978－4－7556－1298－5 C0030